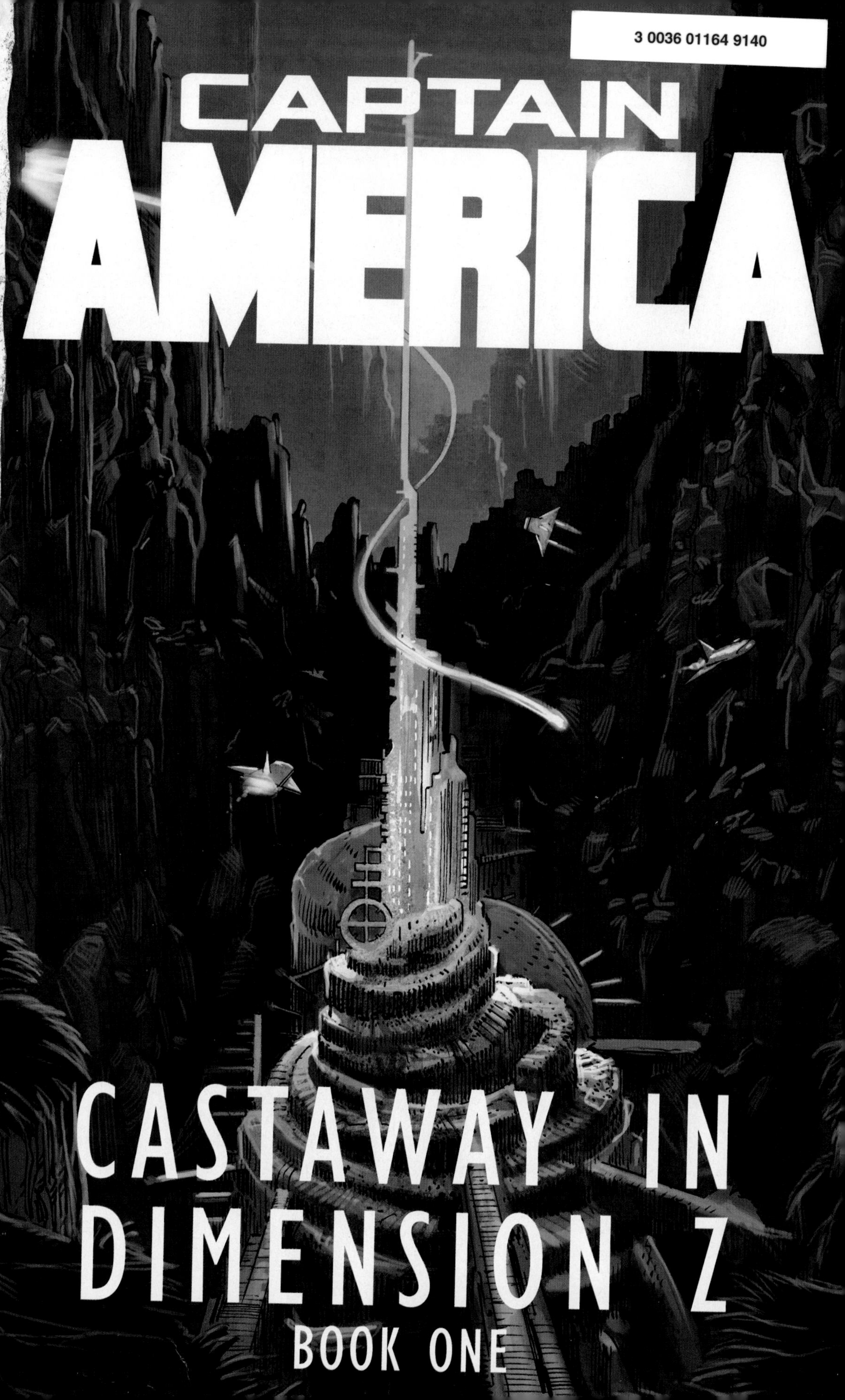
CAPTAIN
AMERICA
CASTAWAY IN
DIMENSION Z
BOOK ONE

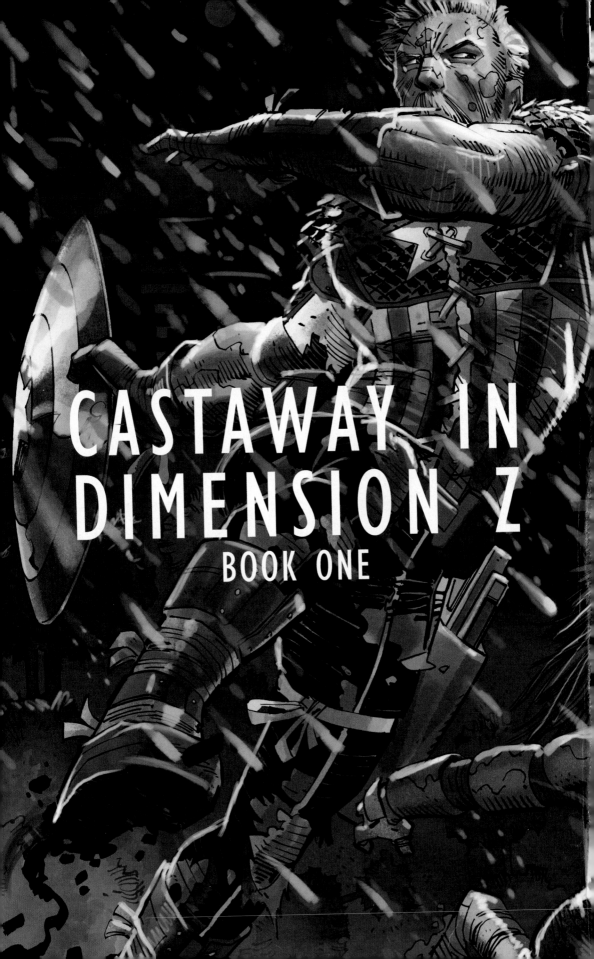

CASTAWAY IN DIMENSION Z
BOOK ONE

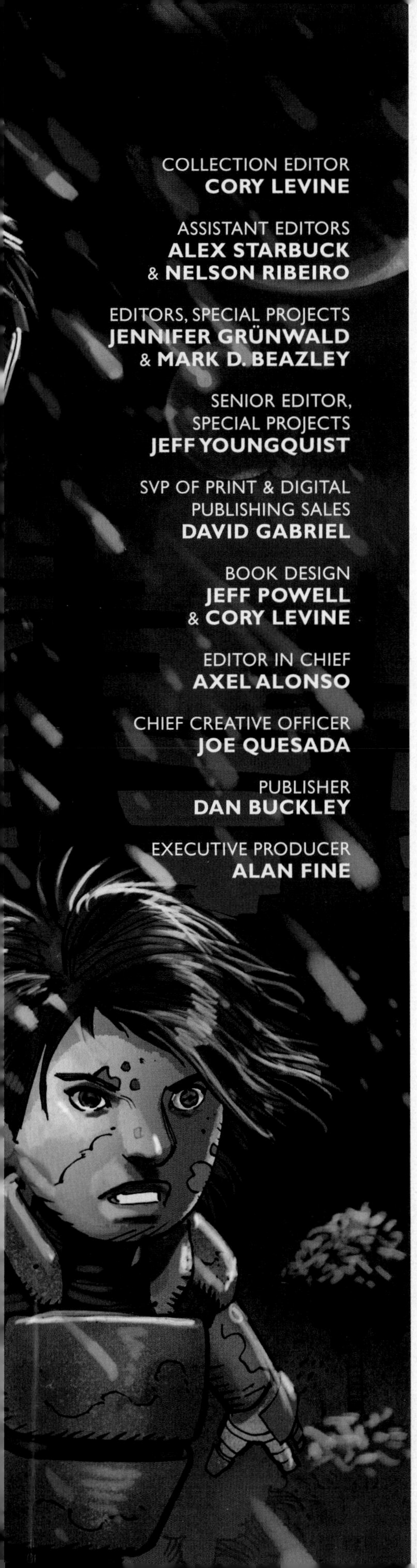

COLLECTION EDITOR
CORY LEVINE

ASSISTANT EDITORS
ALEX STARBUCK
& **NELSON RIBEIRO**

EDITORS, SPECIAL PROJECTS
JENNIFER GRÜNWALD
& **MARK D. BEAZLEY**

SENIOR EDITOR,
SPECIAL PROJECTS
JEFF YOUNGQUIST

SVP OF PRINT & DIGITAL
PUBLISHING SALES
DAVID GABRIEL

BOOK DESIGN
JEFF POWELL
& **CORY LEVINE**

EDITOR IN CHIEF
AXEL ALONSO

CHIEF CREATIVE OFFICER
JOE QUESADA

PUBLISHER
DAN BUCKLEY

EXECUTIVE PRODUCER
ALAN FINE

WRITER
RICK REMENDER

PENCILER
JOHN ROMITA JR.

INKERS
KLAUS JANSON (#1-4),
TOM PALMER (#5)
& **SCOTT HANNA** (#5)

COLORISTS
DEAN WHITE (#1-5)
& **LEE LOUGHRIDGE** (#2-5)
WITH **DAN BROWN** (#2)

LETTERER
VC'S JOE CARAMAGNA

COVER ARTISTS
JOHN ROMITA JR., KLAUS JANSON,
DEAN WHITE & **MORRY HOLLOWELL**

ASSISTANT EDITOR
JAKE THOMAS

EDITORS
TOM BREVOORT
WITH **LAUREN SANKOVITCH**

CAPTAIN AMERICA CREATED BY
JOE SIMON & **JACK KIRBY**

CAPTAIN AMERICA VOL. 1: CASTAWAY IN DIMENSION Z BOOK 1. Contains material originally published in magazine form as CAPTAIN AMERICA #1-5. First printing 2013. ISBN# 978-0-7851-6826-3. Published by MARVEL WORLDWIDE, INC., a subsidiary of MARVEL ENTERTAINMENT, LLC. OFFICE OF PUBLICATION: 135 West 50th Street, New York, NY 10020. **Printed in the U.S.A.** ALAN FINE, EVP - Office of the President, Marvel Worldwide, Inc. and EVP & CMO Marvel Characters B.V.; DAN BUCKLEY, Publisher & President - Print, Animation & Digital Divisions; JOE QUESADA, Chief Creative Officer; TOM BREVOORT, SVP of Publishing; DAVID BOGART, SVP of Operations & Procurement, Publishing; C.B. CEBULSKI, SVP of Creator & Content Development; DAVID GABRIEL, SVP of Print & Digital Publishing Sales; JIM O'KEEFE, VP of Operations & Logistics; DAN CARR, Executive Director of Publishing Technology; SUSAN CRESPI, Editorial Operations Manager; ALEX MORALES, Publishing Operations Manager; STAN LEE, Chairman Emeritus. For information regarding advertising in Marvel Comics or on Marvel.com, please contact Niza Disla, Director of Marvel Partnerships, at ndisla@marvel.com. For Marvel subscription inquiries, please call 800-217-9158. **Manufactured between 4/15/2013 and 5/27/2013 by R.R. DONNELLEY, INC., SALEM, VA, USA.**

10 9 8 7 6 5 4 3 2 1

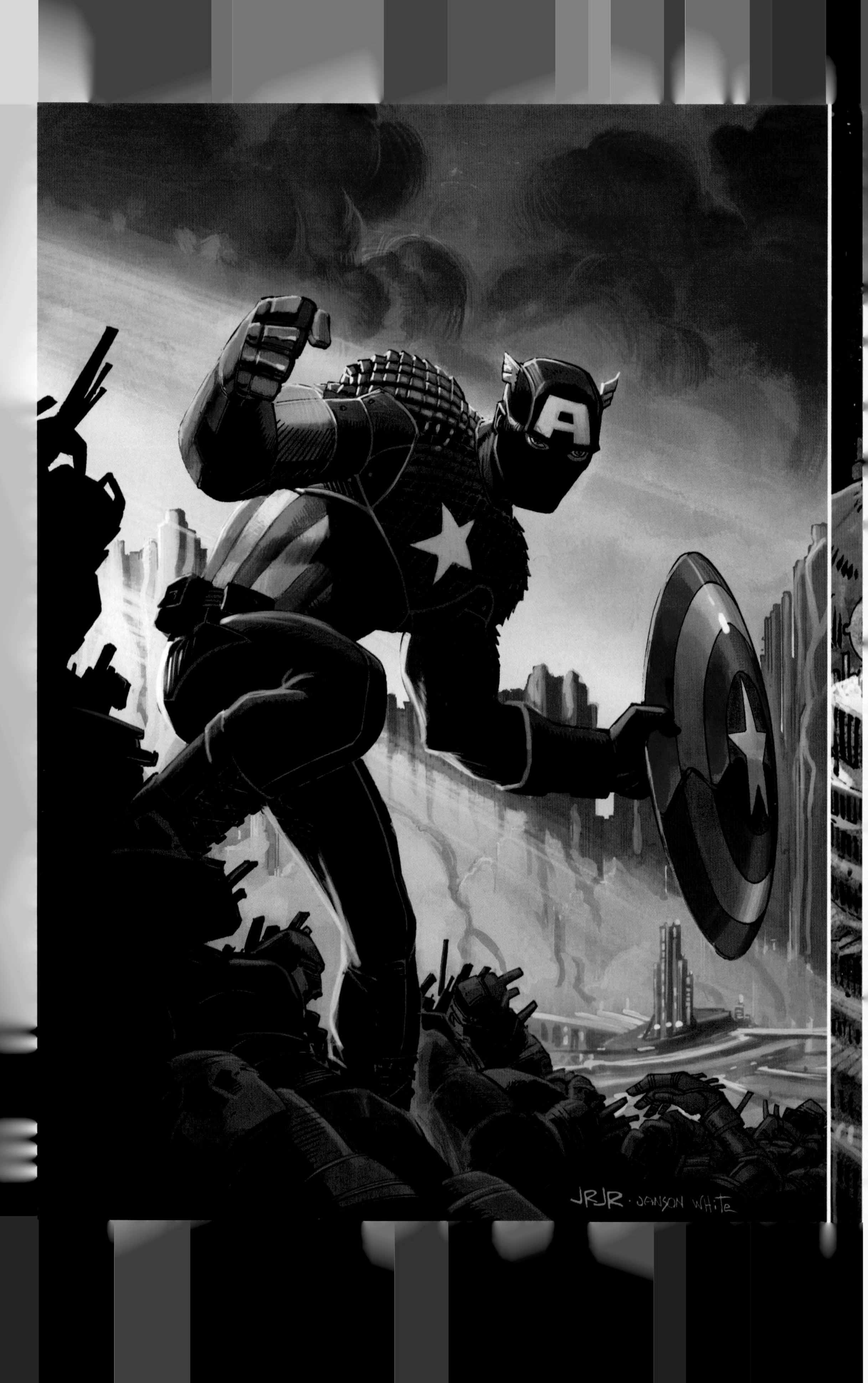
JRJR · JANSON WHITE

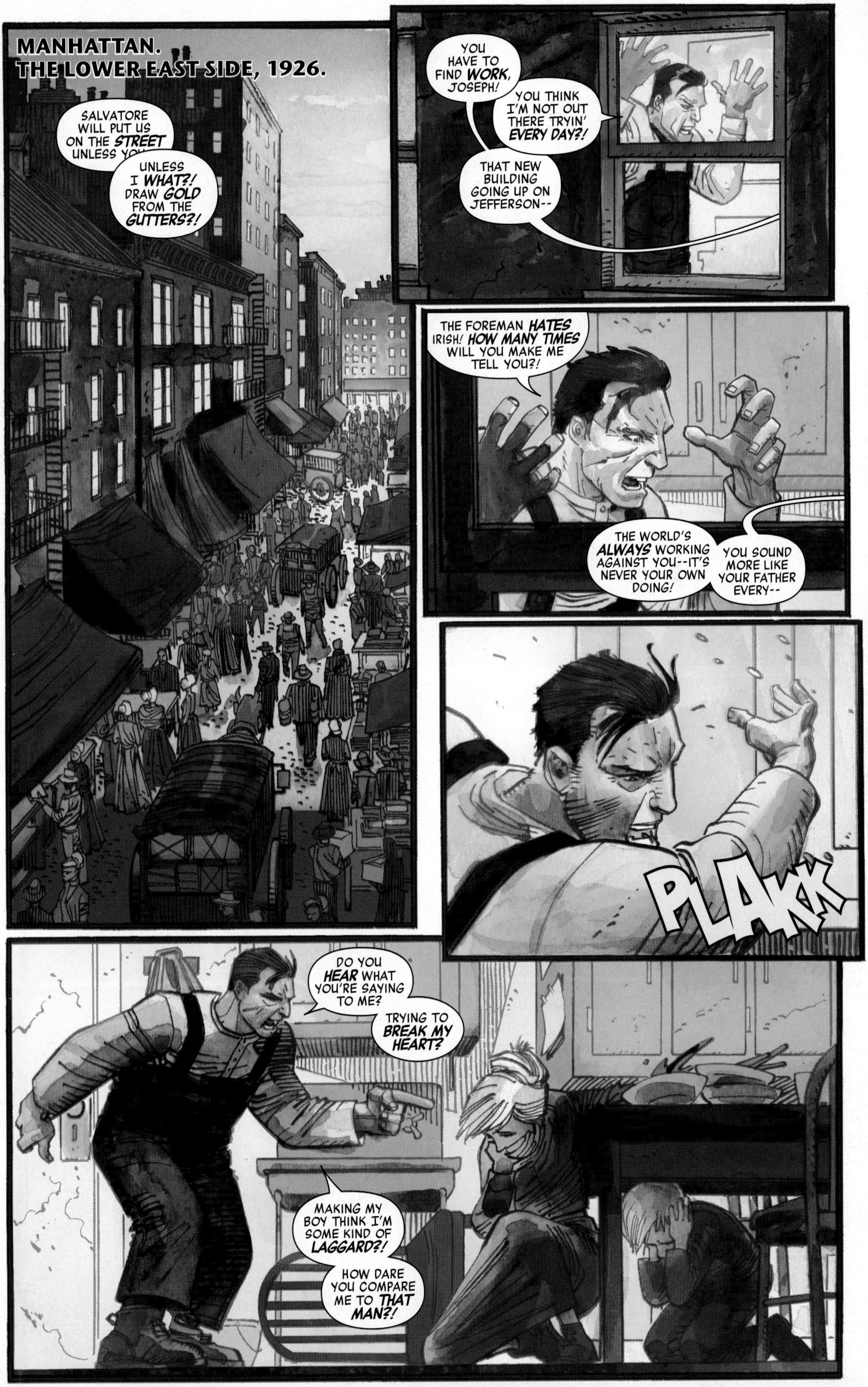
MANHATTAN.
THE LOWER EAST SIDE, 1926.
SALVATORE WILL PUT US ON THE STREET UNLESS YOU--
UNLESS I WHAT?! DRAW GOLD FROM THE GUTTERS?!
YOU HAVE TO FIND WORK, JOSEPH!
YOU THINK I'M NOT OUT THERE TRYIN' EVERY DAY?!
THAT NEW BUILDING GOING UP ON JEFFERSON--
THE FOREMAN HATES IRISH! HOW MANY TIMES WILL YOU MAKE ME TELL YOU?!
THE WORLD'S ALWAYS WORKING AGAINST YOU--IT'S NEVER YOUR OWN DOING!
YOU SOUND MORE LIKE YOUR FATHER EVERY--
PLAKK
DO YOU HEAR WHAT YOU'RE SAYING TO ME?
TRYING TO BREAK MY HEART?
MAKING MY BOY THINK I'M SOME KIND OF LAGGARD?!
HOW DARE YOU COMPARE ME TO THAT MAN?!

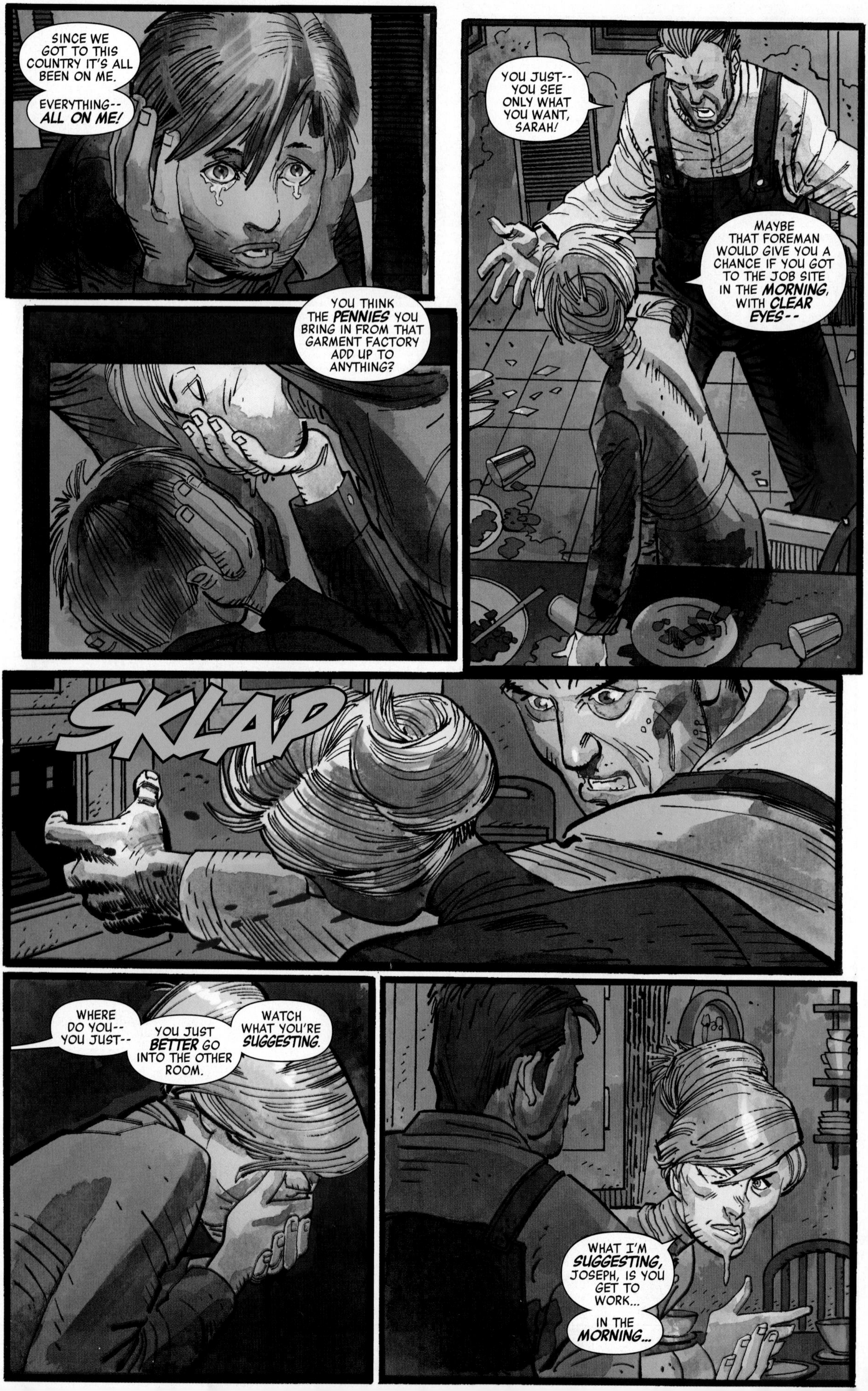
SINCE WE GOT TO THIS COUNTRY IT'S ALL BEEN ON ME.
EVERYTHING-- ALL ON ME!
YOU JUST-- YOU SEE ONLY WHAT YOU WANT, SARAH!
MAYBE THAT FOREMAN WOULD GIVE YOU A CHANCE IF YOU GOT TO THE JOB SITE IN THE MORNING, WITH CLEAR EYES--
YOU THINK THE PENNIES YOU BRING IN FROM THAT GARMENT FACTORY ADD UP TO ANYTHING?
SKLAP
WHERE DO YOU-- YOU JUST--
YOU JUST BETTER GO INTO THE OTHER ROOM.
WATCH WHAT YOU'RE SUGGESTING.
WHAT I'M SUGGESTING, JOSEPH, IS YOU GET TO WORK...
IN THE MORNING...

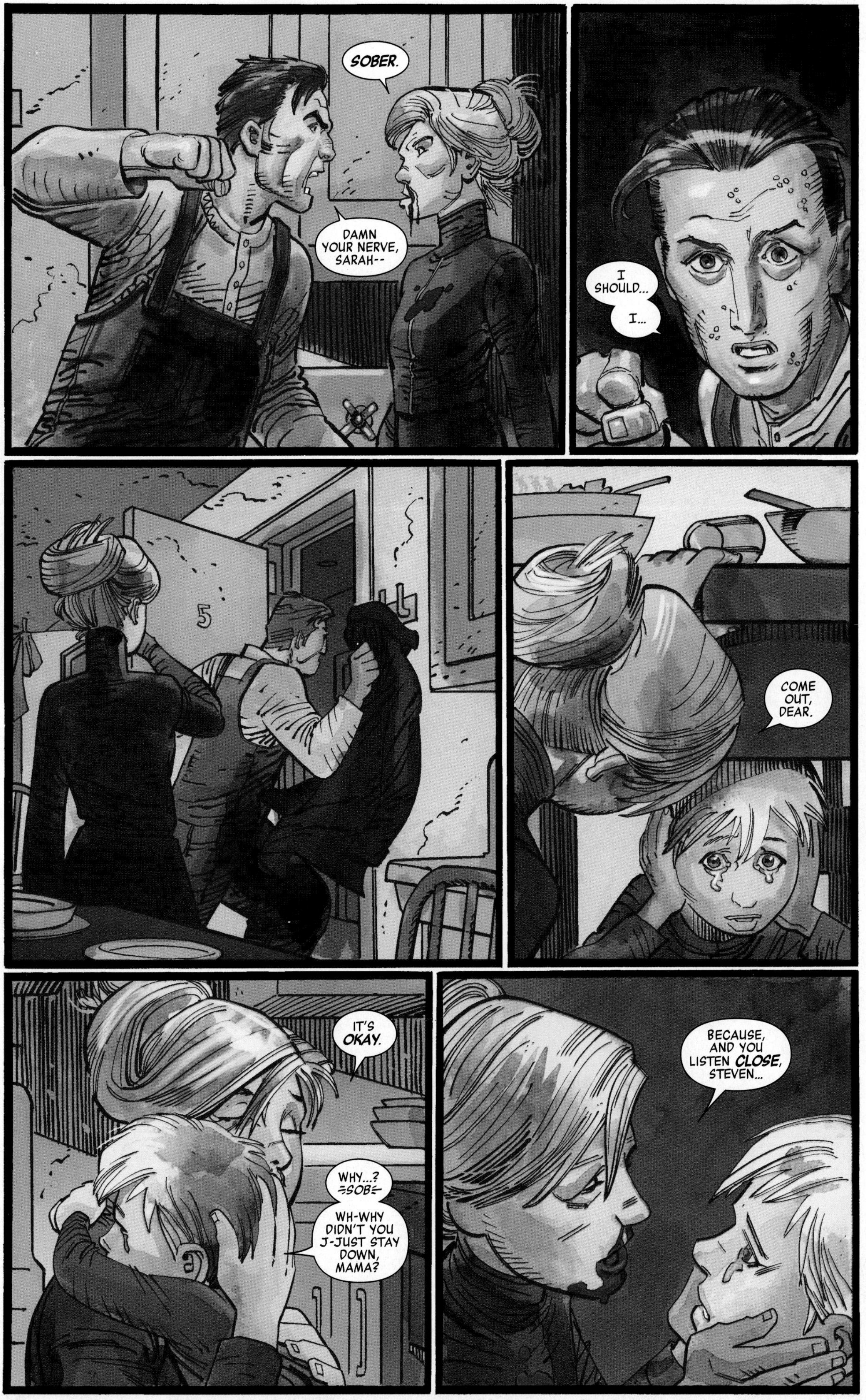
SOBER.
DAMN YOUR NERVE, SARAH--
I SHOULD...
I...
COME OUT, DEAR.
IT'S OKAY.
WHY...? =SOB=
WH-WHY DIDN'T YOU J-JUST STAY DOWN, MAMA?
BECAUSE, AND YOU LISTEN CLOSE, STEVEN...

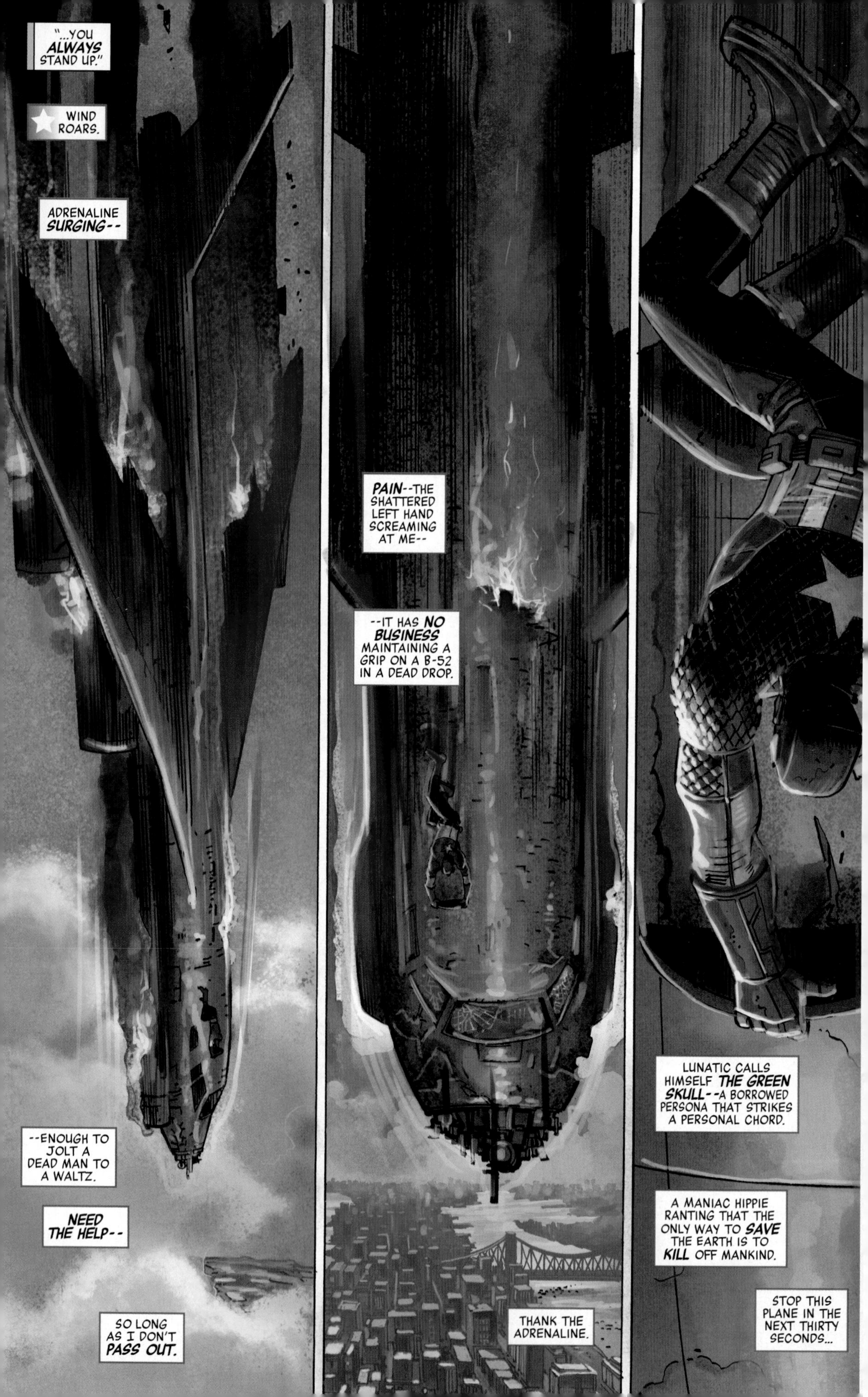

"...YOU ALWAYS STAND UP."
WIND ROARS.
ADRENALINE SURGING--
--ENOUGH TO JOLT A DEAD MAN TO A WALTZ.
NEED THE HELP--
SO LONG AS I DON'T PASS OUT.
PAIN--THE SHATTERED LEFT HAND SCREAMING AT ME--
--IT HAS NO BUSINESS MAINTAINING A GRIP ON A B-52 IN A DEAD DROP.
THANK THE ADRENALINE.
LUNATIC CALLS HIMSELF THE GREEN SKULL--A BORROWED PERSONA THAT STRIKES A PERSONAL CHORD.
A MANIAC HIPPIE RANTING THAT THE ONLY WAY TO SAVE THE EARTH IS TO KILL OFF MANKIND.
STOP THIS PLANE IN THE NEXT THIRTY SECONDS...

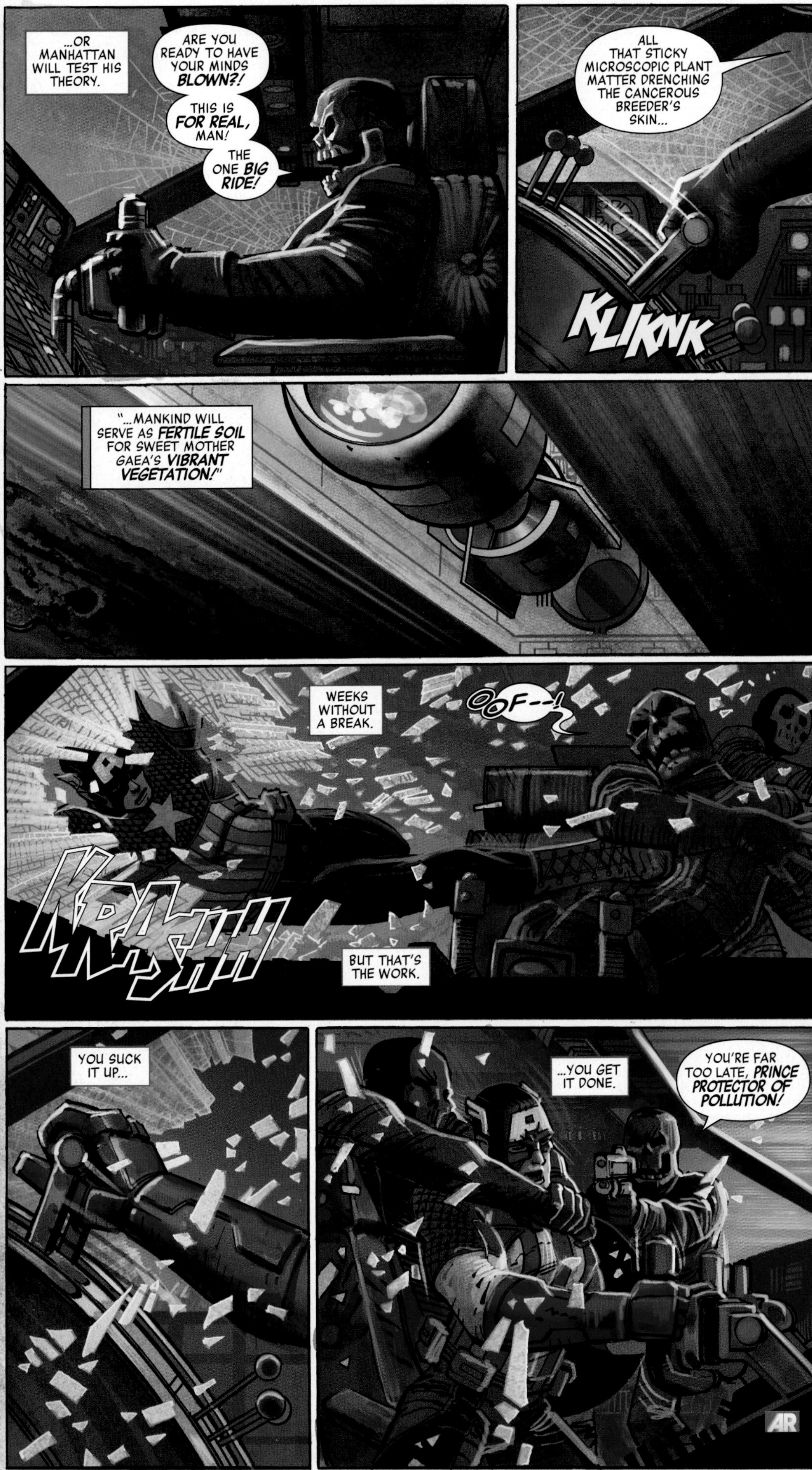

...OR MANHATTAN WILL TEST HIS THEORY.
ARE YOU READY TO HAVE YOUR MINDS BLOWN?!
THIS IS FOR REAL, MAN!
THE ONE BIG RIDE!
ALL THAT STICKY MICROSCOPIC PLANT MATTER DRENCHING THE CANCEROUS BREEDER'S SKIN...
KLIKNK
"...MANKIND WILL SERVE AS FERTILE SOIL FOR SWEET MOTHER GAEA'S VIBRANT VEGETATION!"
WEEKS WITHOUT A BREAK.
OOF--!
BUT THAT'S THE WORK.
YOU SUCK IT UP...
...YOU GET IT DONE.
YOU'RE FAR TOO LATE, PRINCE PROTECTOR OF POLLUTION!

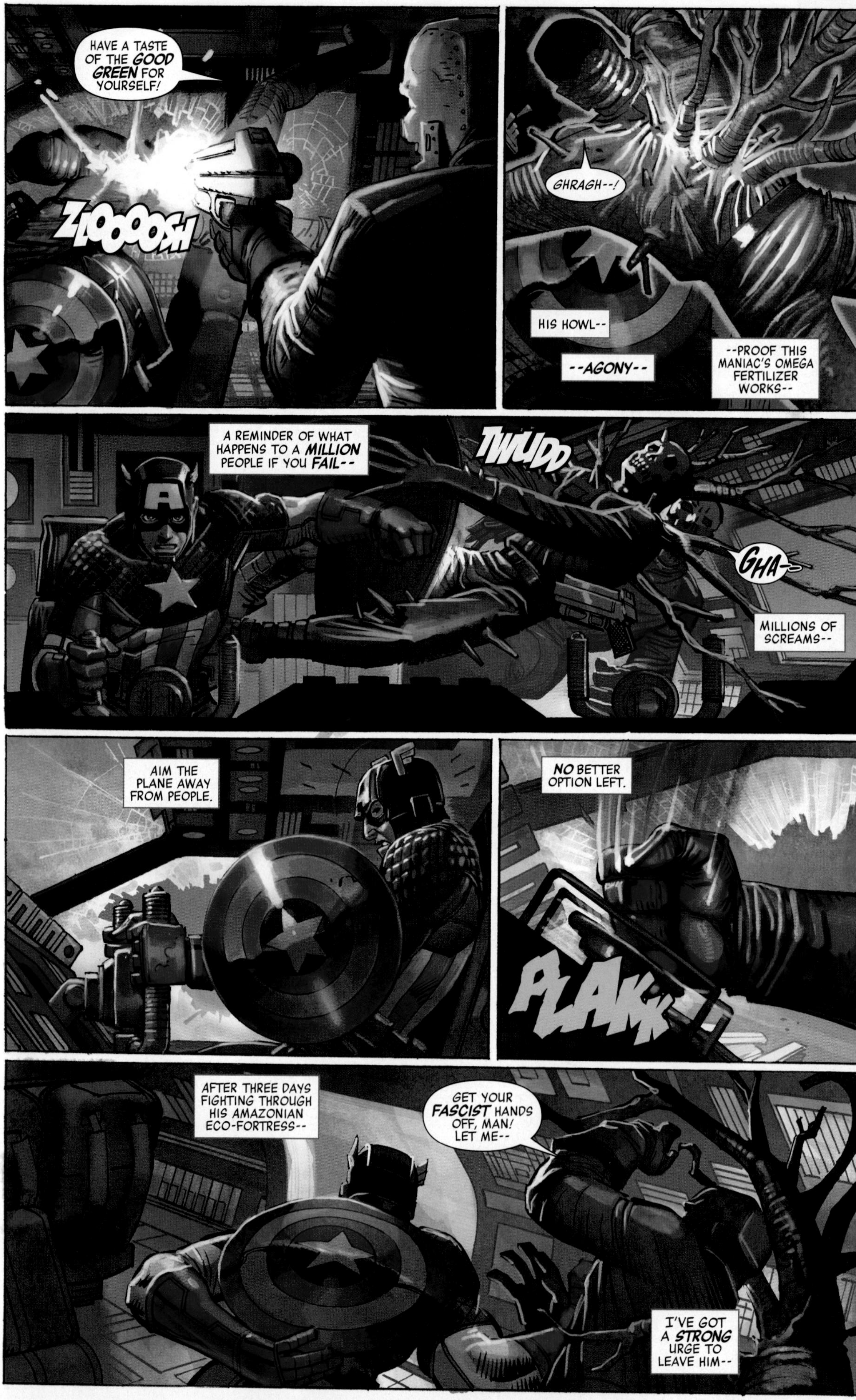
HAVE A TASTE OF THE GOOD GREEN FOR YOURSELF!
ZIOOOOSH
GHRAGH--!
HIS HOWL--
--AGONY--
--PROOF THIS MANIAC'S OMEGA FERTILIZER WORKS--
A REMINDER OF WHAT HAPPENS TO A MILLION PEOPLE IF YOU FAIL--
TWUDD
GHA-
MILLIONS OF SCREAMS--
AIM THE PLANE AWAY FROM PEOPLE.
NO BETTER OPTION LEFT.
PLAKK
AFTER THREE DAYS FIGHTING THROUGH HIS AMAZONIAN ECO-FORTRESS--
GET YOUR FASCIST HANDS OFF, MAN! LET ME--
I'VE GOT A STRONG URGE TO LEAVE HIM--

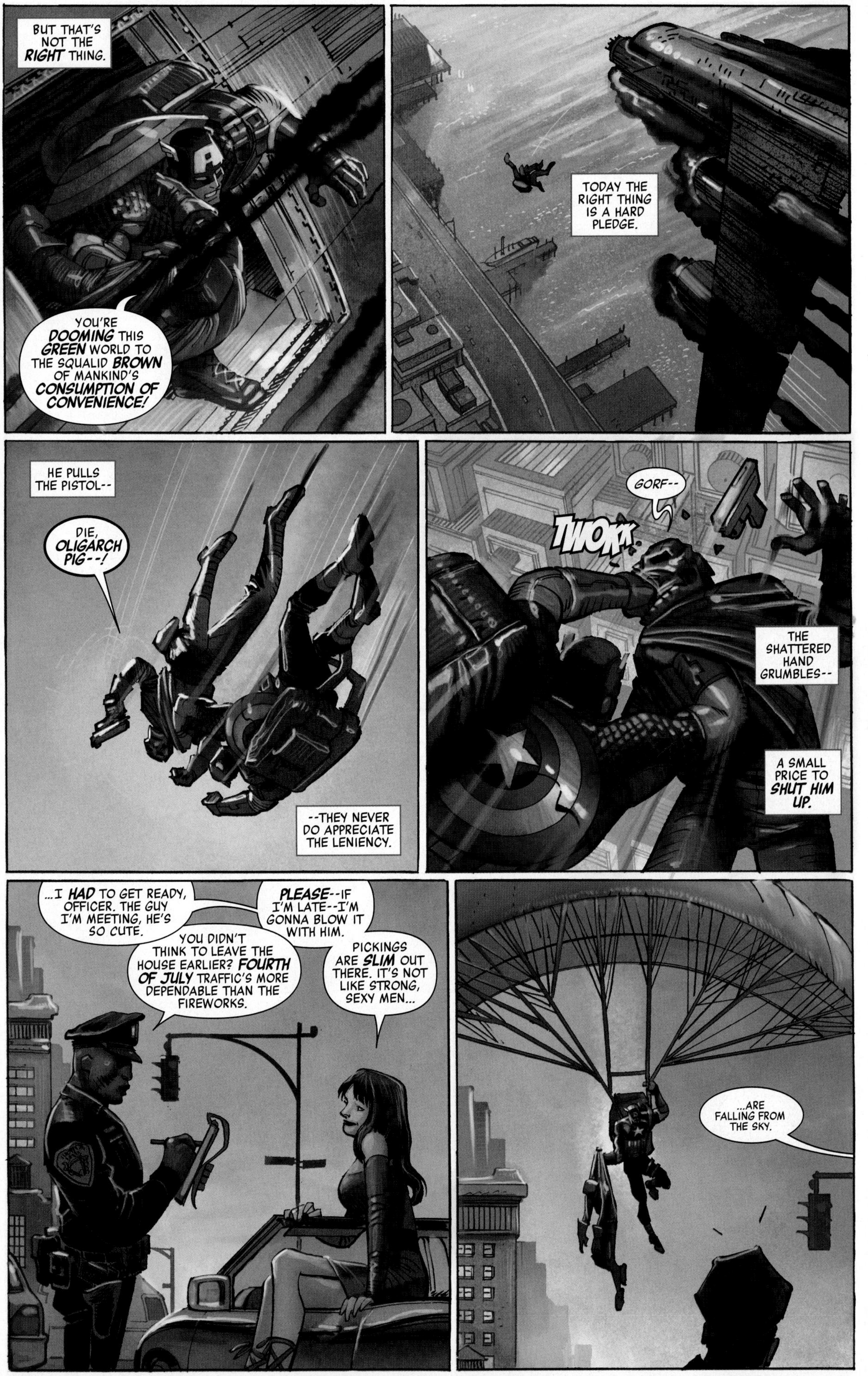

BUT THAT'S NOT THE RIGHT THING.
YOU'RE DOOMING THIS GREEN WORLD TO THE SQUALID BROWN OF MANKIND'S CONSUMPTION OF CONVENIENCE!
TODAY THE RIGHT THING IS A HARD PLEDGE.
HE PULLS THE PISTOL--
DIE, OLIGARCH PIG--!
--THEY NEVER DO APPRECIATE THE LENIENCY.
GORF--
TWOKK
THE SHATTERED HAND GRUMBLES--
A SMALL PRICE TO SHUT HIM UP.
...I HAD TO GET READY, OFFICER. THE GUY I'M MEETING, HE'S SO CUTE.
PLEASE--IF I'M LATE--I'M GONNA BLOW IT WITH HIM.
YOU DIDN'T THINK TO LEAVE THE HOUSE EARLIER? FOURTH OF JULY TRAFFIC'S MORE DEPENDABLE THAN THE FIREWORKS.
PICKINGS ARE SLIM OUT THERE. IT'S NOT LIKE STRONG, SEXY MEN...
...ARE FALLING FROM THE SKY.

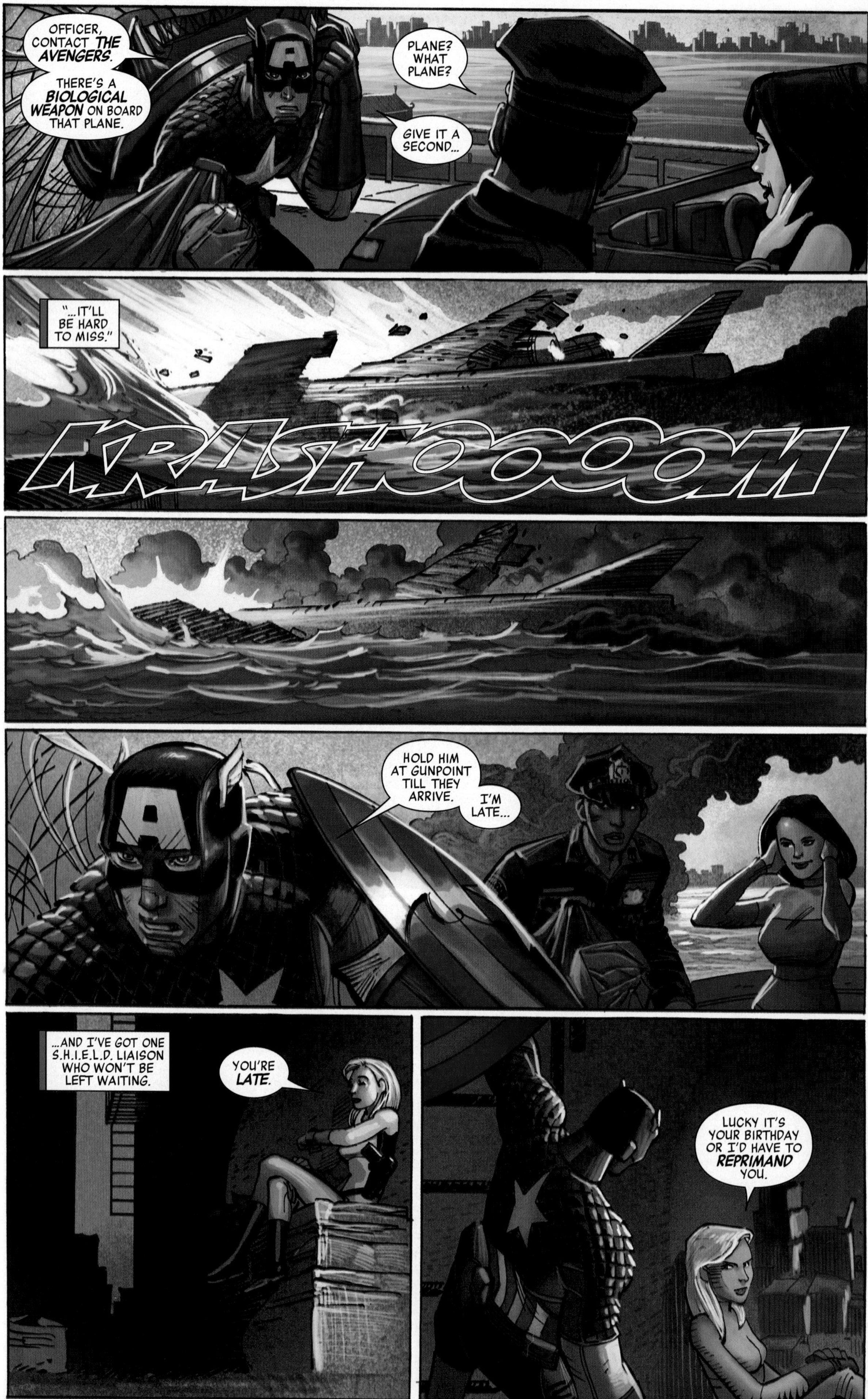
OFFICER, CONTACT THE AVENGERS.
THERE'S A BIOLOGICAL WEAPON ON BOARD THAT PLANE.
PLANE? WHAT PLANE?
GIVE IT A SECOND...
"...IT'LL BE HARD TO MISS."
KRASHOOOOM
HOLD HIM AT GUNPOINT TILL THEY ARRIVE.
I'M LATE...
...AND I'VE GOT ONE S.H.I.E.L.D. LIAISON WHO WON'T BE LEFT WAITING.
YOU'RE LATE.
LUCKY IT'S YOUR BIRTHDAY OR I'D HAVE TO REPRIMAND YOU.

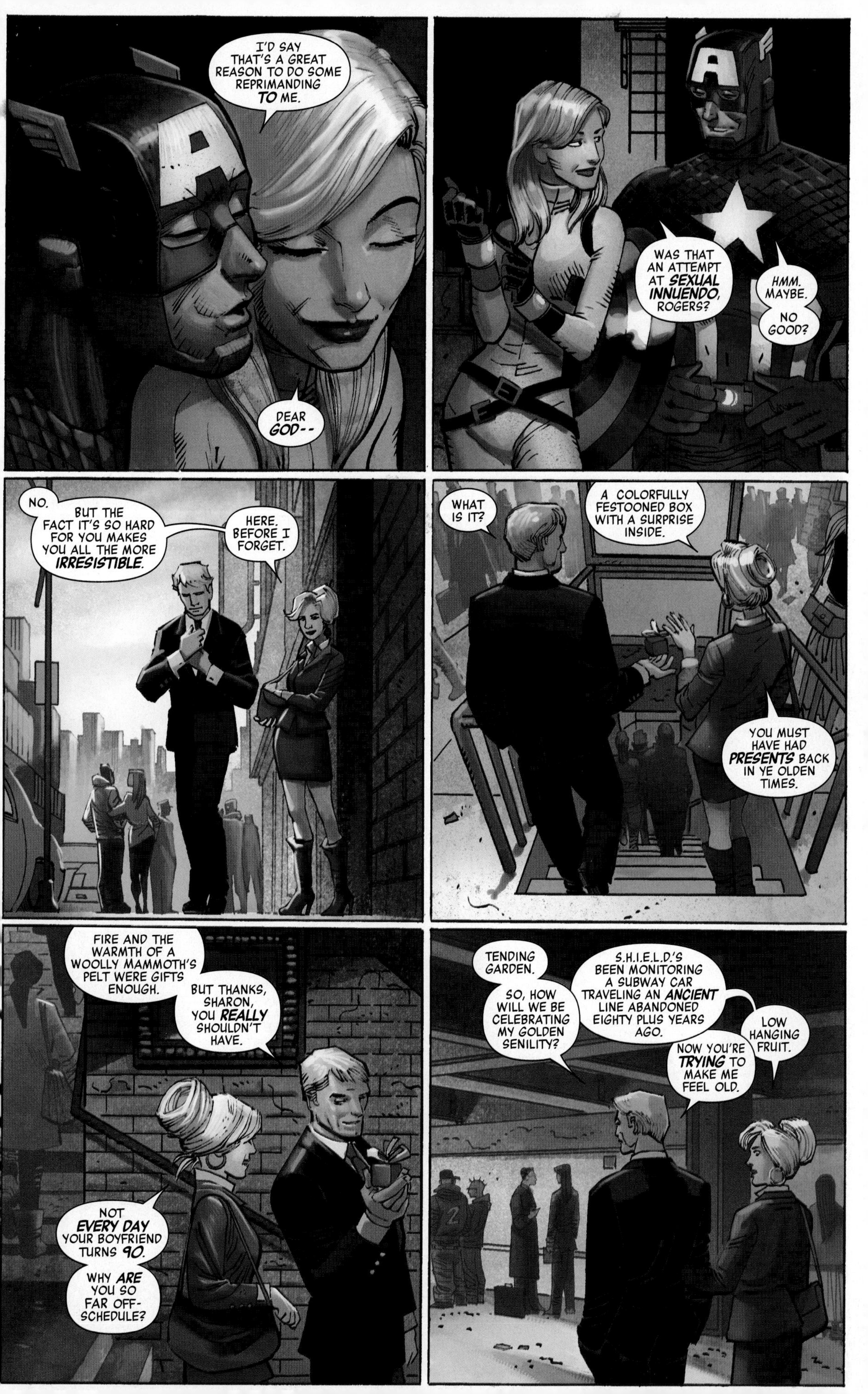
I'D SAY THAT'S A GREAT REASON TO DO SOME REPRIMANDING TO ME.
DEAR GOD--
WAS THAT AN ATTEMPT AT SEXUAL INNUENDO, ROGERS?
HMM. MAYBE.
NO GOOD?
NO.
BUT THE FACT IT'S SO HARD FOR YOU MAKES YOU ALL THE MORE IRRESISTIBLE.
HERE. BEFORE I FORGET.
WHAT IS IT?
A COLORFULLY FESTOONED BOX WITH A SURPRISE INSIDE.
YOU MUST HAVE HAD PRESENTS BACK IN YE OLDEN TIMES.
FIRE AND THE WARMTH OF A WOOLLY MAMMOTH'S PELT WERE GIFTS ENOUGH.
BUT THANKS, SHARON, YOU REALLY SHOULDN'T HAVE.
NOT EVERY DAY YOUR BOYFRIEND TURNS 90.
WHY ARE YOU SO FAR OFF-SCHEDULE?
TENDING GARDEN.
SO, HOW WILL WE BE CELEBRATING MY GOLDEN SENILITY?
S.H.I.E.L.D.'S BEEN MONITORING A SUBWAY CAR TRAVELING AN ANCIENT LINE ABANDONED EIGHTY PLUS YEARS AGO.
LOW HANGING FRUIT.
NOW YOU'RE TRYING TO MAKE ME FEEL OLD.

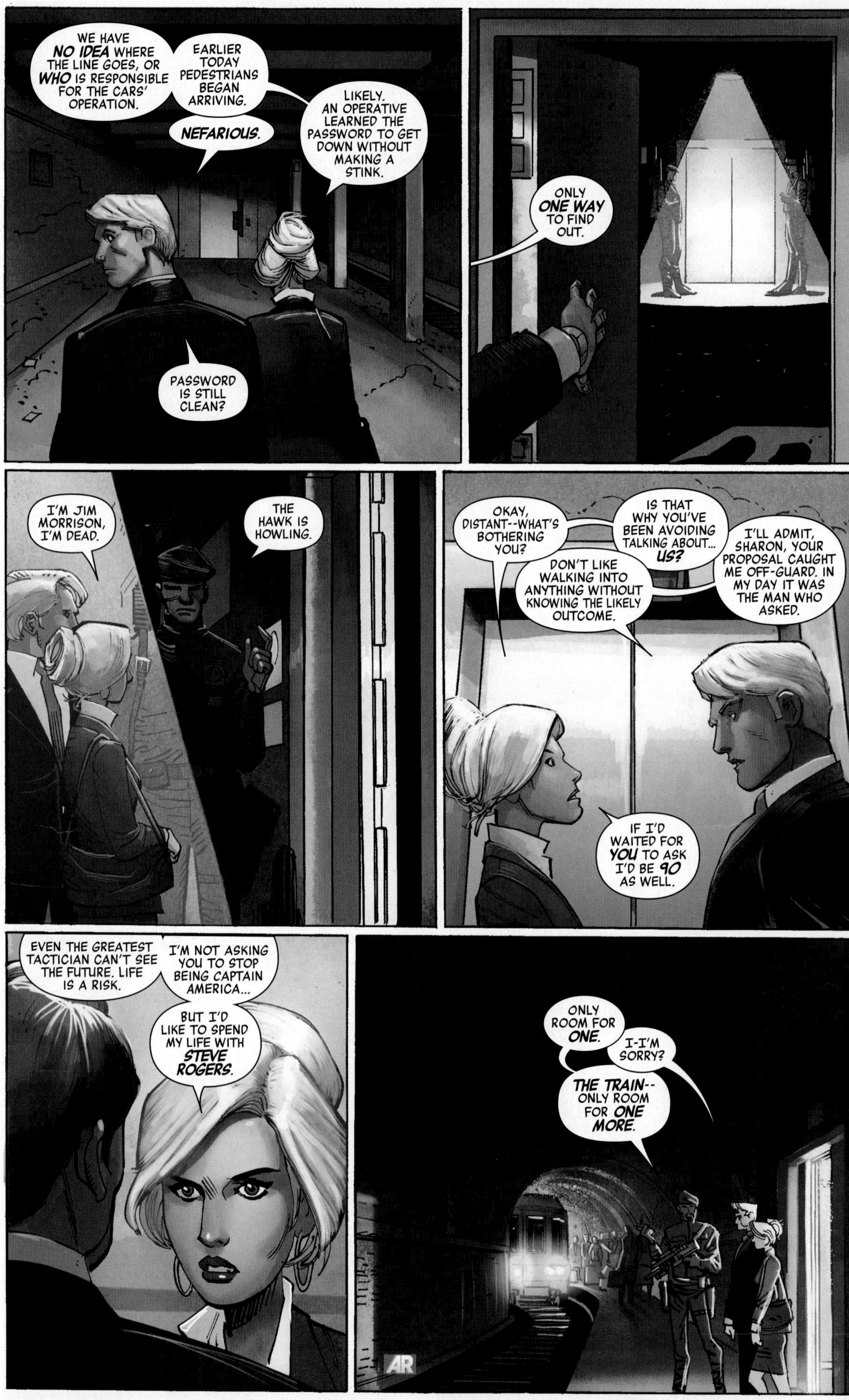
WE HAVE NO IDEA WHERE THE LINE GOES, OR WHO IS RESPONSIBLE FOR THE CARS' OPERATION.
EARLIER TODAY PEDESTRIANS BEGAN ARRIVING.
NEFARIOUS.
LIKELY. AN OPERATIVE LEARNED THE PASSWORD TO GET DOWN WITHOUT MAKING A STINK.
PASSWORD IS STILL CLEAN?
ONLY ONE WAY TO FIND OUT.
I'M JIM MORRISON, I'M DEAD.
THE HAWK IS HOWLING.
OKAY, DISTANT--WHAT'S BOTHERING YOU?
IS THAT WHY YOU'VE BEEN AVOIDING TALKING ABOUT... US?
DON'T LIKE WALKING INTO ANYTHING WITHOUT KNOWING THE LIKELY OUTCOME.
I'LL ADMIT, SHARON, YOUR PROPOSAL CAUGHT ME OFF-GUARD. IN MY DAY IT WAS THE MAN WHO ASKED.
IF I'D WAITED FOR YOU TO ASK I'D BE 90 AS WELL.
EVEN THE GREATEST TACTICIAN CAN'T SEE THE FUTURE. LIFE IS A RISK.
I'M NOT ASKING YOU TO STOP BEING CAPTAIN AMERICA...
BUT I'D LIKE TO SPEND MY LIFE WITH STEVE ROGERS.
ONLY ROOM FOR ONE.
I-I'M SORRY?
THE TRAIN-- ONLY ROOM FOR ONE MORE.
AR

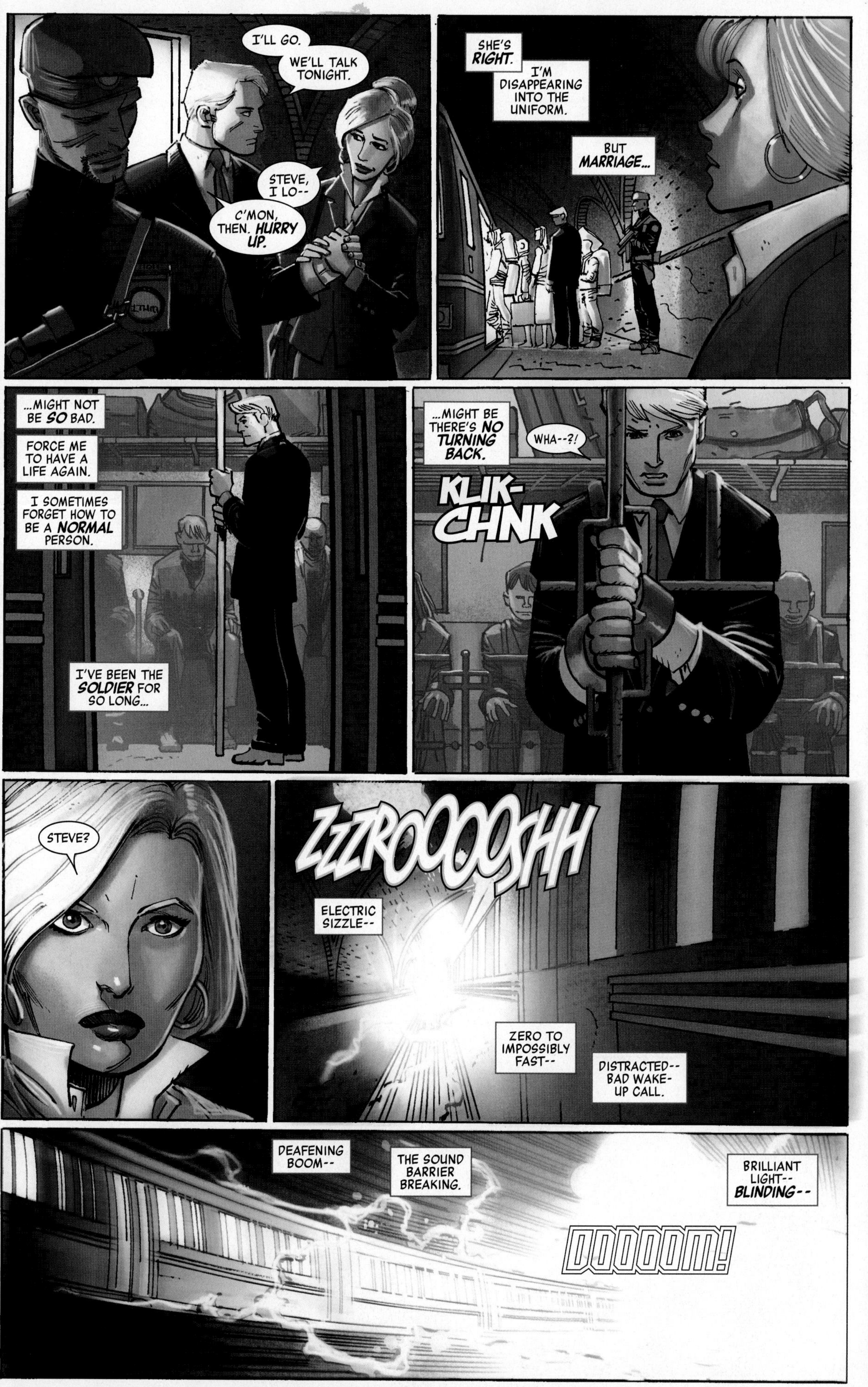

I'LL GO.
WE'LL TALK TONIGHT.
STEVE, I LO--
C'MON, THEN. HURRY UP.
SHE'S RIGHT.
I'M DISAPPEARING INTO THE UNIFORM.
BUT MARRIAGE...
...MIGHT NOT BE SO BAD.
FORCE ME TO HAVE A LIFE AGAIN.
I SOMETIMES FORGET HOW TO BE A NORMAL PERSON.
I'VE BEEN THE SOLDIER FOR SO LONG...
...MIGHT BE THERE'S NO TURNING BACK.
WHA--?!
KLIK-CHNK
STEVE?
ZZZROOOOOSHH
ELECTRIC SIZZLE--
ZERO TO IMPOSSIBLY FAST--
DISTRACTED--BAD WAKE-UP CALL.
DEAFENING BOOM--
THE SOUND BARRIER BREAKING.
BRILLIANT LIGHT--BLINDING--
DOOOOOM!

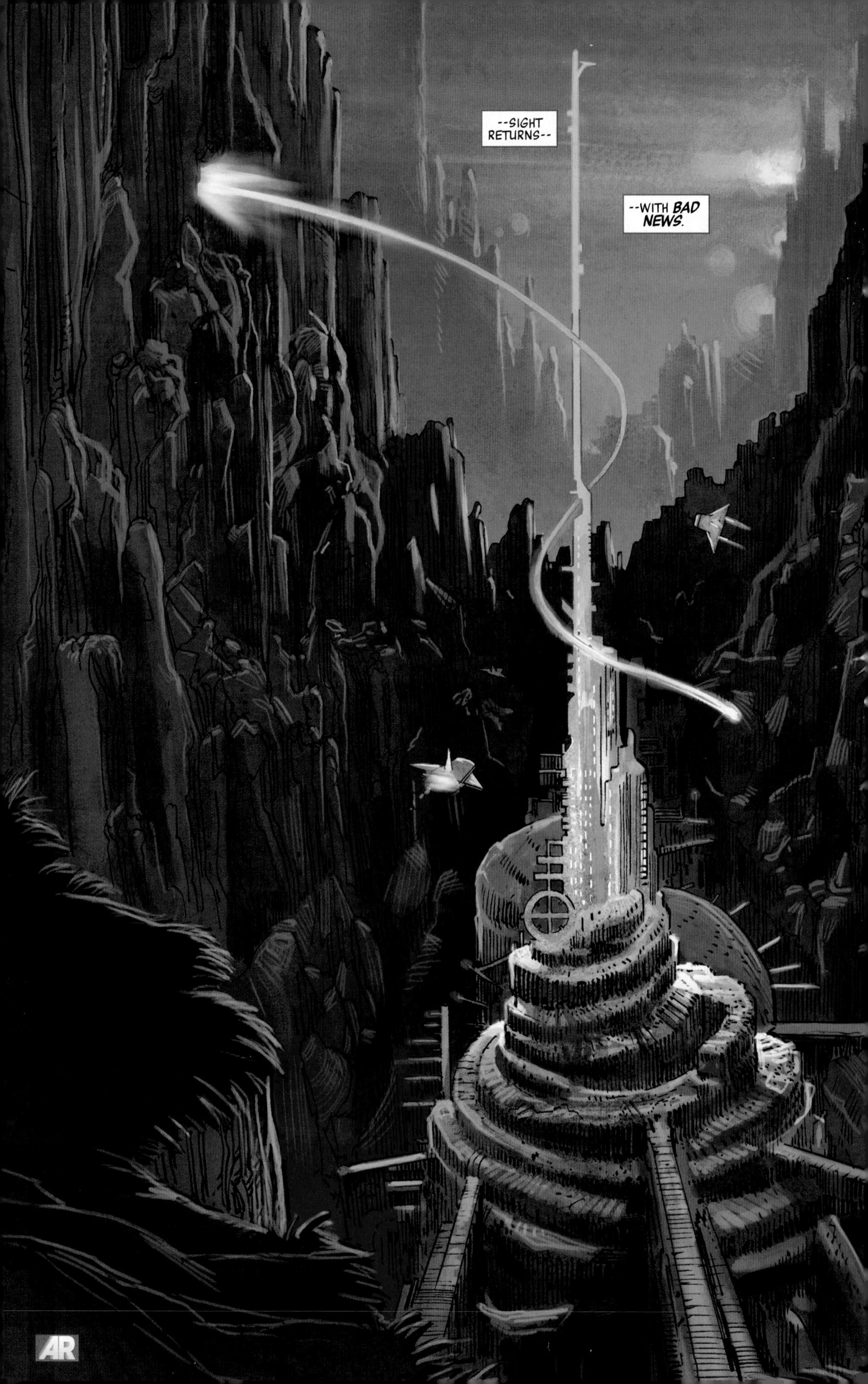
--SIGHT RETURNS--
--WITH BAD NEWS.

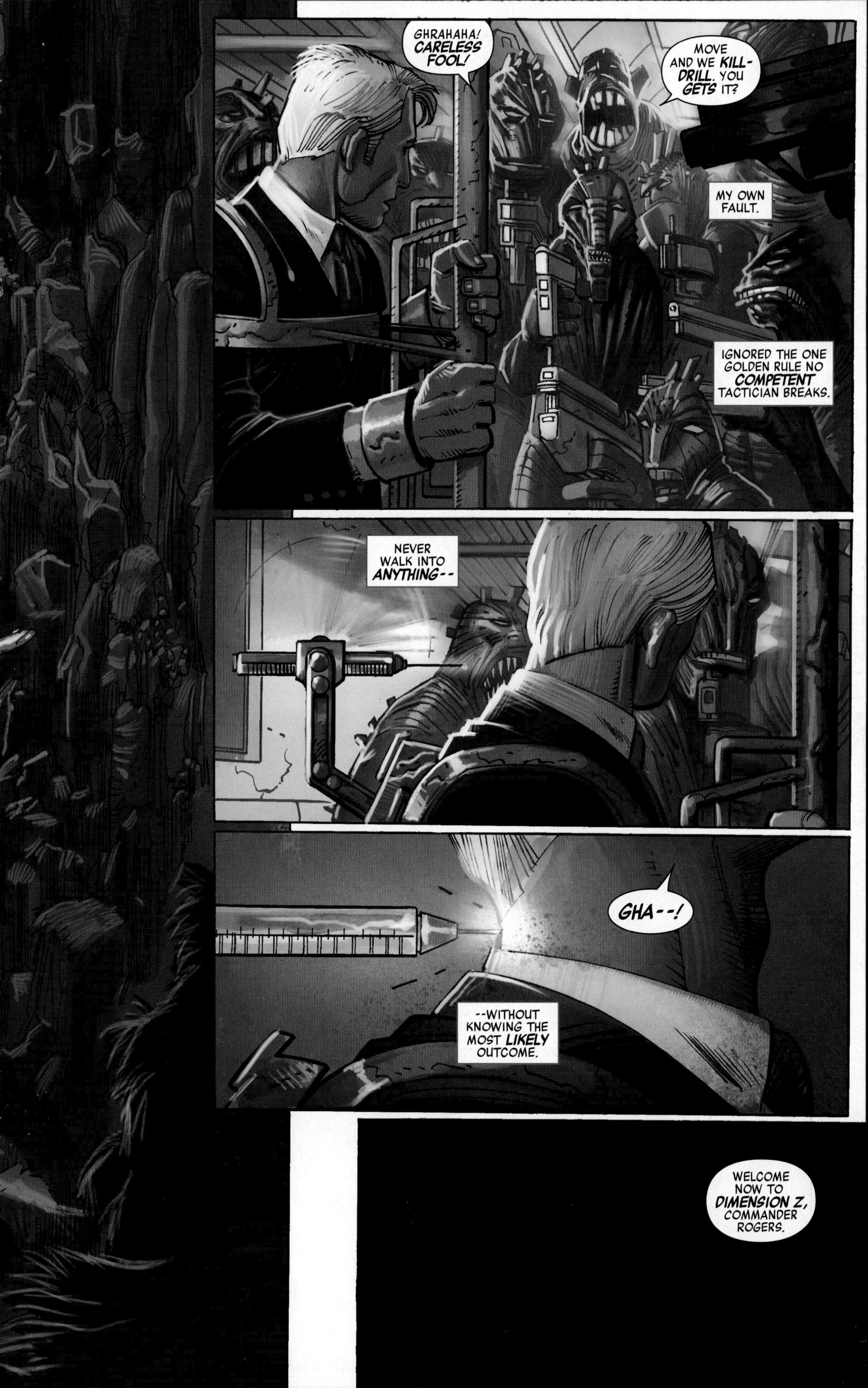
GHRAHAHA! CARELESS FOOL!
MOVE AND WE KILL-DRILL. YOU GETS IT?
MY OWN FAULT.
IGNORED THE ONE GOLDEN RULE NO COMPETENT TACTICIAN BREAKS.
NEVER WALK INTO ANYTHING--
GHA--!
--WITHOUT KNOWING THE MOST LIKELY OUTCOME.
WELCOME NOW TO DIMENSION Z, COMMANDER ROGERS.

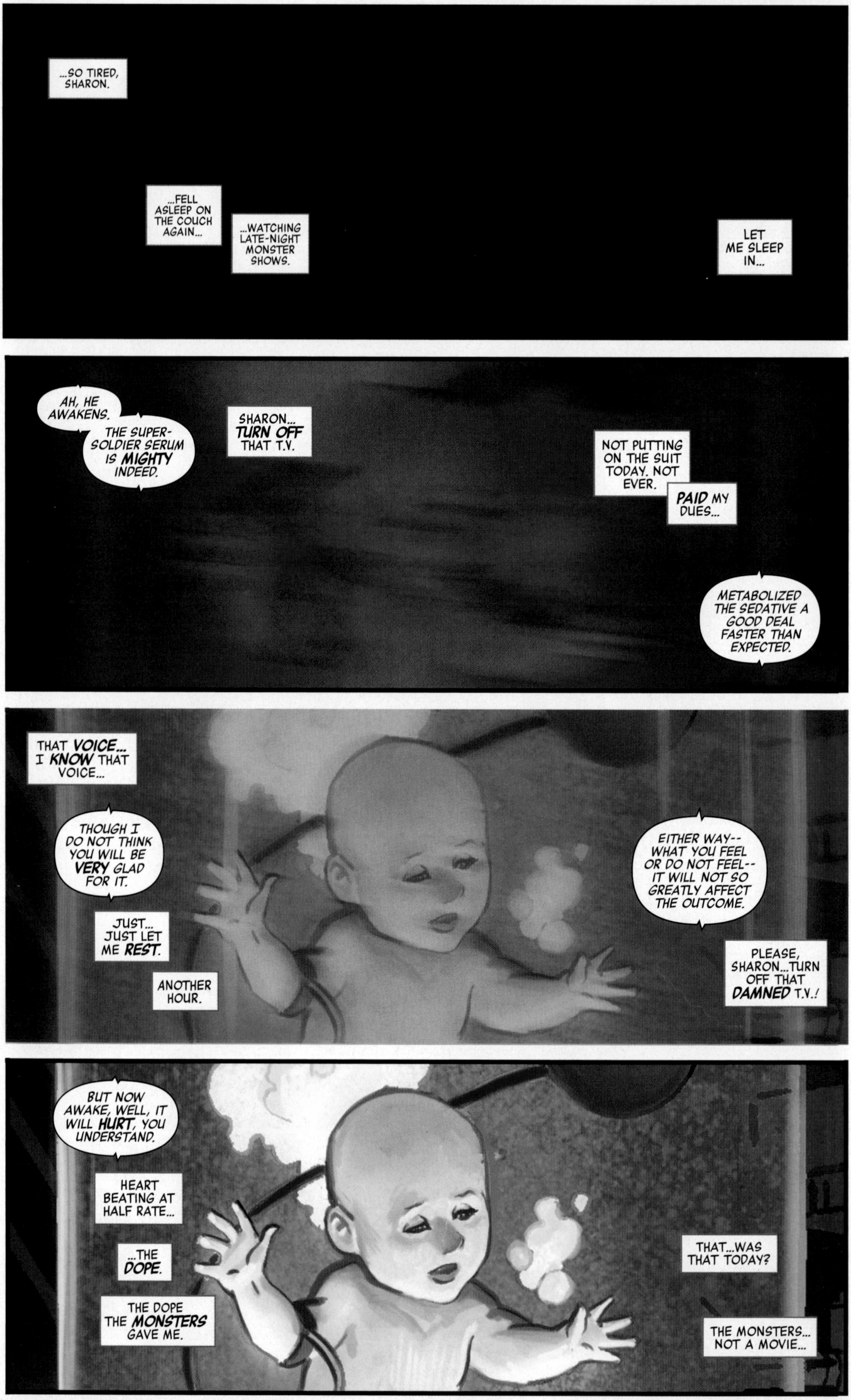
...SO TIRED, SHARON.
...FELL ASLEEP ON THE COUCH AGAIN...
...WATCHING LATE-NIGHT MONSTER SHOWS.
LET ME SLEEP IN...
AH, HE AWAKENS.
THE SUPER-SOLDIER SERUM IS MIGHTY INDEED.
SHARON... TURN OFF THAT T.V.
NOT PUTTING ON THE SUIT TODAY. NOT EVER.
PAID MY DUES...
METABOLIZED THE SEDATIVE A GOOD DEAL FASTER THAN EXPECTED.
THAT VOICE... I KNOW THAT VOICE...
THOUGH I DO NOT THINK YOU WILL BE VERY GLAD FOR IT.
JUST... JUST LET ME REST.
ANOTHER HOUR.
EITHER WAY-- WHAT YOU FEEL OR DO NOT FEEL-- IT WILL NOT SO GREATLY AFFECT THE OUTCOME.
PLEASE, SHARON...TURN OFF THAT DAMNED T.V.!
BUT NOW AWAKE, WELL, IT WILL HURT, YOU UNDERSTAND.
HEART BEATING AT HALF RATE...
...THE DOPE.
THE DOPE THE MONSTERS GAVE ME.
THAT...WAS THAT TODAY?
THE MONSTERS... NOT A MOVIE...

...THE MONSTERS WERE REAL.

YOU CAN'T KNOW THE JOY I FELT TO SEE YOU'D FOLLOWED THE TRAIL I LEFT.

I HAVE BEEN SO EAGERLY ANTICIPATING YOUR ARRIVAL, AND FOR SOME TIME.

YOU ARE OVERCONFIDENT, ROGERS.

MADE THIS ALL TOO EASY.

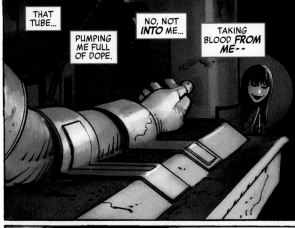

THAT TUBE...

PUMPING ME FULL OF DOPE.

NO, NOT INTO ME...

TAKING BLOOD FROM ME--

I WOULD BE LYING TO TELL YOU I WON'T FEEL SOME JOY WATCHING YOU WRITHE.

AND YOU WILL WRITHE.

DEAR, GOD--

WE SHOULD WASTE NO TIME.

AND IT HITS ME--

GHRAH-YERAGHH!

SYNTHESIZED WITH A HUMAN TONE--

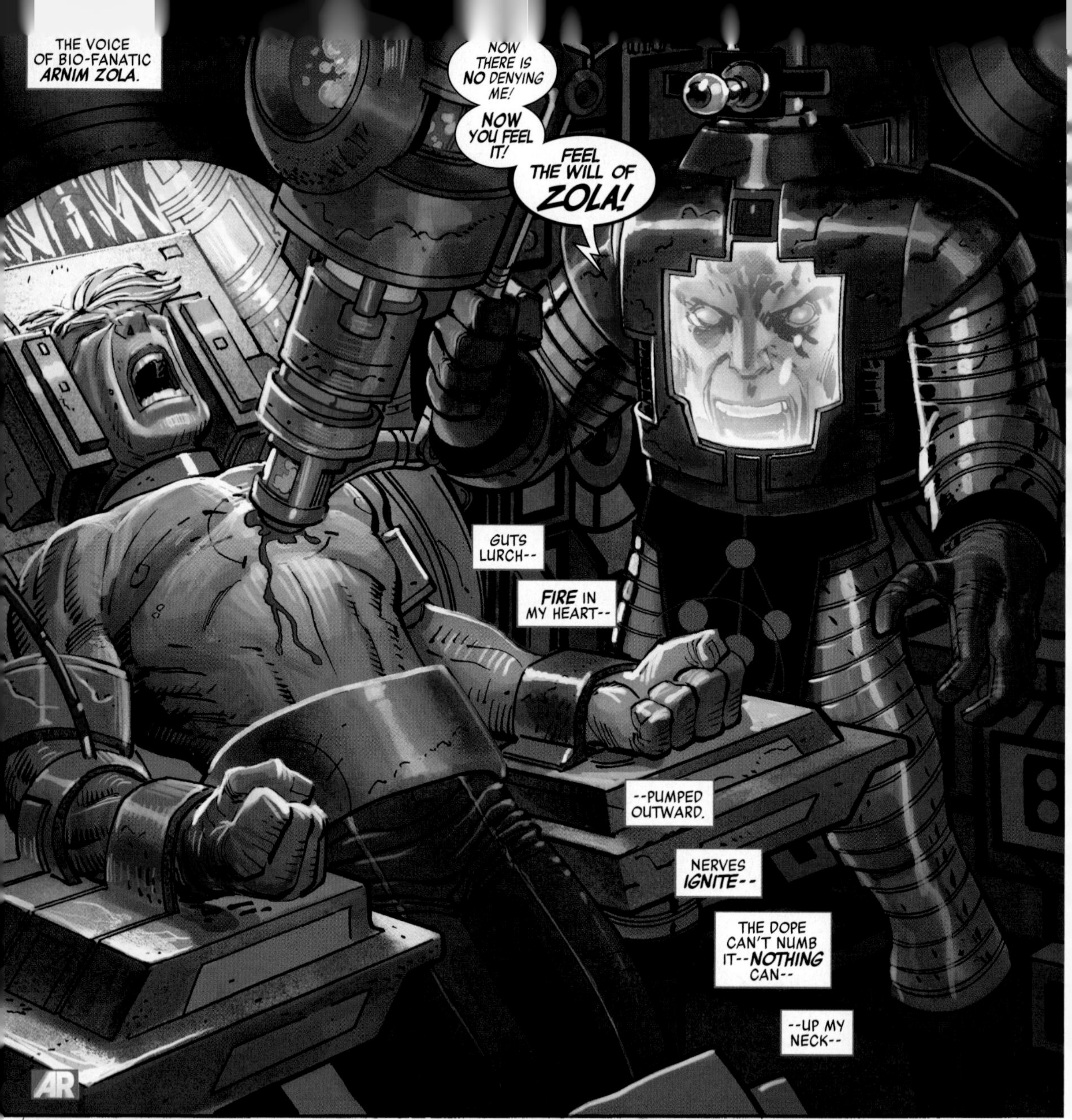
THE VOICE OF BIO-FANATIC ARNIM ZOLA.
NOW THERE IS NO DENYING ME!
NOW YOU FEEL IT!
FEEL THE WILL OF ZOLA!
GUTS LURCH--
FIRE IN MY HEART--
--PUMPED OUTWARD.
NERVES IGNITE--
THE DOPE CAN'T NUMB IT--NOTHING CAN--
--UP MY NECK--

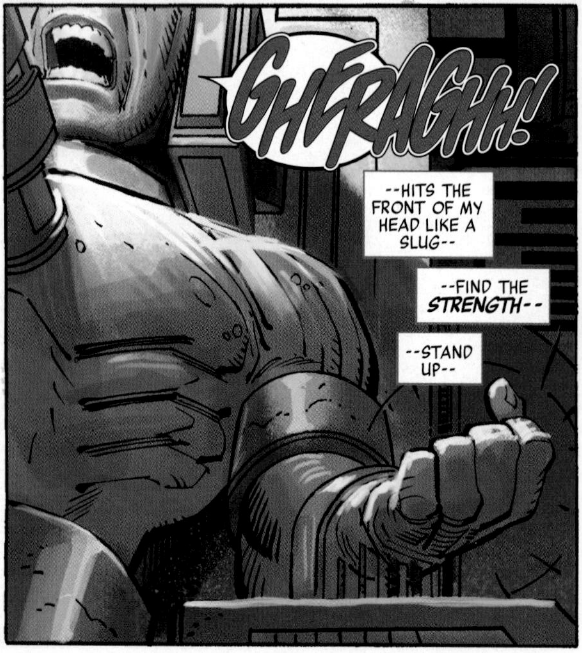
GHERAGHH!
--HITS THE FRONT OF MY HEAD LIKE A SLUG--
--FIND THE STRENGTH--
--STAND UP--

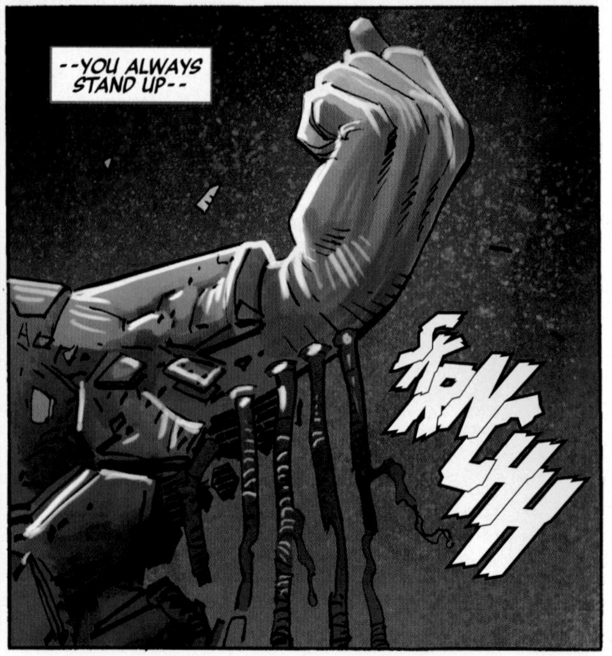
--YOU ALWAYS STAND UP--
SKRNCHH

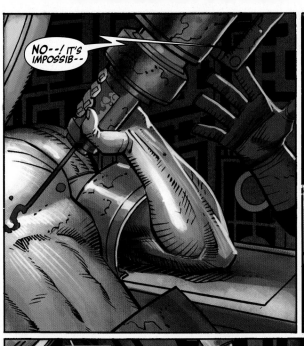

NO--! IT'S IMPOSSIB--

TWOK

AGH--!

GET UP--

--STAY AWAKE--

PAIN OVERLOAD--

--STAY AWAKE--

I TRIED TO TELL! WHY LEAVE HIS BODY WITH ARMS?!

MUSCLES DON'T RESPOND--

--ASLEEP FROM THE DOPE.

PUSH THROUGH THE MUD--

--GET OUT--

GET AWAY FROM HERE--

STOP HIM!

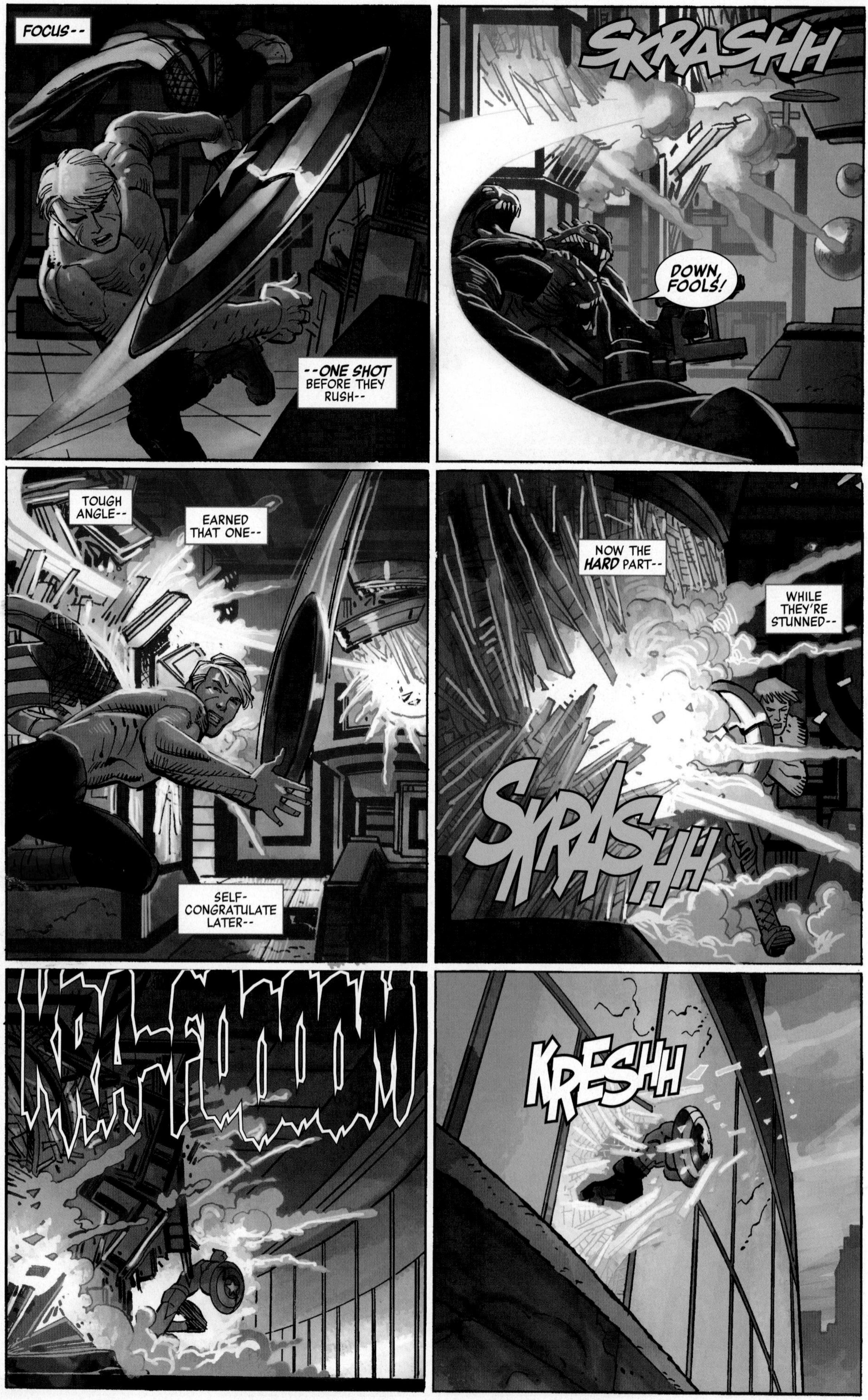
FOCUS--
--ONE SHOT BEFORE THEY RUSH--
SKRASHH
DOWN, FOOLS!
TOUGH ANGLE--
EARNED THAT ONE--
SELF-CONGRATULATE LATER--
NOW THE HARD PART--
WHILE THEY'RE STUNNED--
SKRASHH
KRESHH

I'VE HAD SOME PRACTICE--

--BUT IT'S A *LUCKY* FALL.

OOF--!

FAPP

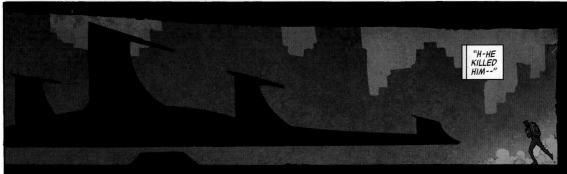

"H-HE KILLED HIM--"

--KILLED *MY BOY.*

DECADES DESIGNING HIM--

--GONE.

MY PERFECT SON...

...HE KILLED YOUR BABY BROTHER, DEAR JET.

PAPA...?

I ONLY WANTED THE SUPER-SOLDIER SERUM FOR YOU BOTH...

...AND NOW MY BOY IS DEAD.

LISTEN TO ME, MUTATES OF ZOLANDIA--

I WANT CAPTAIN AMERICA BROUGHT TO ME!

ALIVE AND UNHARMED!

"HE WILL LIVE TO SUFFER *BEYOND IMAGINING.*"

VOOOOSH

FIREWORKS--

--TUNNEL VISION--

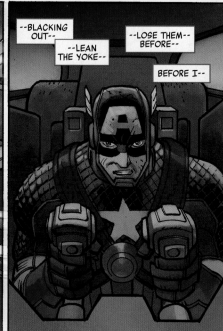

--BLACKING OUT--

--LEAN THE YOKE--

--LOSE THEM-- BEFORE--

BEFORE I--

DKH-BOOOOOOOM

CAN'T--

GET--

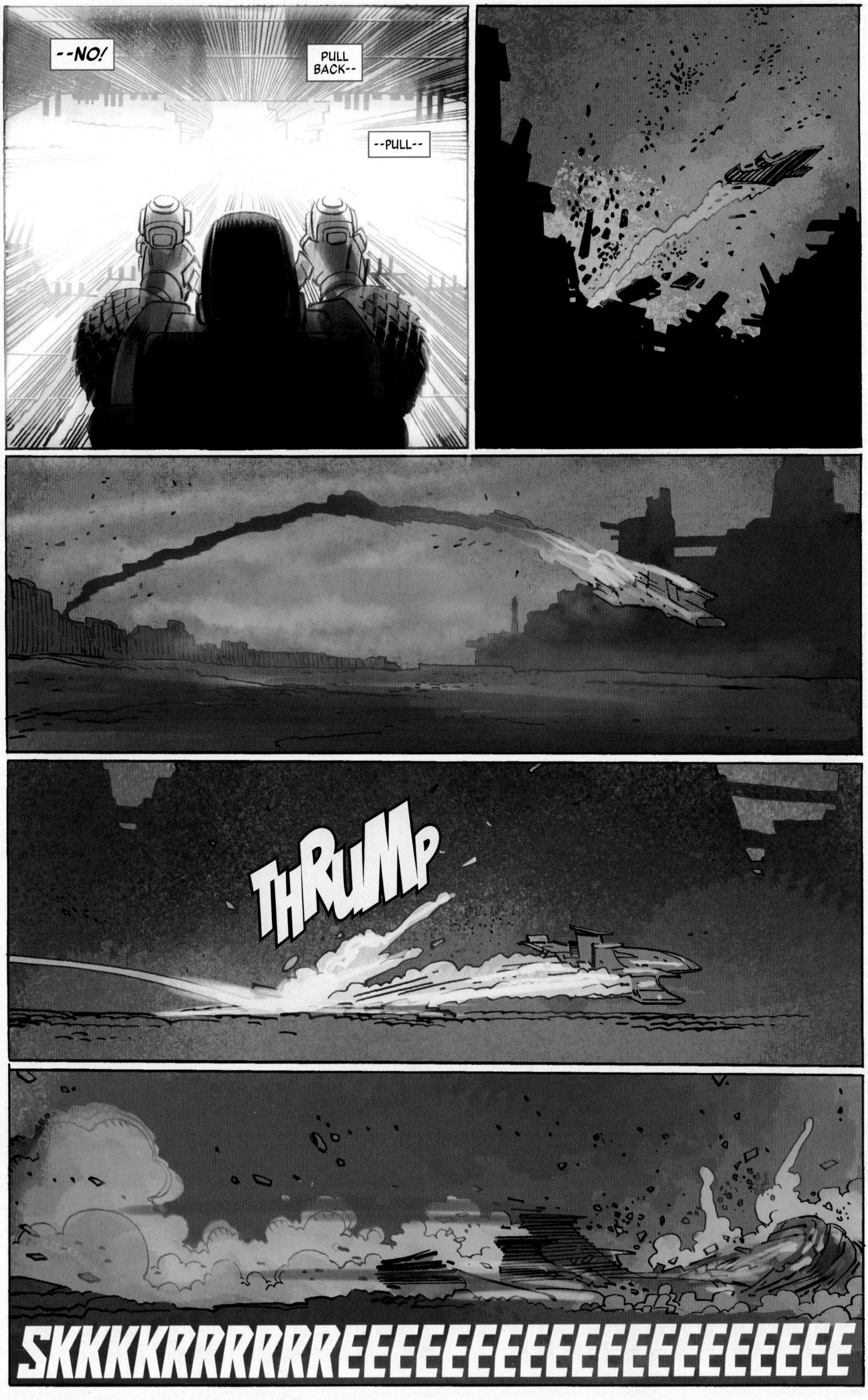
--NO!
PULL BACK--
--PULL--
THRUMP
SKKKKRRRRRRREEEEEEEEEEEEEEEEEEEEE

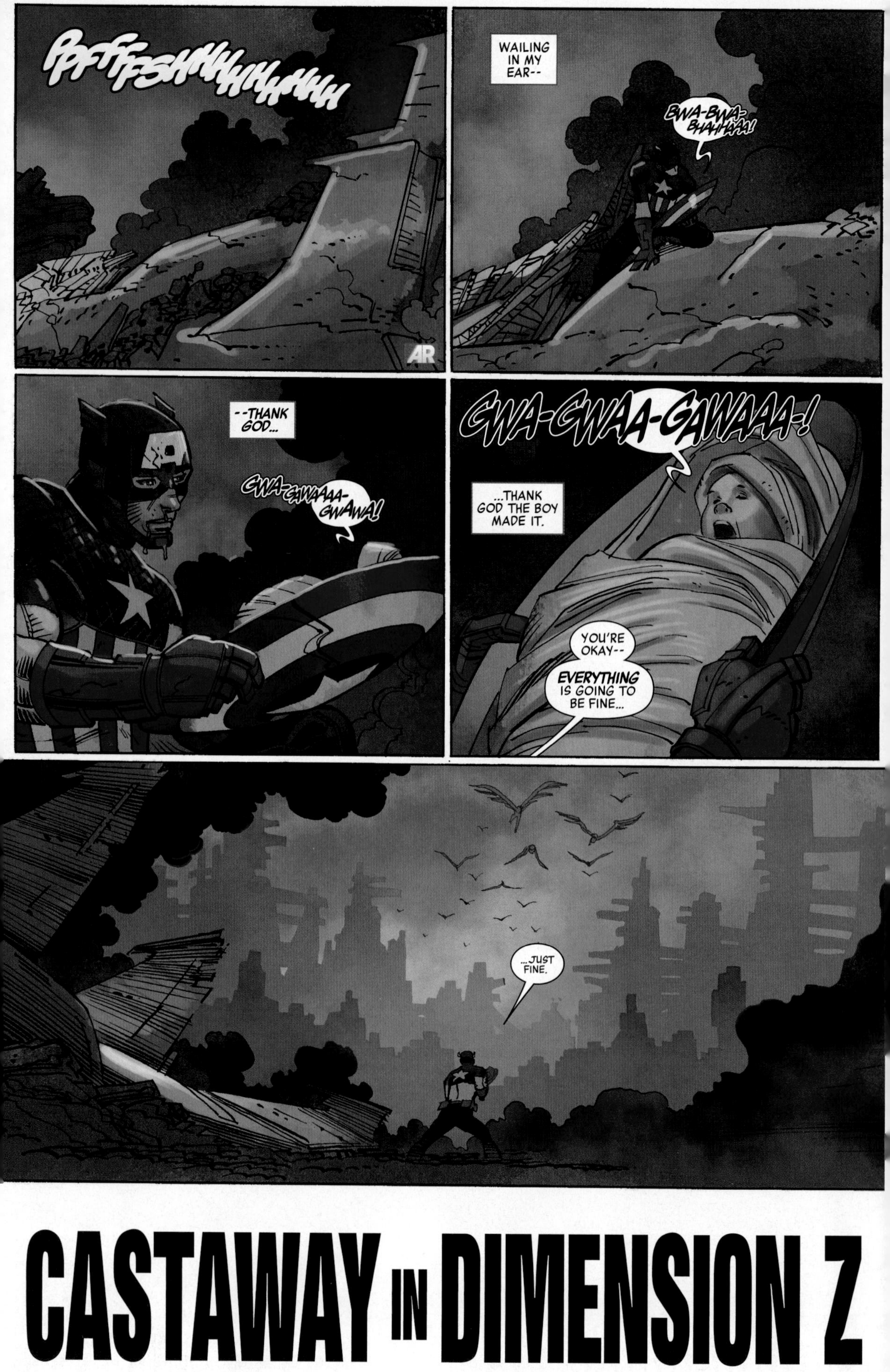
PPFFFSHHHHHHHHHH
WAILING IN MY EAR--
BWA-BWA-BHAHHAAA!
--THANK GOD...
GWA-GAWAAAA-GWAWA!
GWA-GWAA-GAWAAA-!
...THANK GOD THE BOY MADE IT.
YOU'RE OKAY--
EVERYTHING IS GOING TO BE FINE...
...JUST FINE.

CASTAWAY IN DIMENSION Z

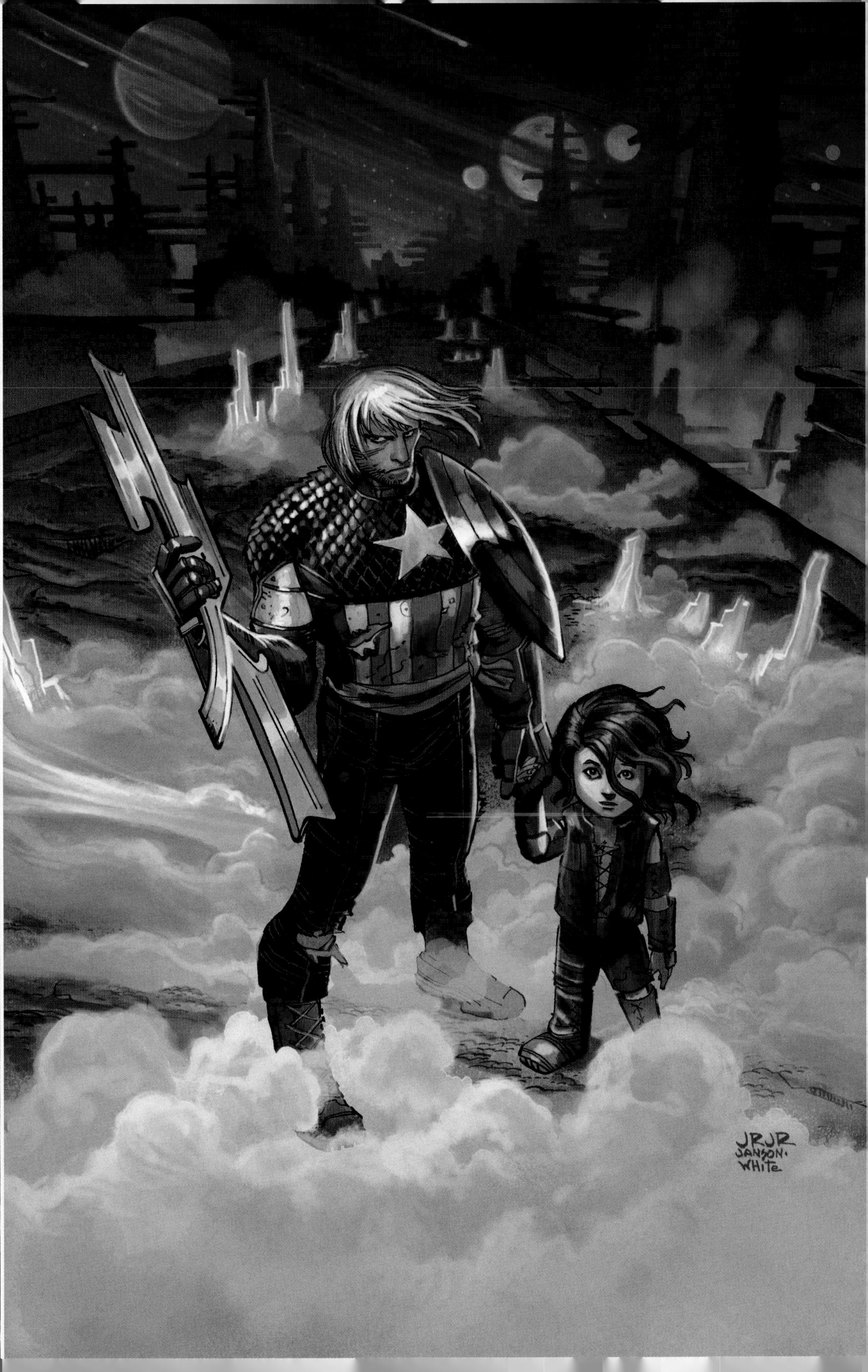
JRJR
JANSON.
WHITE

ONE YEAR LATER.

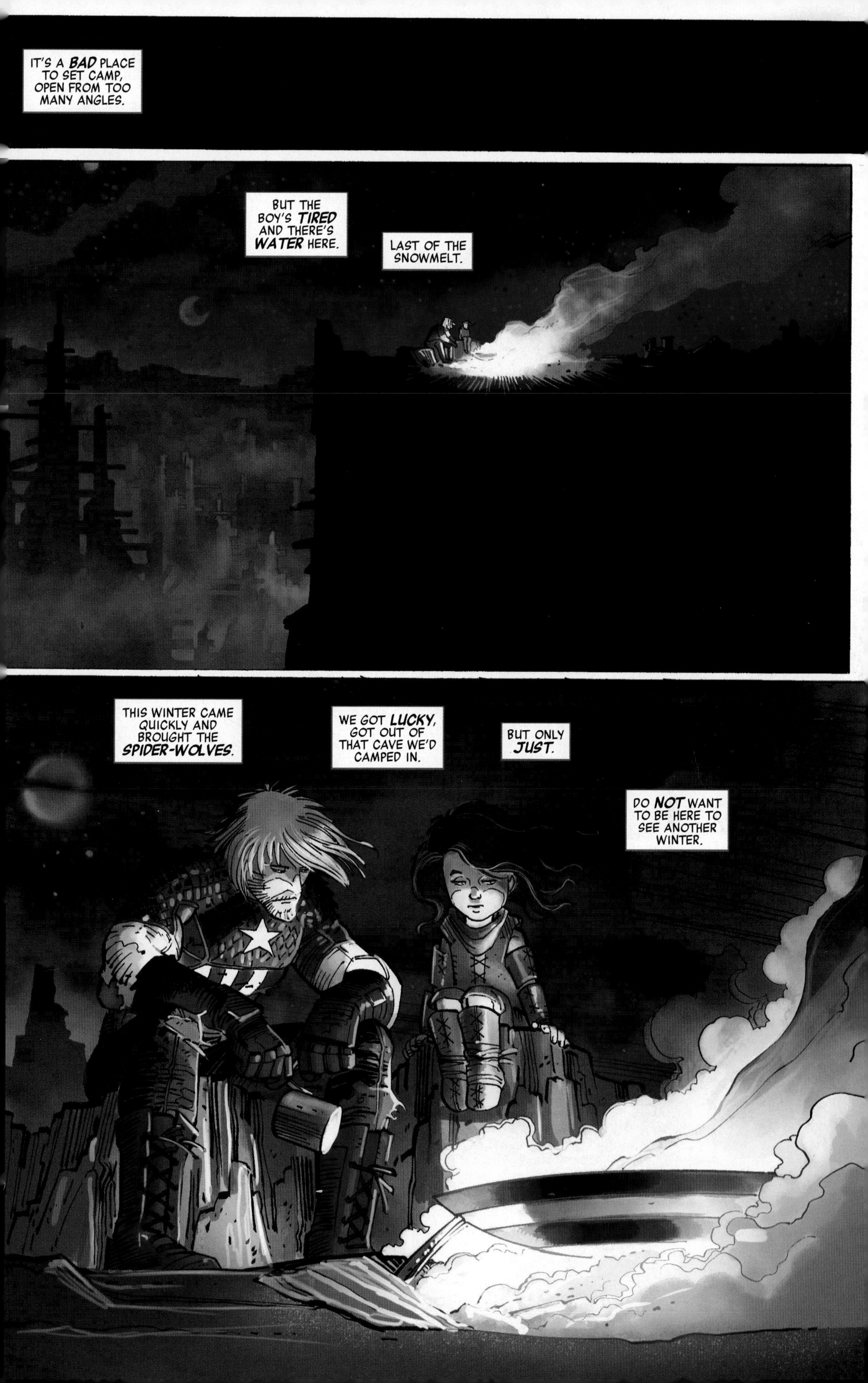
IT'S A BAD PLACE TO SET CAMP, OPEN FROM TOO MANY ANGLES.
BUT THE BOY'S TIRED AND THERE'S WATER HERE.
LAST OF THE SNOWMELT.
THIS WINTER CAME QUICKLY AND BROUGHT THE SPIDER-WOLVES.
WE GOT LUCKY, GOT OUT OF THAT CAVE WE'D CAMPED IN.
BUT ONLY JUST.
DO NOT WANT TO BE HERE TO SEE ANOTHER WINTER.

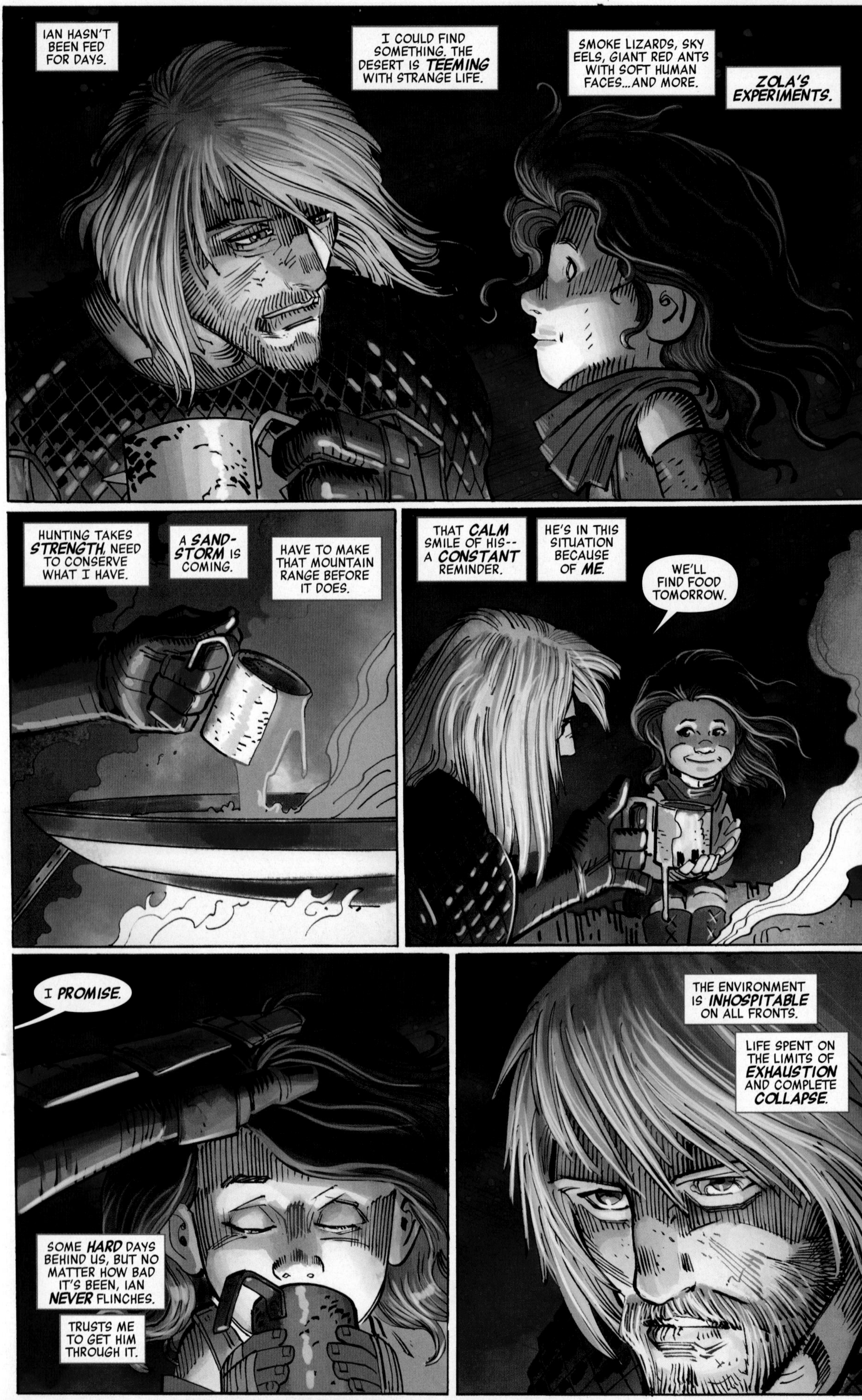
IAN HASN'T BEEN FED FOR DAYS.
I COULD FIND SOMETHING. THE DESERT IS TEEMING WITH STRANGE LIFE.
SMOKE LIZARDS, SKY EELS, GIANT RED ANTS WITH SOFT HUMAN FACES...AND MORE.
ZOLA'S EXPERIMENTS.
HUNTING TAKES STRENGTH, NEED TO CONSERVE WHAT I HAVE.
A SAND-STORM IS COMING.
HAVE TO MAKE THAT MOUNTAIN RANGE BEFORE IT DOES.
THAT CALM SMILE OF HIS-- A CONSTANT REMINDER.
HE'S IN THIS SITUATION BECAUSE OF ME.
WE'LL FIND FOOD TOMORROW.
I PROMISE.
SOME HARD DAYS BEHIND US, BUT NO MATTER HOW BAD IT'S BEEN, IAN NEVER FLINCHES.
TRUSTS ME TO GET HIM THROUGH IT.
THE ENVIRONMENT IS INHOSPITABLE ON ALL FRONTS.
LIFE SPENT ON THE LIMITS OF EXHAUSTION AND COMPLETE COLLAPSE.

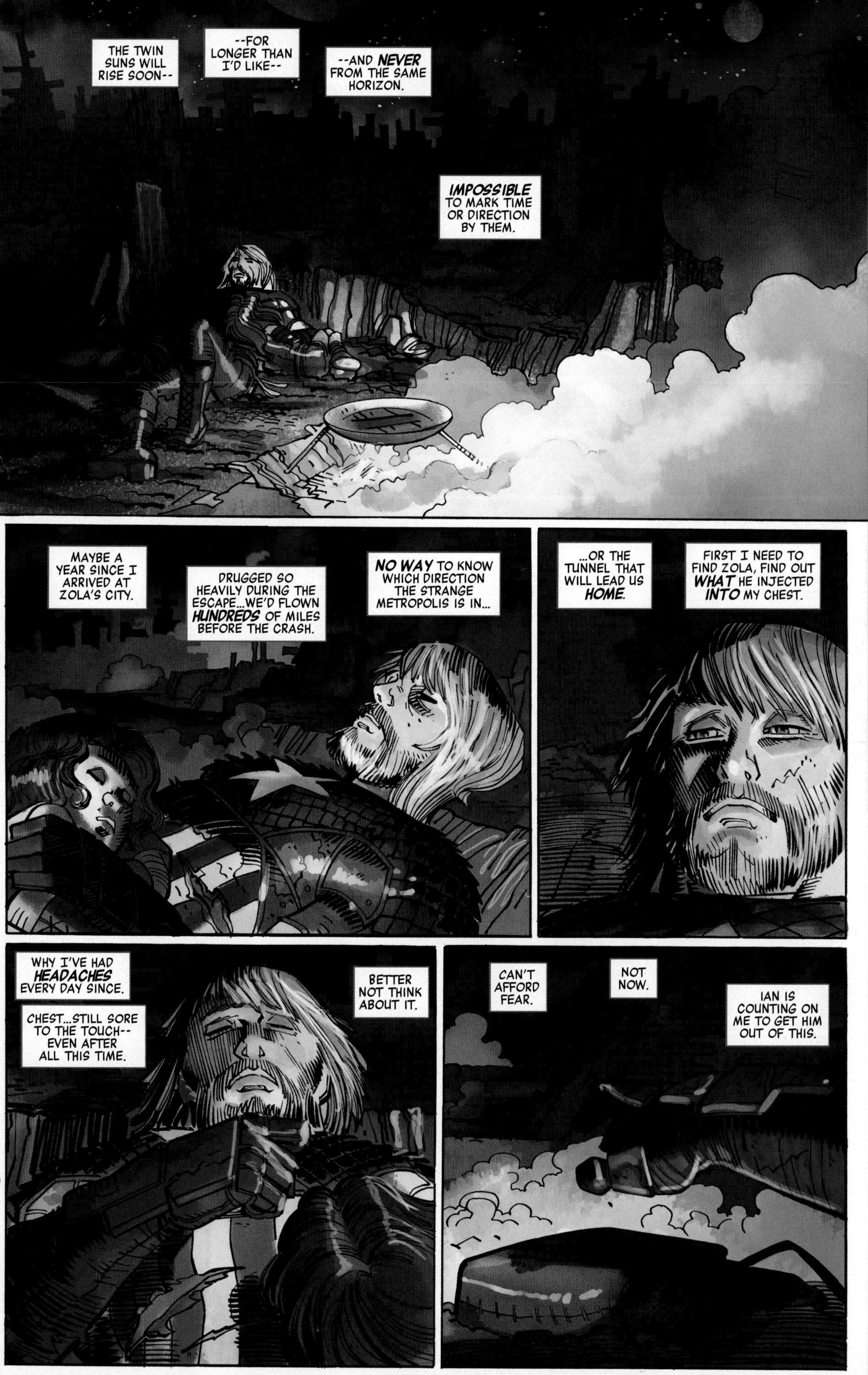
THE TWIN SUNS WILL RISE SOON--
--FOR LONGER THAN I'D LIKE--
--AND NEVER FROM THE SAME HORIZON.
IMPOSSIBLE TO MARK TIME OR DIRECTION BY THEM.
MAYBE A YEAR SINCE I ARRIVED AT ZOLA'S CITY.
DRUGGED SO HEAVILY DURING THE ESCAPE...WE'D FLOWN HUNDREDS OF MILES BEFORE THE CRASH.
NO WAY TO KNOW WHICH DIRECTION THE STRANGE METROPOLIS IS IN...
...OR THE TUNNEL THAT WILL LEAD US HOME.
FIRST I NEED TO FIND ZOLA, FIND OUT WHAT HE INJECTED INTO MY CHEST.
WHY I'VE HAD HEADACHES EVERY DAY SINCE.
CHEST...STILL SORE TO THE TOUCH--EVEN AFTER ALL THIS TIME.
BETTER NOT THINK ABOUT IT.
CAN'T AFFORD FEAR.
NOT NOW.
IAN IS COUNTING ON ME TO GET HIM OUT OF THIS.

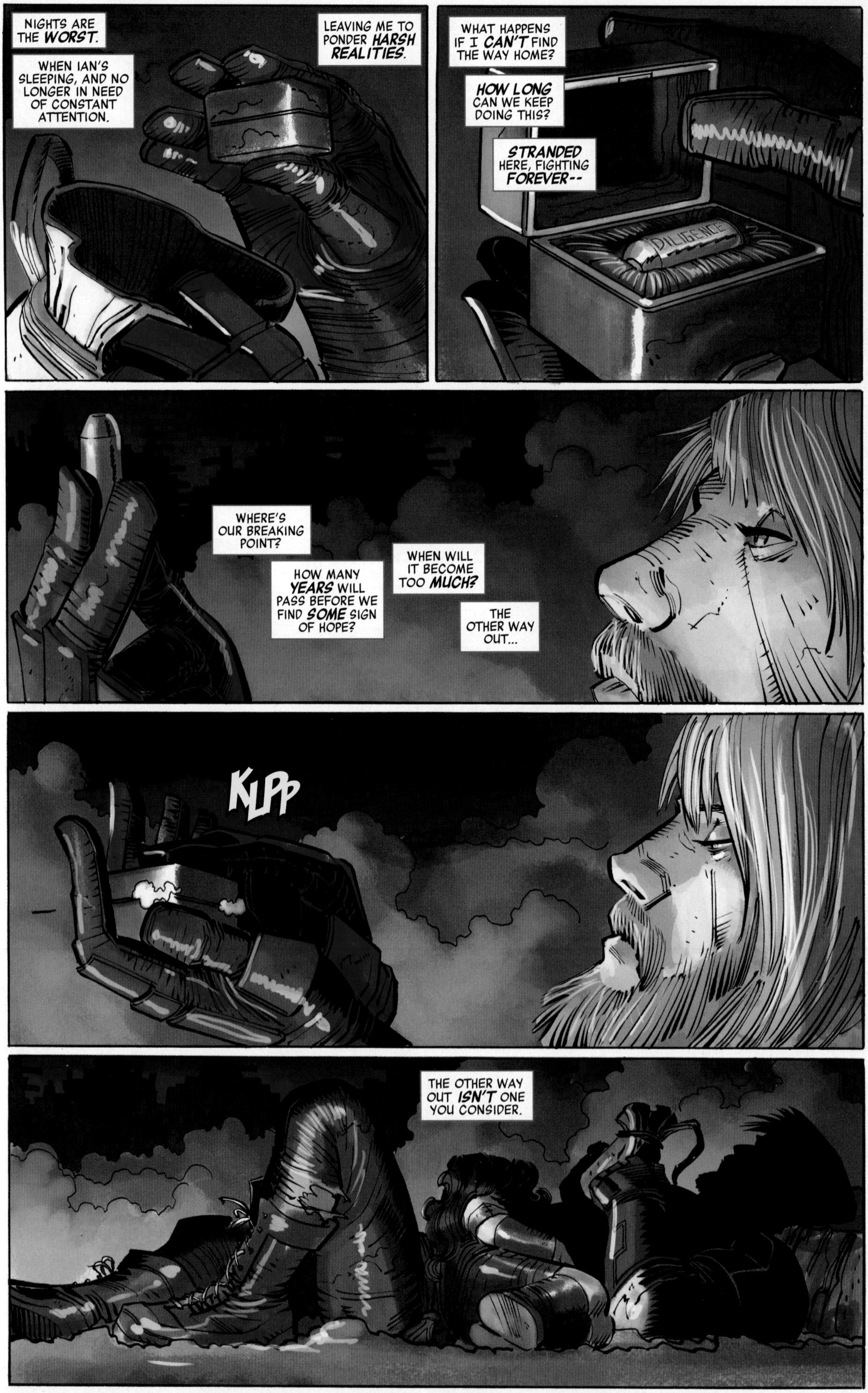
NIGHTS ARE THE **WORST**.
WHEN IAN'S SLEEPING, AND NO LONGER IN NEED OF CONSTANT ATTENTION.
LEAVING ME TO PONDER **HARSH REALITIES**.
WHAT HAPPENS IF I **CAN'T** FIND THE WAY HOME?
HOW LONG CAN WE KEEP DOING THIS?
STRANDED HERE, FIGHTING **FOREVER**--
DILIGENCE
WHERE'S OUR BREAKING POINT?
HOW MANY **YEARS** WILL PASS BEFORE WE FIND **SOME** SIGN OF HOPE?
WHEN WILL IT BECOME TOO **MUCH?**
THE OTHER WAY OUT...
KLPP
THE OTHER WAY OUT **ISN'T** ONE YOU CONSIDER.

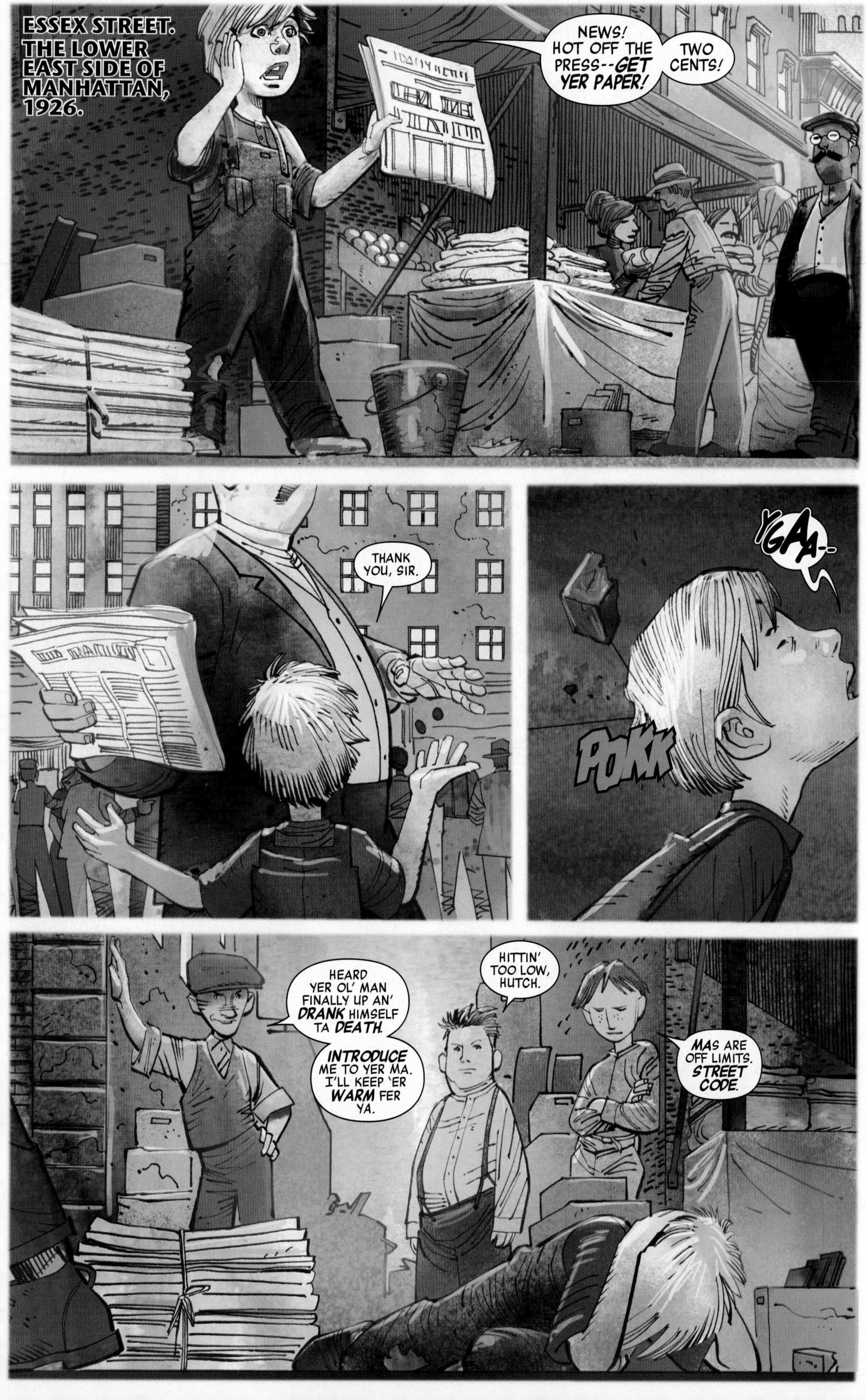
ESSEX STREET. THE LOWER EAST SIDE OF MANHATTAN, 1926.
NEWS! HOT OFF THE PRESS--GET YER PAPER!
TWO CENTS!
THANK YOU, SIR.
YGAA--
POKK
HEARD YER OL' MAN FINALLY UP AN' DRANK HIMSELF TA DEATH.
INTRODUCE ME TO YER MA. I'LL KEEP 'ER WARM FER YA.
HITTIN' TOO LOW, HUTCH.
MAS ARE OFF LIMITS. STREET CODE.

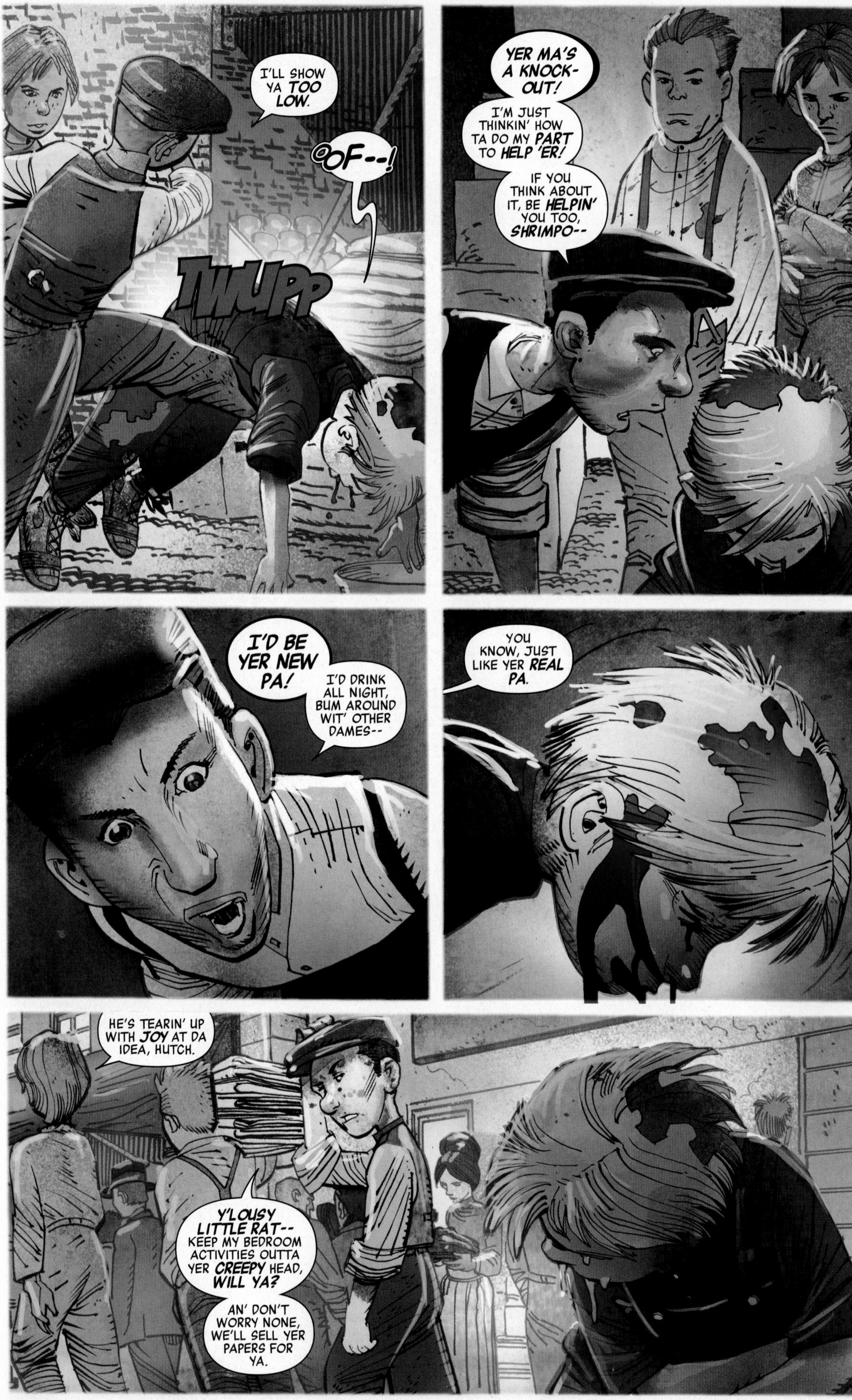

I'LL SHOW YA TOO LOW.
OOF--!
TWUPP
YER MA'S A KNOCK-OUT!
I'M JUST THINKIN' HOW TA DO MY PART TO HELP 'ER!
IF YOU THINK ABOUT IT, BE HELPIN' YOU TOO, SHRIMPO--
I'D BE YER NEW PA!
I'D DRINK ALL NIGHT, BUM AROUND WIT' OTHER DAMES--
YOU KNOW, JUST LIKE YER REAL PA.
HE'S TEARIN' UP WITH JOY AT DA IDEA, HUTCH.
Y'LOUSY LITTLE RAT-- KEEP MY BEDROOM ACTIVITIES OUTTA YER CREEPY HEAD, WILL YA?
AN' DON'T WORRY NONE, WE'LL SELL YER PAPERS FOR YA.

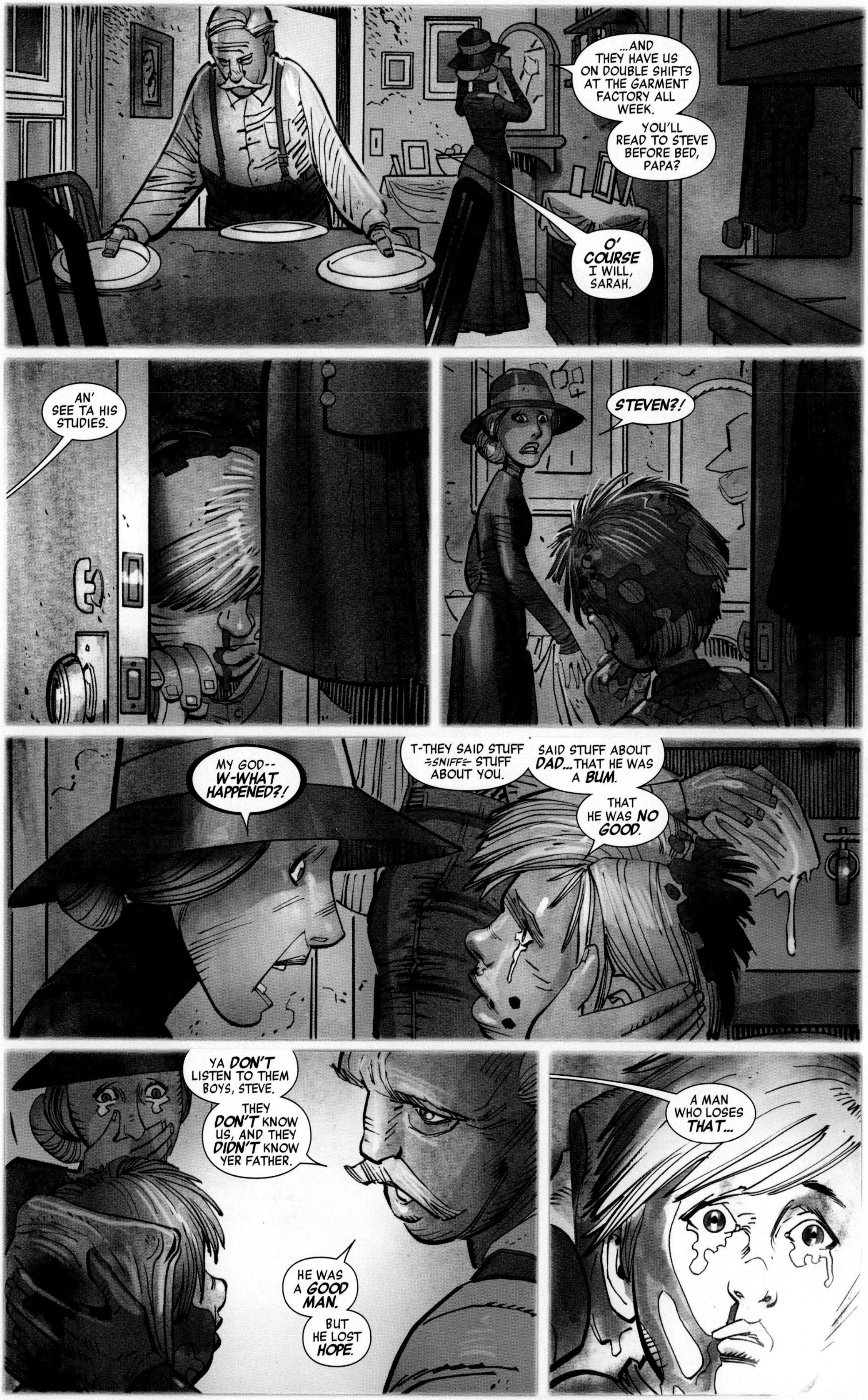
...AND THEY HAVE US ON DOUBLE SHIFTS AT THE GARMENT FACTORY ALL WEEK.
YOU'LL READ TO STEVE BEFORE BED, PAPA?
O' COURSE I WILL, SARAH.
AN' SEE TA HIS STUDIES.
STEVEN?!
MY GOD-- W-WHAT HAPPENED?!
T-THEY SAID STUFF =SNIFF= STUFF ABOUT YOU.
SAID STUFF ABOUT DAD... THAT HE WAS A BUM.
THAT HE WAS NO GOOD.
YA DON'T LISTEN TO THEM BOYS, STEVE.
THEY DON'T KNOW US, AND THEY DIDN'T KNOW YER FATHER.
HE WAS A GOOD MAN.
BUT HE LOST HOPE.
A MAN WHO LOSES THAT...

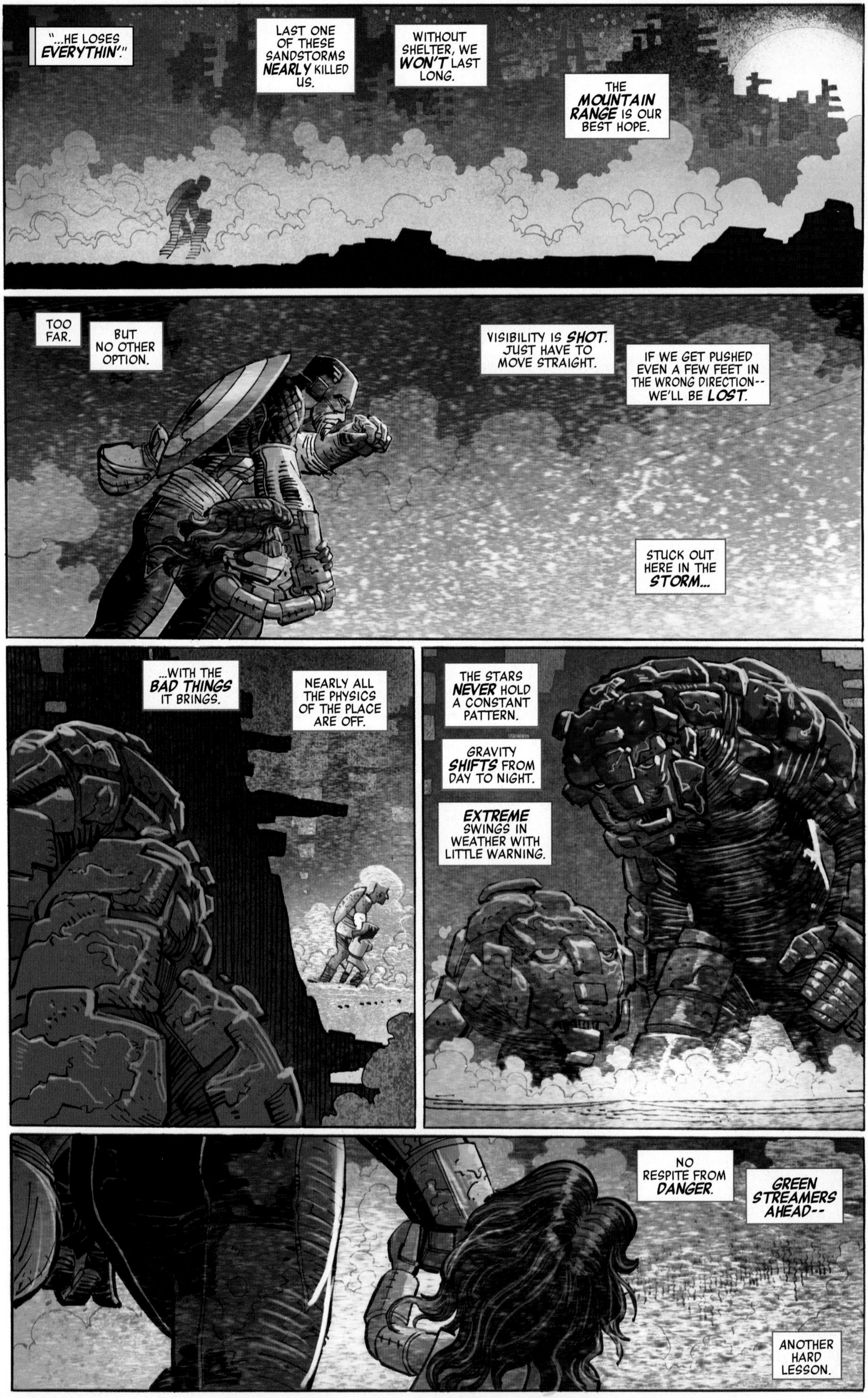
"...HE LOSES EVERYTHIN'."
LAST ONE OF THESE SANDSTORMS NEARLY KILLED US.
WITHOUT SHELTER, WE WON'T LAST LONG.
THE MOUNTAIN RANGE IS OUR BEST HOPE.
TOO FAR.
BUT NO OTHER OPTION.
VISIBILITY IS SHOT. JUST HAVE TO MOVE STRAIGHT.
IF WE GET PUSHED EVEN A FEW FEET IN THE WRONG DIRECTION-- WE'LL BE LOST.
STUCK OUT HERE IN THE STORM...
...WITH THE BAD THINGS IT BRINGS.
NEARLY ALL THE PHYSICS OF THE PLACE ARE OFF.
THE STARS NEVER HOLD A CONSTANT PATTERN.
GRAVITY SHIFTS FROM DAY TO NIGHT.
EXTREME SWINGS IN WEATHER WITH LITTLE WARNING.
NO RESPITE FROM DANGER.
GREEN STREAMERS AHEAD--
ANOTHER HARD LESSON.

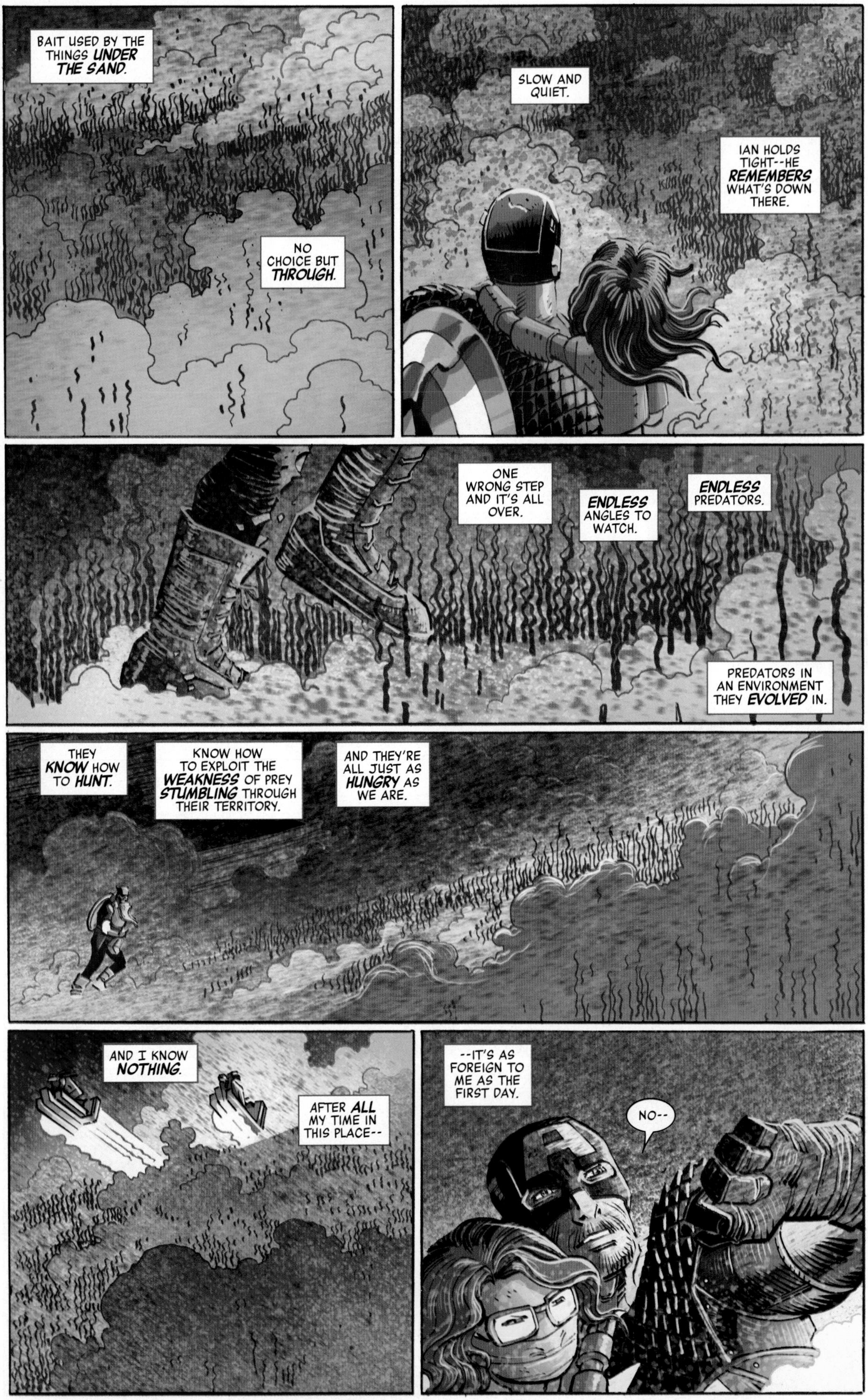
BAIT USED BY THE THINGS UNDER THE SAND.
NO CHOICE BUT THROUGH.
SLOW AND QUIET.
IAN HOLDS TIGHT--HE REMEMBERS WHAT'S DOWN THERE.
ONE WRONG STEP AND IT'S ALL OVER.
ENDLESS ANGLES TO WATCH.
ENDLESS PREDATORS.
PREDATORS IN AN ENVIRONMENT THEY EVOLVED IN.
THEY KNOW HOW TO HUNT.
KNOW HOW TO EXPLOIT THE WEAKNESS OF PREY STUMBLING THROUGH THEIR TERRITORY.
AND THEY'RE ALL JUST AS HUNGRY AS WE ARE.
AND I KNOW NOTHING.
AFTER ALL MY TIME IN THIS PLACE--
--IT'S AS FOREIGN TO ME AS THE FIRST DAY.
NO--

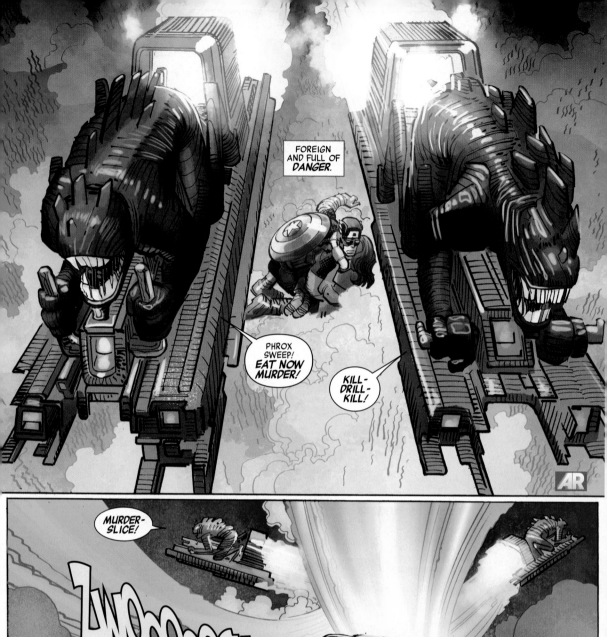

FOREIGN AND FULL OF DANGER.

PHROX SWEEP! EAT NOW MURDER!

KILL-DRILL-KILL!

MURDER-SLICE!

ZWOOOOOSH

GO.

LIKE RUNNING FROM A SNIPER THROUGH A MINE FIELD--

--SAME BASIC RULES--

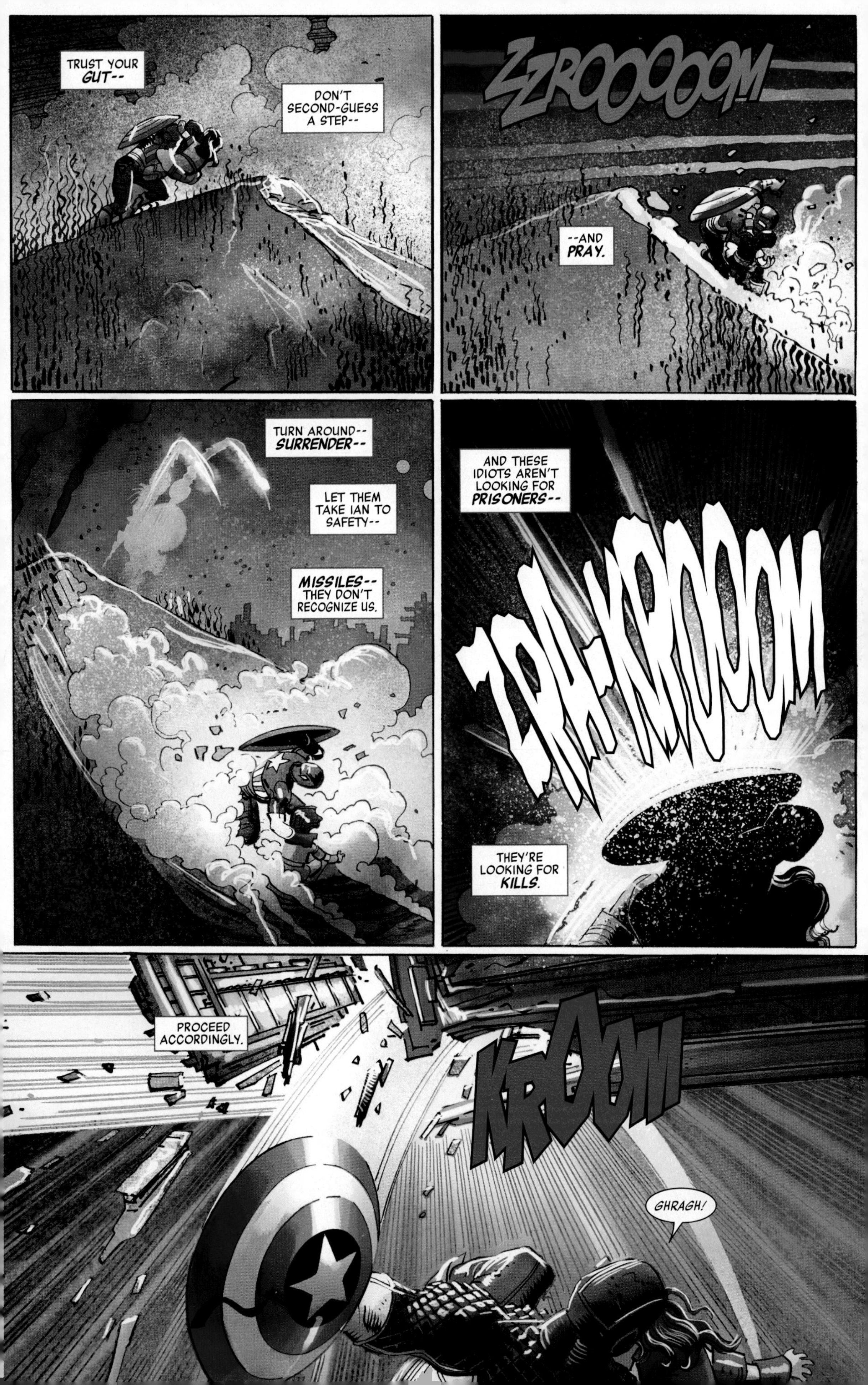
TRUST YOUR GUT--
DON'T SECOND-GUESS A STEP--
ZZROOOOOM
--AND PRAY.
TURN AROUND-- SURRENDER--
LET THEM TAKE IAN TO SAFETY--
MISSILES-- THEY DON'T RECOGNIZE US.
AND THESE IDIOTS AREN'T LOOKING FOR PRISONERS--
ZRAK-KROOOM
THEY'RE LOOKING FOR KILLS.
PROCEED ACCORDINGLY.
KROOM
GHRAGH!

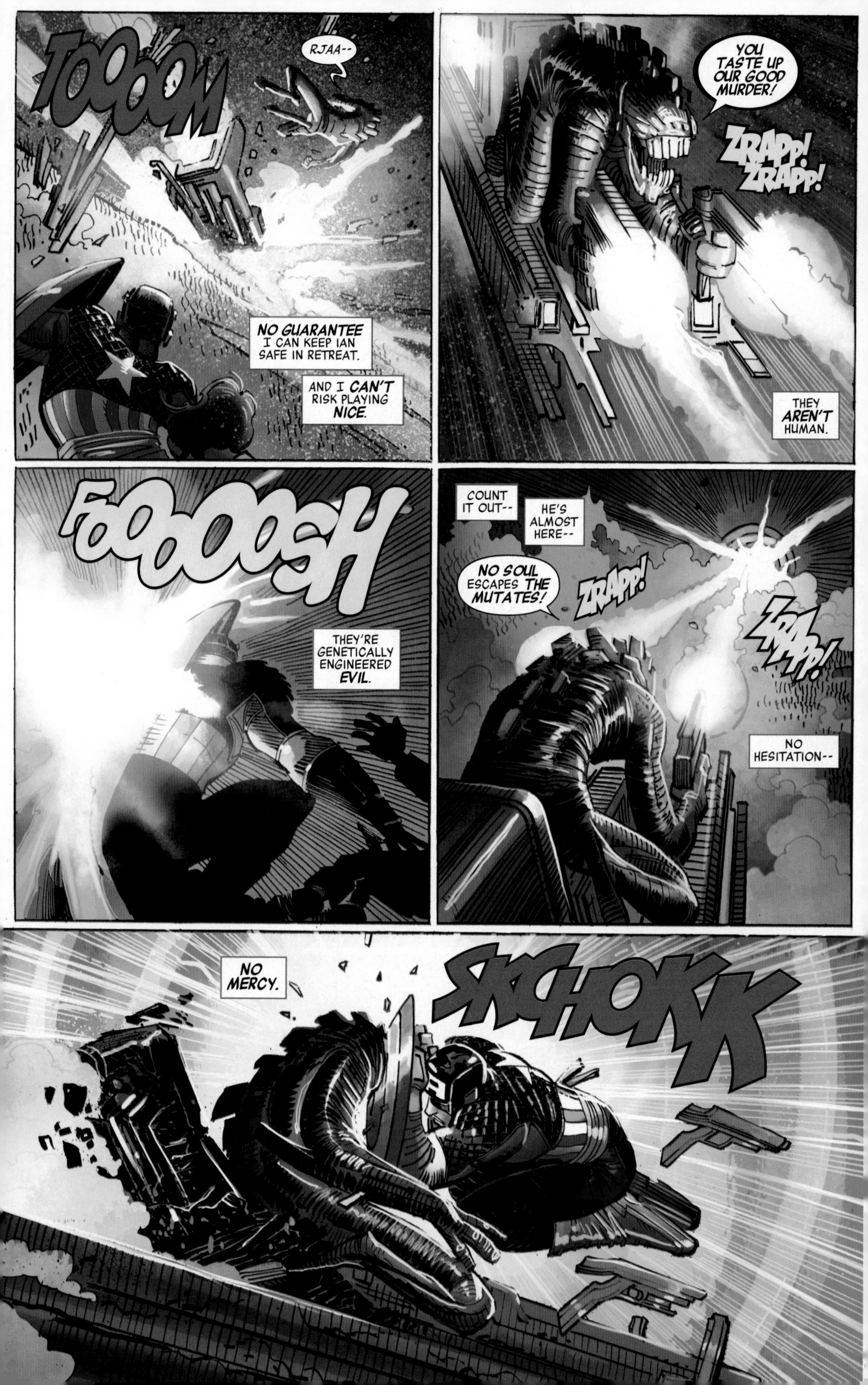
TOOOOM
RJAA--
NO GUARANTEE I CAN KEEP IAN SAFE IN RETREAT.
AND I CAN'T RISK PLAYING NICE.
YOU TASTE UP OUR GOOD MURDER!
ZRAPP! ZRAPP!
THEY AREN'T HUMAN.
FOOOOOSH
THEY'RE GENETICALLY ENGINEERED EVIL.
COUNT IT OUT--
HE'S ALMOST HERE--
NO SOUL ESCAPES THE MUTATES!
ZRAPP!
ZRAPPP!
NO HESITATION--
NO MERCY.
SKCHOKK

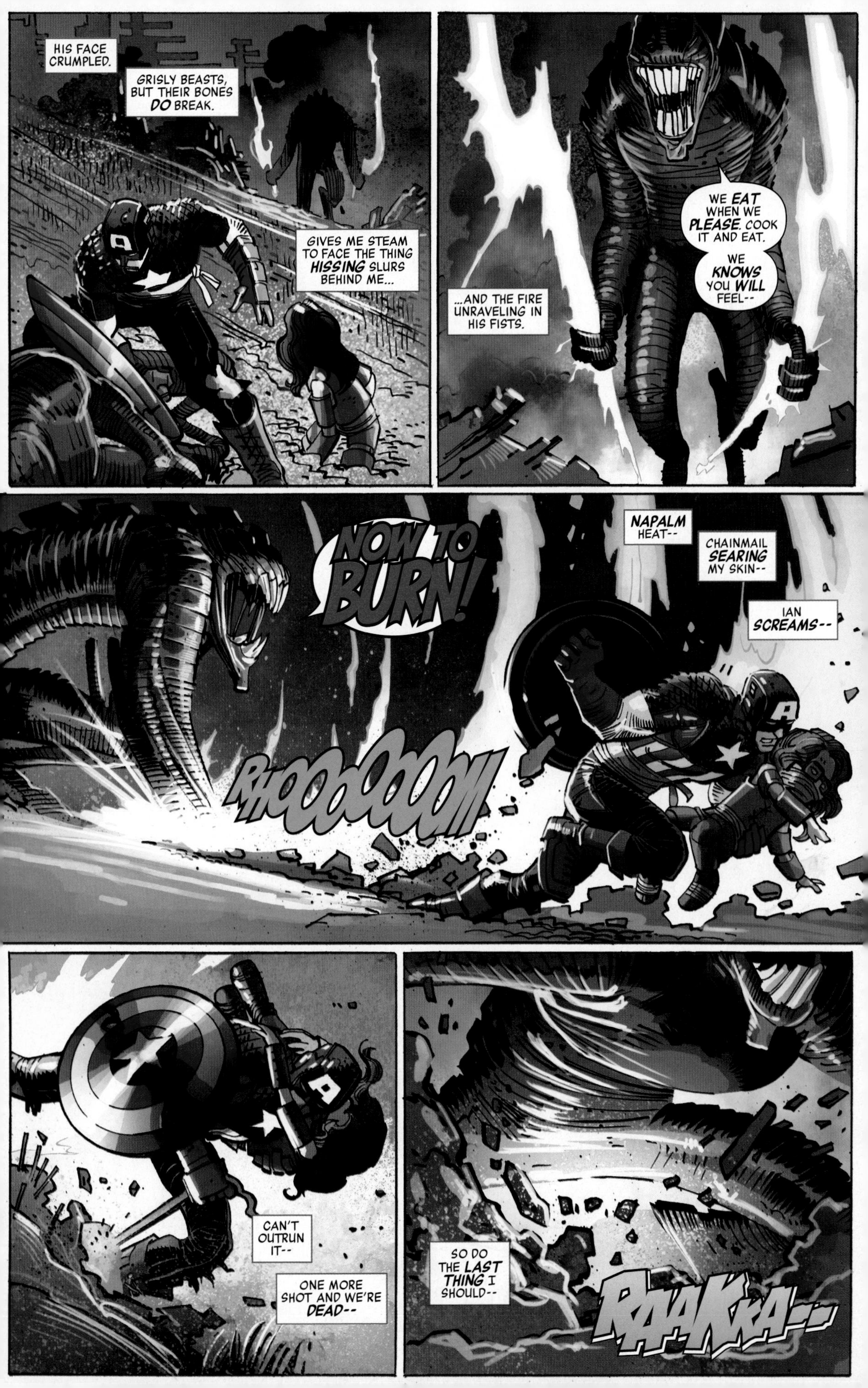

HIS FACE CRUMPLED.
GRISLY BEASTS, BUT THEIR BONES DO BREAK.
GIVES ME STEAM TO FACE THE THING HISSING SLURS BEHIND ME...
...AND THE FIRE UNRAVELING IN HIS FISTS.
WE EAT WHEN WE PLEASE. COOK IT AND EAT.
WE KNOWS YOU WILL FEEL--
NOW TO BURN!
NAPALM HEAT--
CHAINMAIL SEARING MY SKIN--
IAN SCREAMS--
RHOOOOOOOM
CAN'T OUTRUN IT--
ONE MORE SHOT AND WE'RE DEAD--
SO DO THE LAST THING I SHOULD--
RAAKKA--

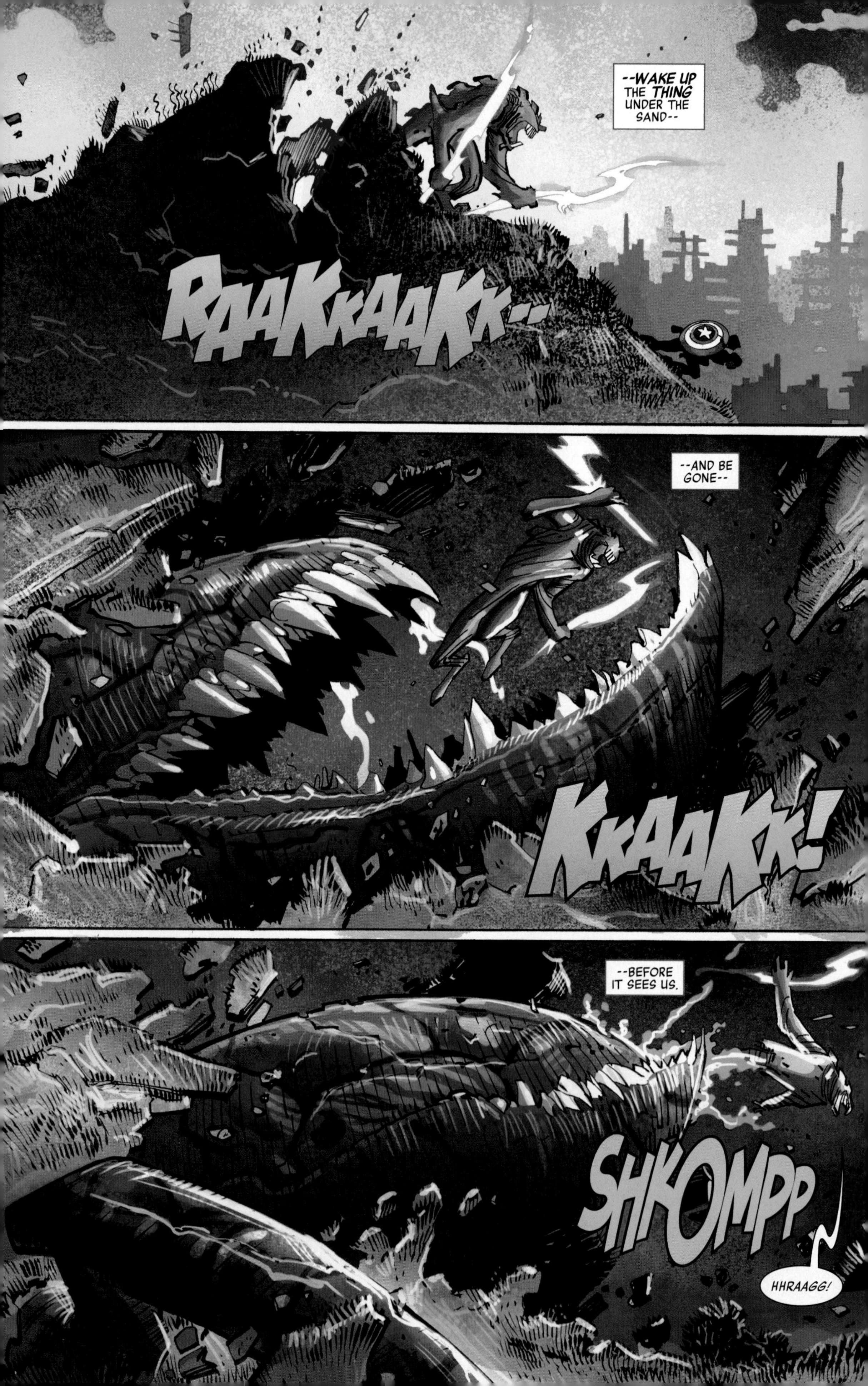
--WAKE UP THE THING UNDER THE SAND--
RAAKKAAKK--
--AND BE GONE--
KKAAKK!
--BEFORE IT SEES US.
SHKOMPP
HHRAAGG!

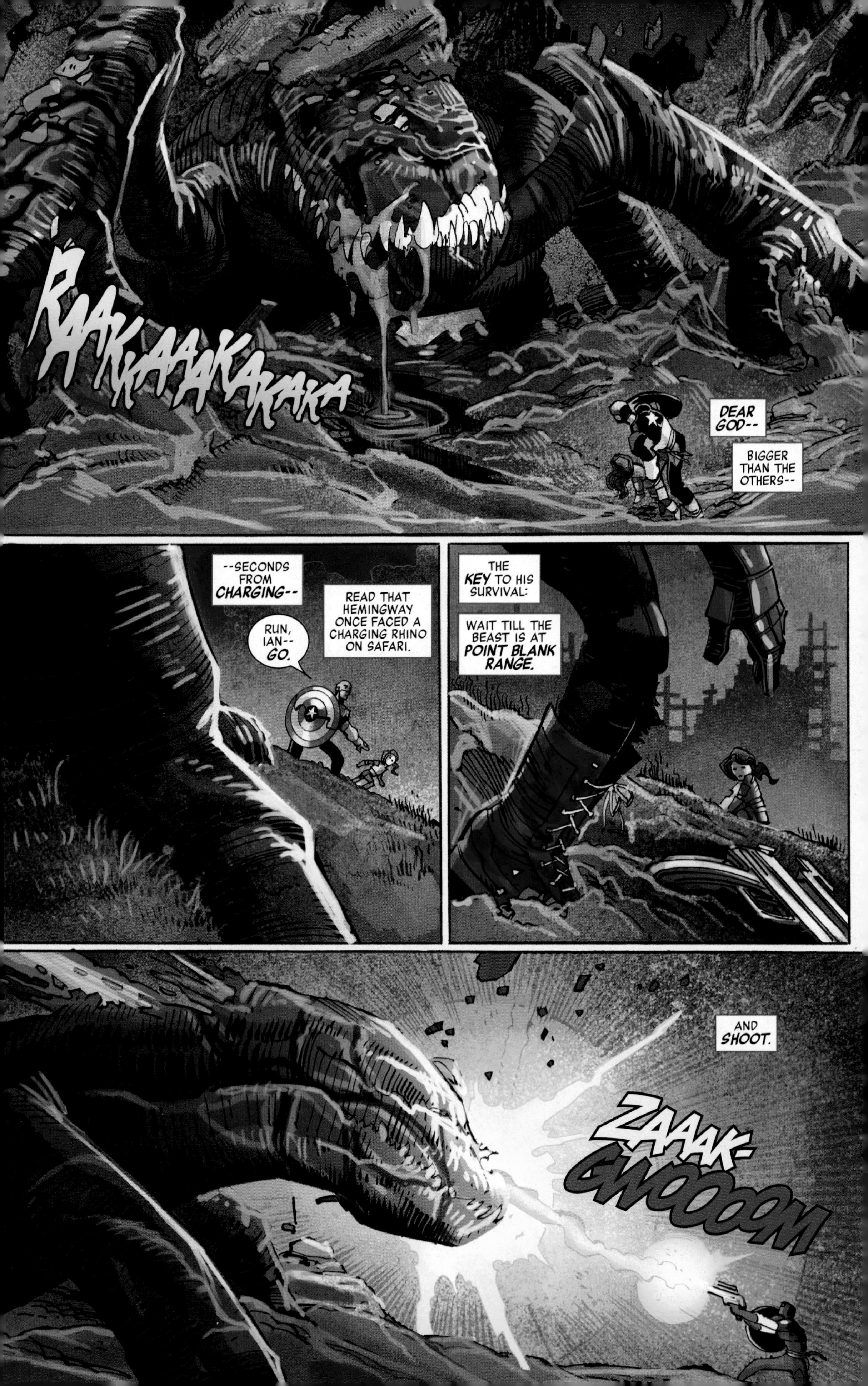
RAAKKAAAKAKAKAKA
DEAR GOD--
BIGGER THAN THE OTHERS--
--SECONDS FROM CHARGING--
RUN, IAN-- GO.
READ THAT HEMINGWAY ONCE FACED A CHARGING RHINO ON SAFARI.
THE KEY TO HIS SURVIVAL:
WAIT TILL THE BEAST IS AT POINT BLANK RANGE.
AND SHOOT.
ZAAAK-GWOOOOM

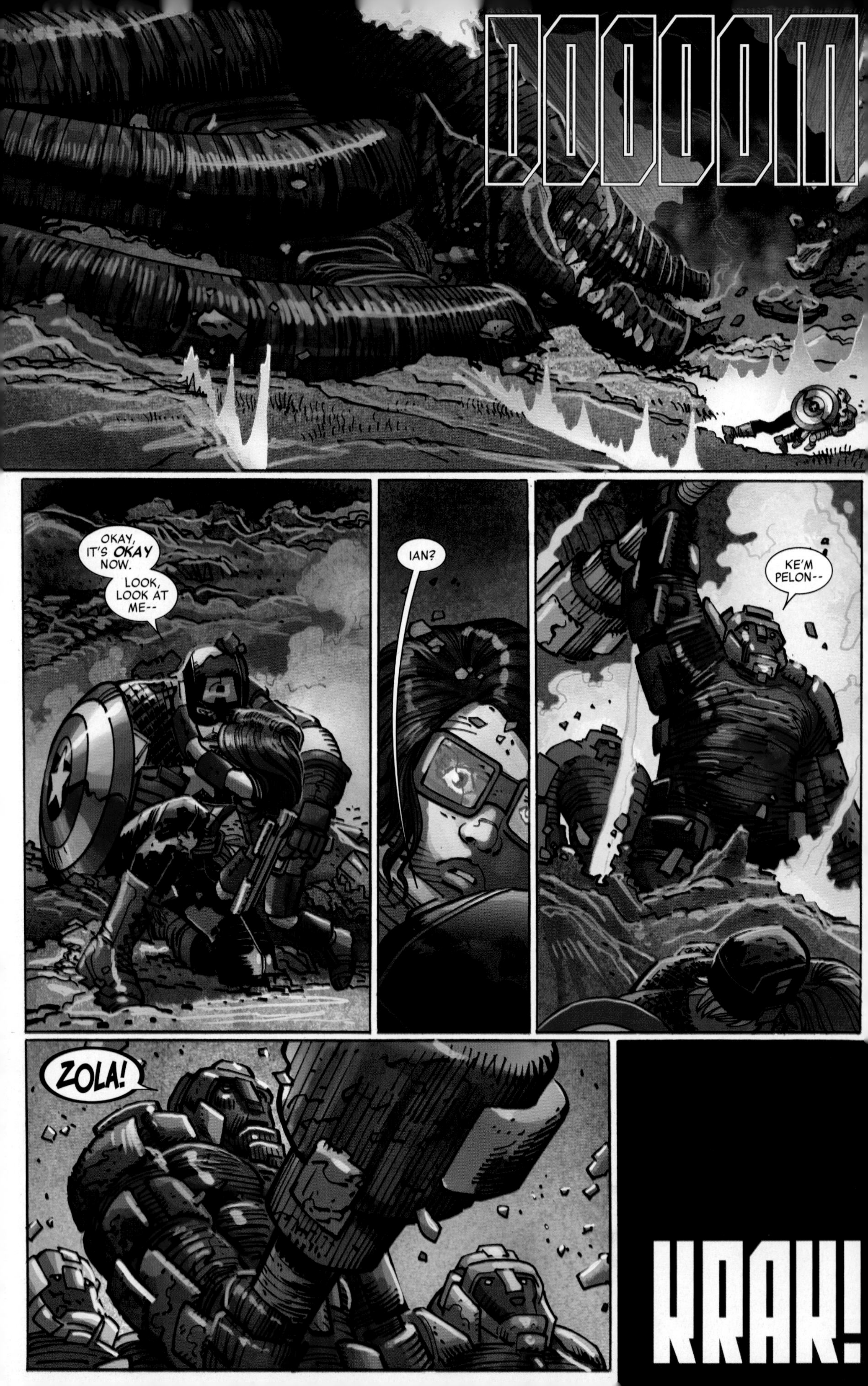
DOOOOM
OKAY, IT'S OKAY NOW.
LOOK, LOOK AT ME--
IAN?
KE'M PELON--
ZOLA!
KRAK!

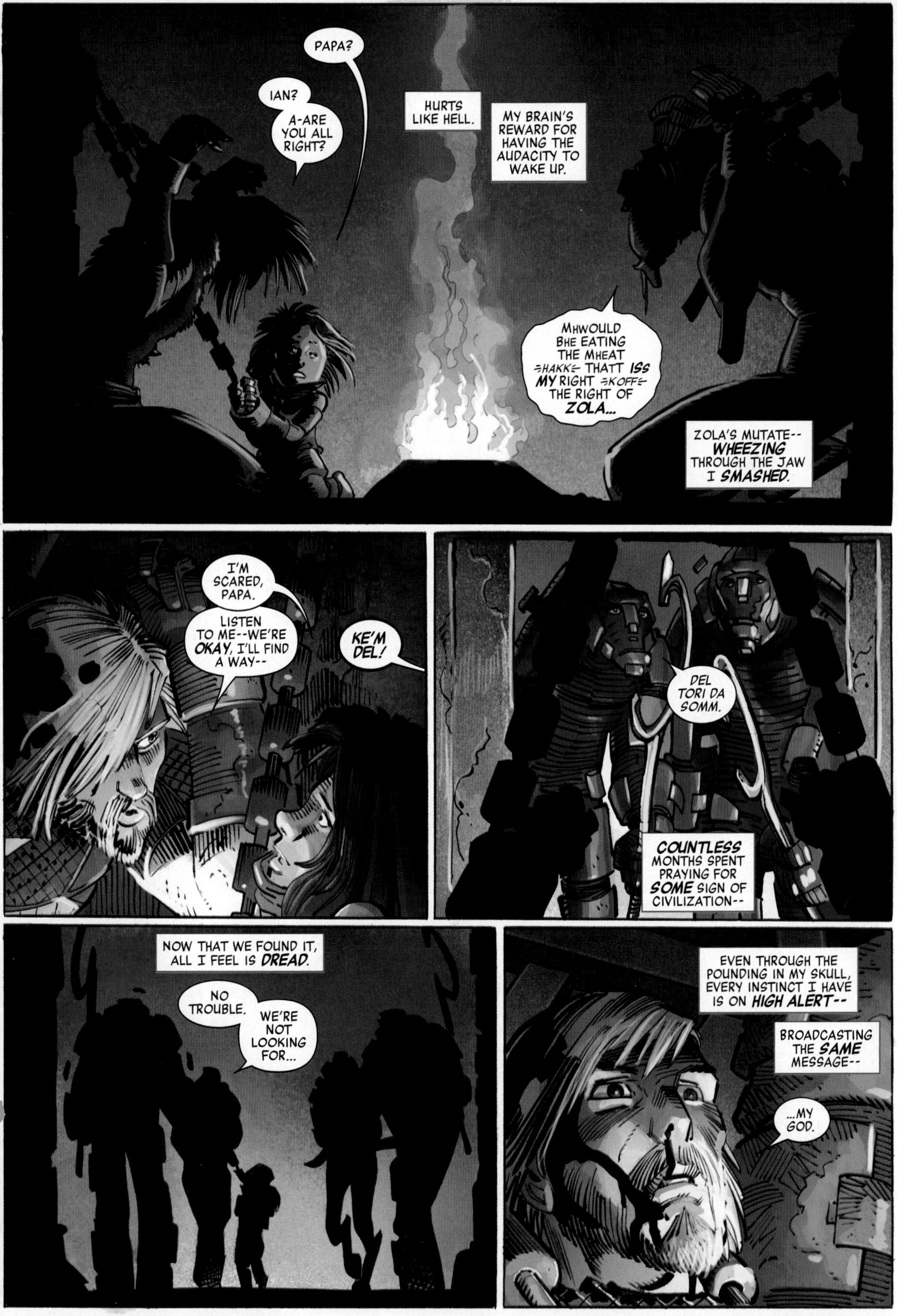
PAPA?
IAN?
A-ARE YOU ALL RIGHT?
HURTS LIKE HELL.
MY BRAIN'S REWARD FOR HAVING THE AUDACITY TO WAKE UP.
MHWOULD BHE EATING THE MHEAT =HAKK= THATT ISS MY RIGHT =KOFF= THE RIGHT OF ZOLA...
ZOLA'S MUTATE--WHEEZING THROUGH THE JAW I SMASHED.
I'M SCARED, PAPA.
LISTEN TO ME--WE'RE OKAY, I'LL FIND A WAY--
KE'M DEL!
DEL TORI DA SOMM.
COUNTLESS MONTHS SPENT PRAYING FOR SOME SIGN OF CIVILIZATION--
NOW THAT WE FOUND IT, ALL I FEEL IS DREAD.
NO TROUBLE.
WE'RE NOT LOOKING FOR...
EVEN THROUGH THE POUNDING IN MY SKULL, EVERY INSTINCT I HAVE IS ON HIGH ALERT--
BROADCASTING THE SAME MESSAGE--
...MY GOD.

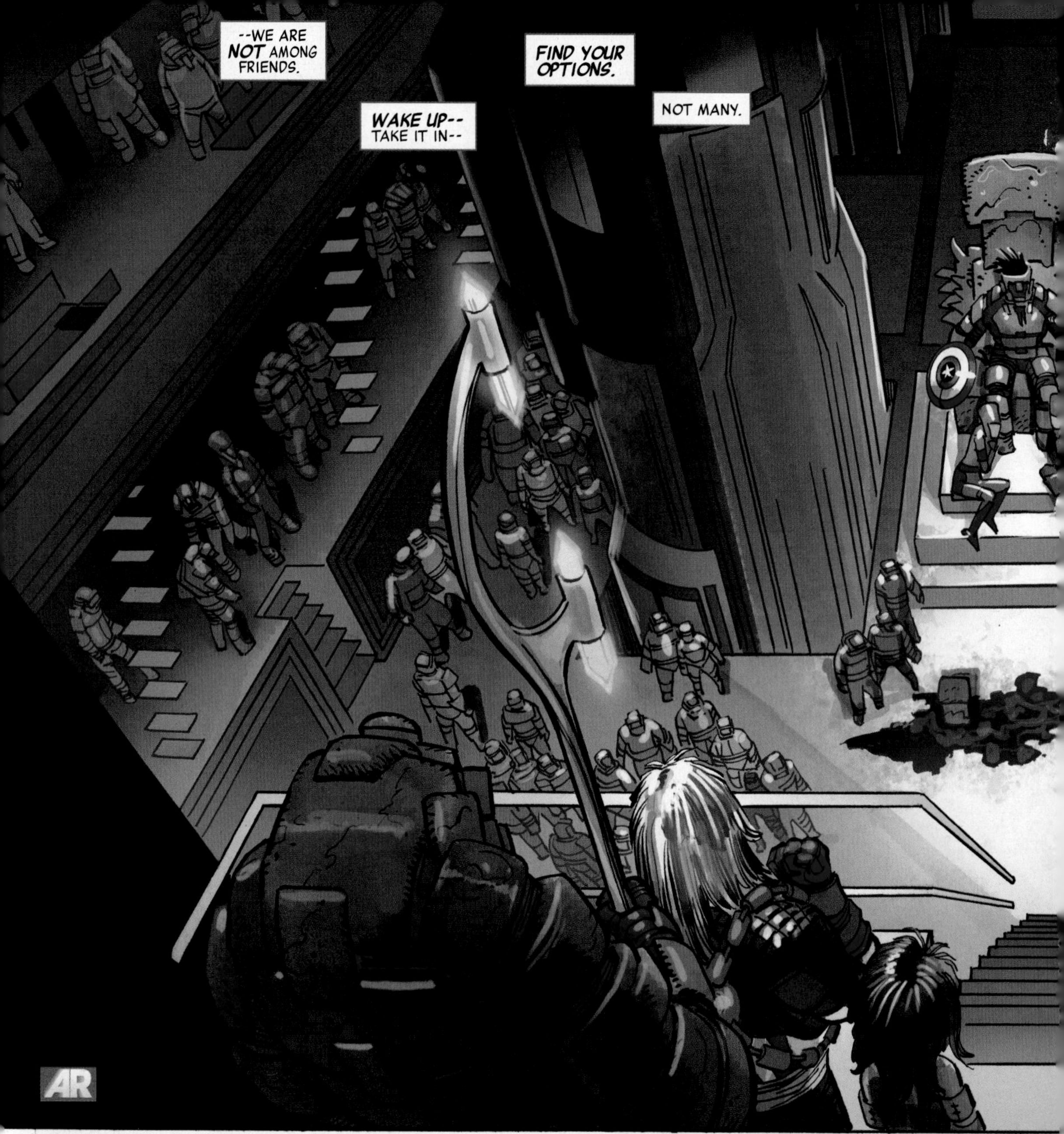
--WE ARE NOT AMONG FRIENDS.
WAKE UP-- TAKE IT IN--
FIND YOUR OPTIONS.
NOT MANY.
AR

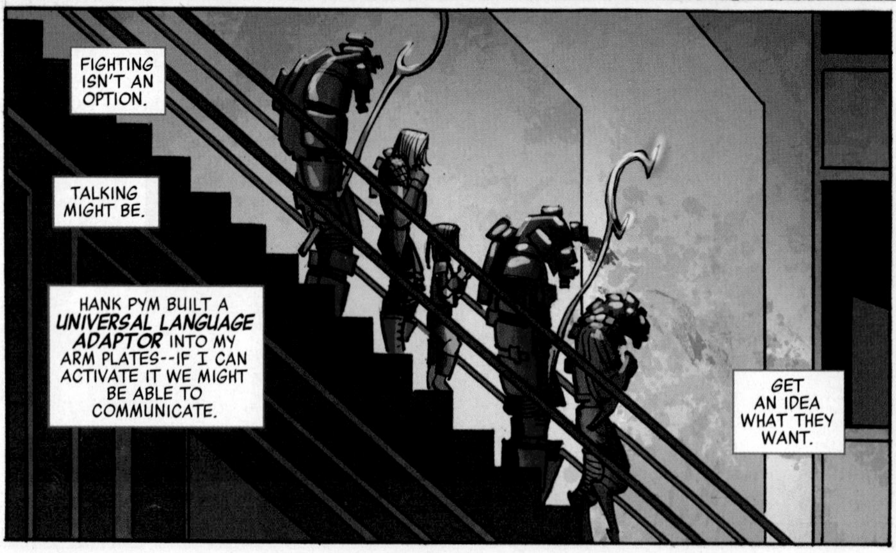
FIGHTING ISN'T AN OPTION.
TALKING MIGHT BE.
HANK PYM BUILT A UNIVERSAL LANGUAGE ADAPTOR INTO MY ARM PLATES--IF I CAN ACTIVATE IT WE MIGHT BE ABLE TO COMMUNICATE.
GET AN IDEA WHAT THEY WANT.

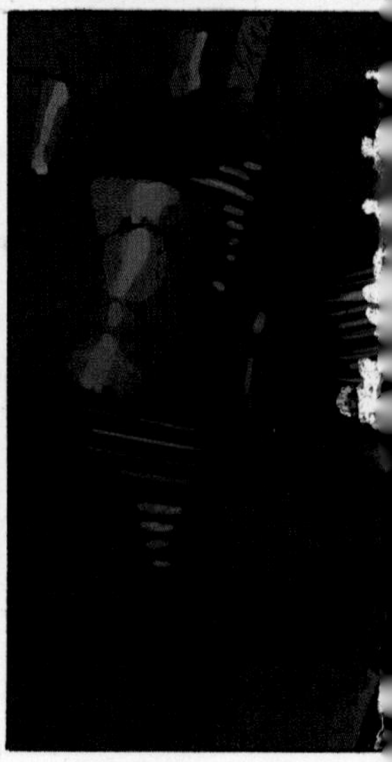

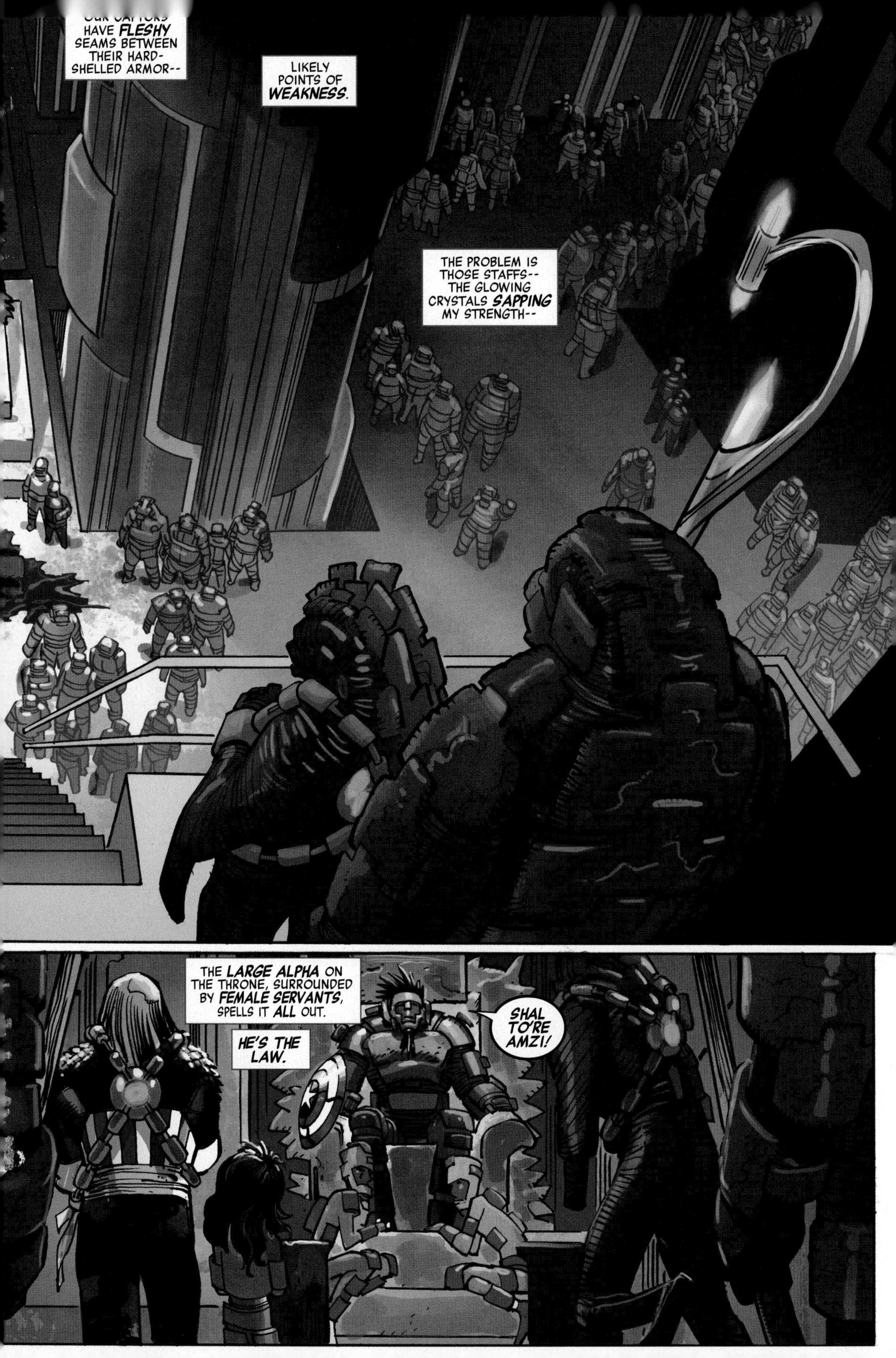
HAVE FLESHY SEAMS BETWEEN THEIR HARD-SHELLED ARMOR--
LIKELY POINTS OF WEAKNESS.
THE PROBLEM IS THOSE STAFFS-- THE GLOWING CRYSTALS SAPPING MY STRENGTH--
THE LARGE ALPHA ON THE THRONE, SURROUNDED BY FEMALE SERVANTS, SPELLS IT ALL OUT.
HE'S THE LAW.
SHAL TO'RE AMZI!

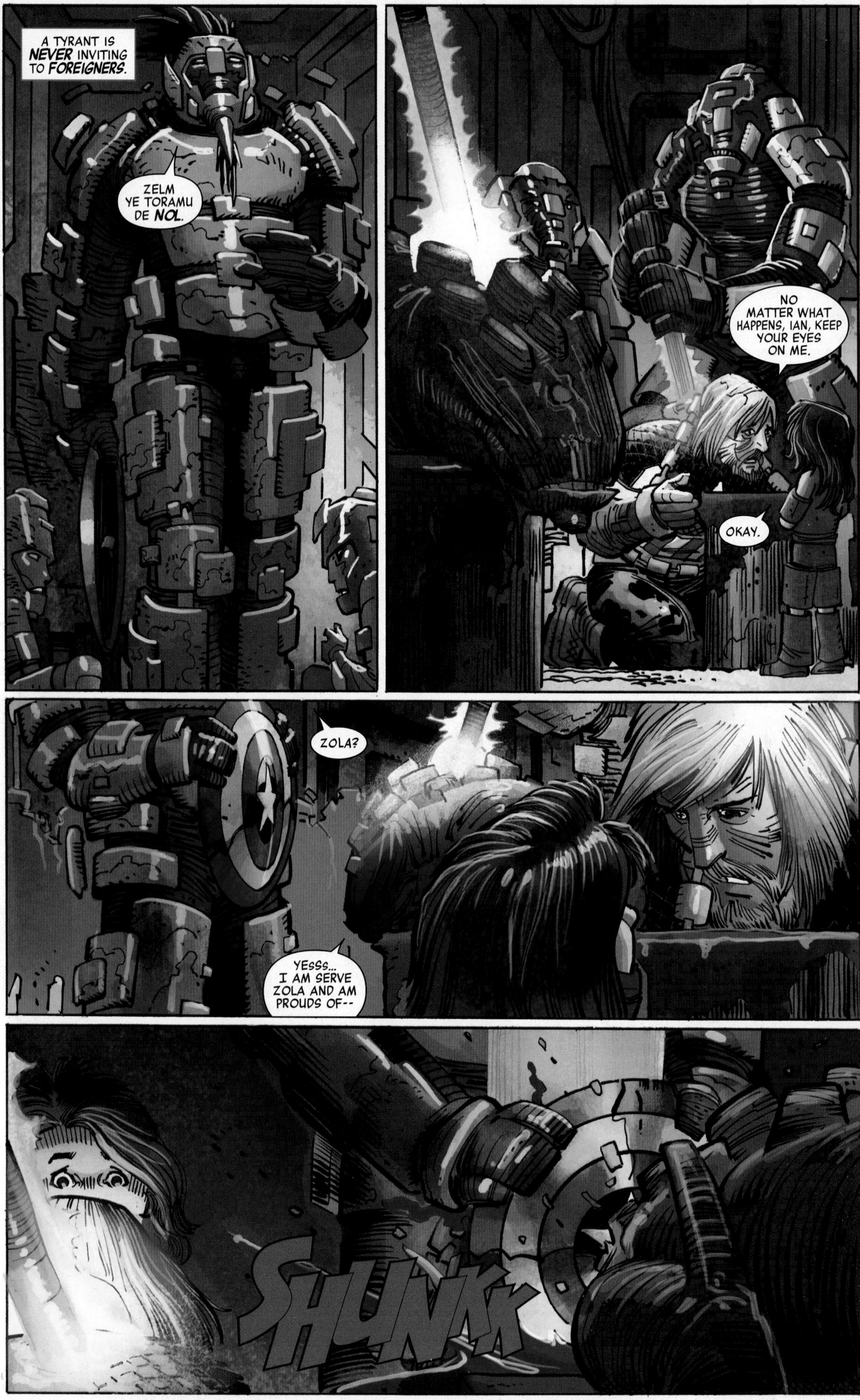
A TYRANT IS NEVER INVITING TO FOREIGNERS.
ZELM YE TORAMU DE NOL.
NO MATTER WHAT HAPPENS, IAN, KEEP YOUR EYES ON ME.
OKAY.
ZOLA?
YESSS... I AM SERVE ZOLA AND AM PROUDS OF--
SHUNKK

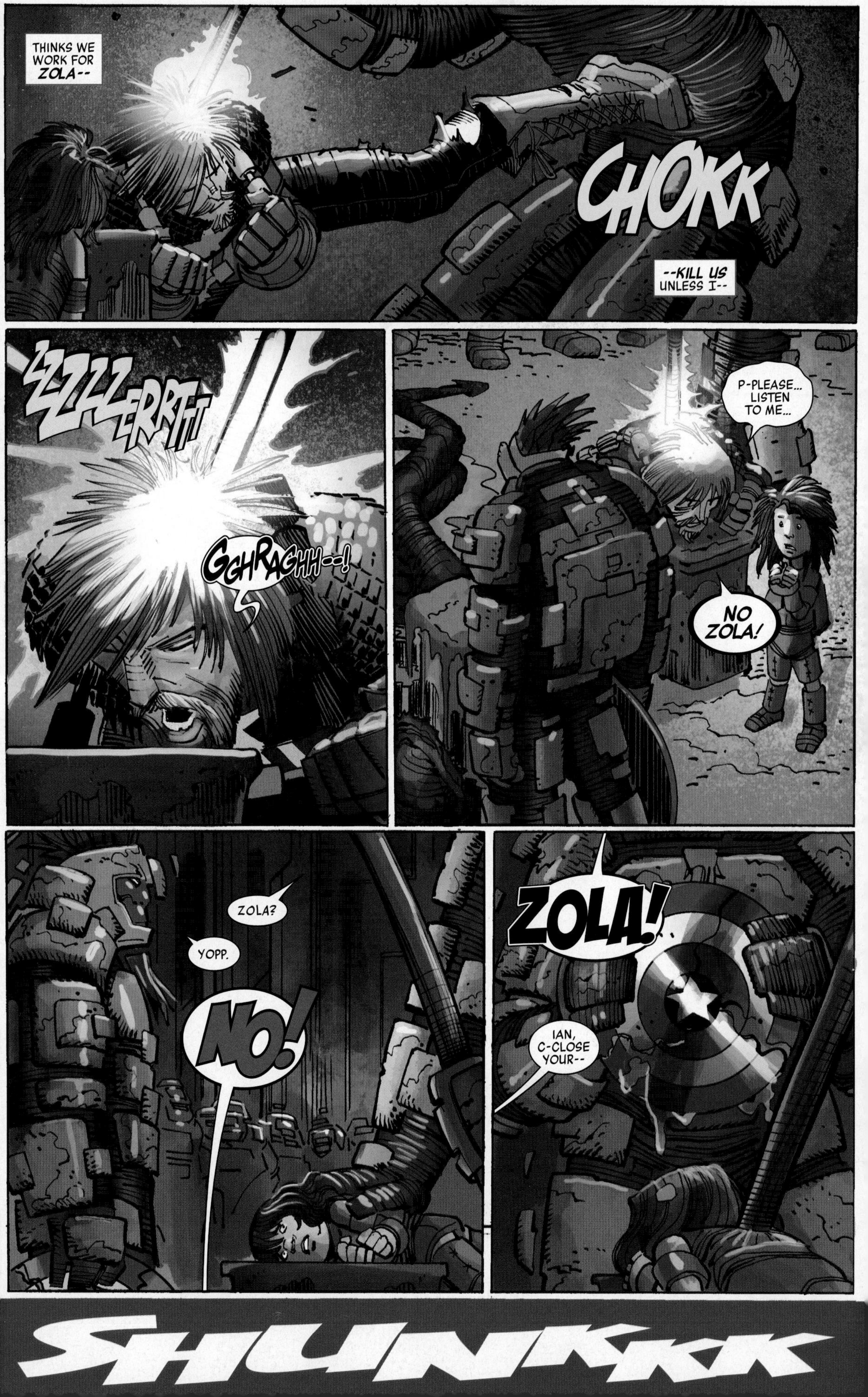
THINKS WE WORK FOR ZOLA--
CHOKK
--KILL US UNLESS I--
ZZZZZERRTTT
GGHRAGHH--!
P-PLEASE... LISTEN TO ME...
NO ZOLA!
ZOLA?
YOPP.
NO!
ZOLA!
IAN, C-CLOSE YOUR--
SHUNKKK

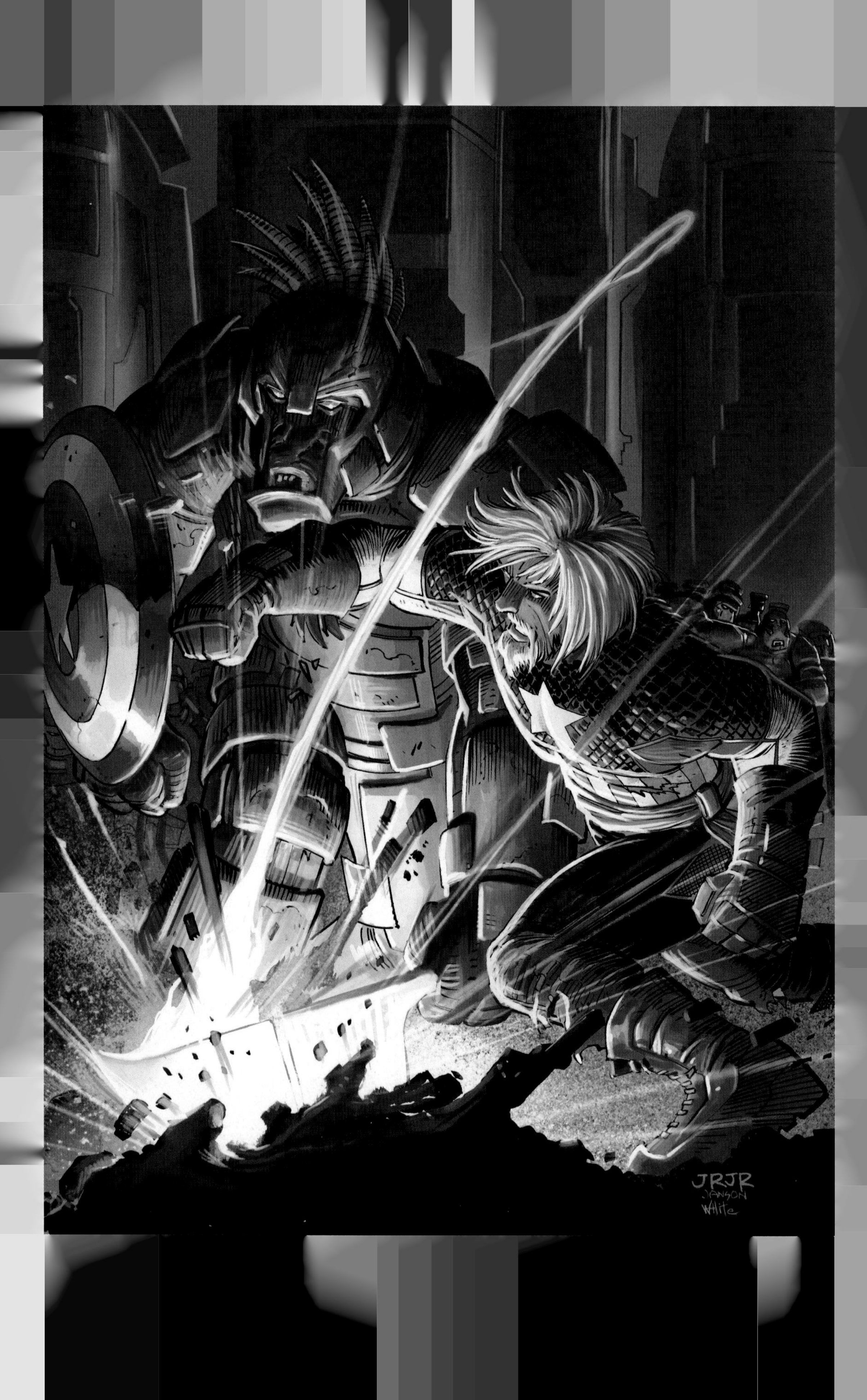
JRJR
JANSON
White

SWITZERLAND,
ZOLA ANCESTRAL CASTLE,
1929...

I HAVEN'T SEEN HILDA SINCE TWO WEEKS BACK, NICHOLAS.

SHE CAME, DID HER USUAL *HALFHEARTED* ATTEMPT AT CLEANING, SHE LEFT. WHEN SHE DID NOT ARRIVE FOR WORK I *ASSUMED* IT WAS FROM *DISGRACE*.

S-SHE'S *NEVER BEEN* GONE FOR SO LONG, ARNIM... *NEVER*.

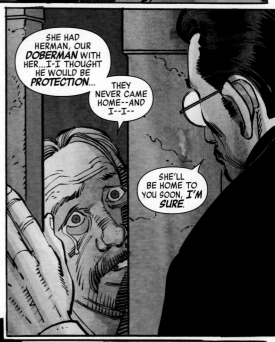

SHE HAD HERMAN, OUR *DOBERMAN* WITH HER...I-I THOUGHT HE WOULD BE *PROTECTION*... THEY NEVER CAME HOME--AND I--I--

SHE'LL BE HOME TO YOU SOON, *I'M SURE*.

YES, YES-- I HEAR YOU, FATHER.

MY EXPLORATION IS GROTESQUE TO A *NOBLEMAN* SUCH AS YOU.

A STRONG BODY IS ACQUIRED THROUGH *STRENUOUS* LABOR AND THE *HEFTING* OF WEIGHT, ISN'T THAT SO?

IN THIS CAPACITY I WAS ALWAYS SURE TO *FAIL YOU*.

YOU *NEVER* COULD UNDERSTAND.

THOSE WITH ADEQUATE INTELLIGENCE AND INVENTIVENESS NEED NOT SEEK OUT EXCELLENCE THROUGH *BRUTE STRENGTH*.

SCIENCE HOLDS THE KEY TO EVERLASTING *HUMAN PERFECTION*.

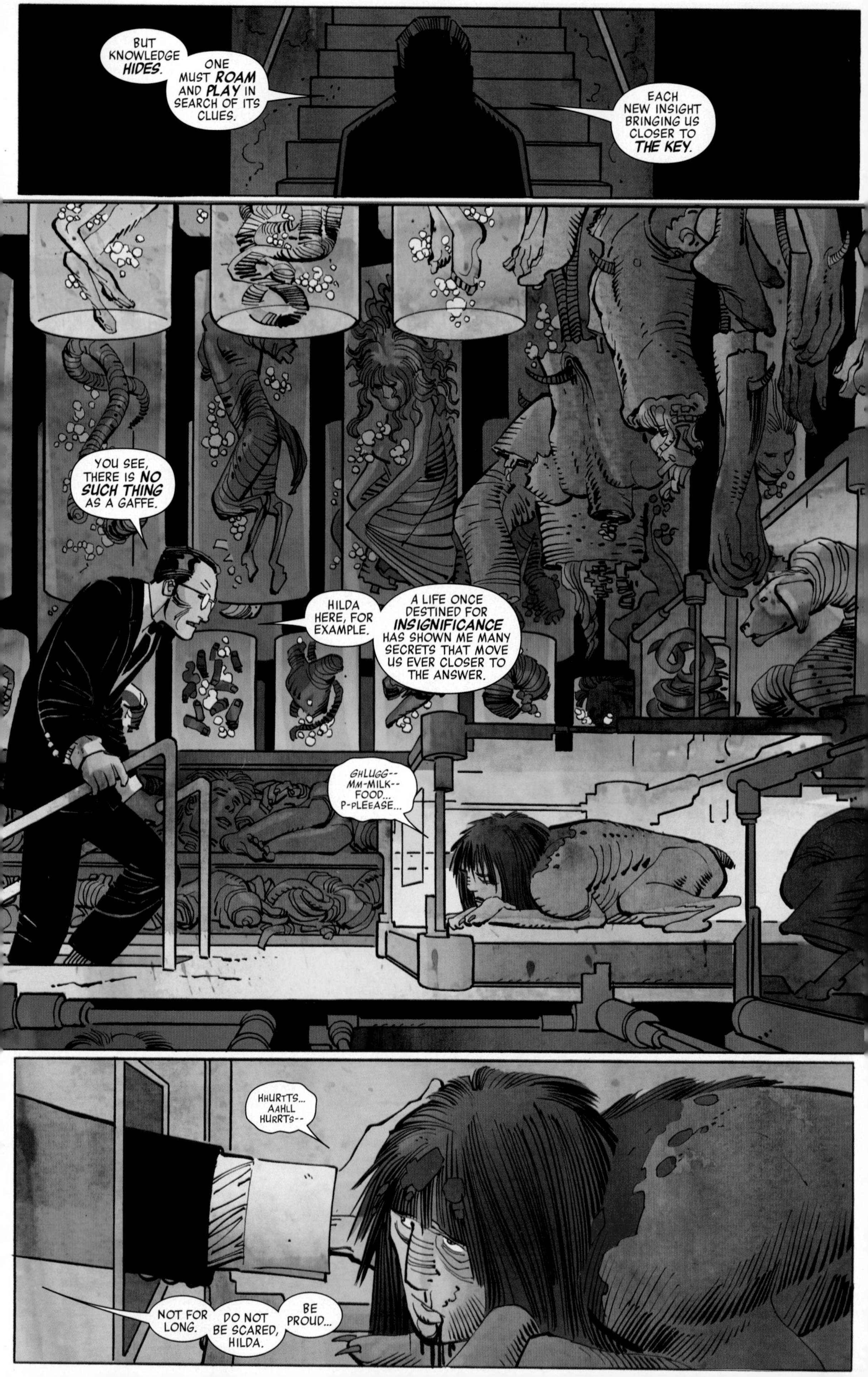
BUT KNOWLEDGE HIDES.
ONE MUST ROAM AND PLAY IN SEARCH OF ITS CLUES.
EACH NEW INSIGHT BRINGING US CLOSER TO THE KEY.
YOU SEE, THERE IS NO SUCH THING AS A GAFFE.
HILDA HERE, FOR EXAMPLE.
A LIFE ONCE DESTINED FOR INSIGNIFICANCE HAS SHOWN ME MANY SECRETS THAT MOVE US EVER CLOSER TO THE ANSWER.
GHLUGG-- MM-MILK-- FOOD... P-PLEEASE...
HHURTTS... AAHLL HURRTS--
NOT FOR LONG.
DO NOT BE SCARED, HILDA.
BE PROUD...

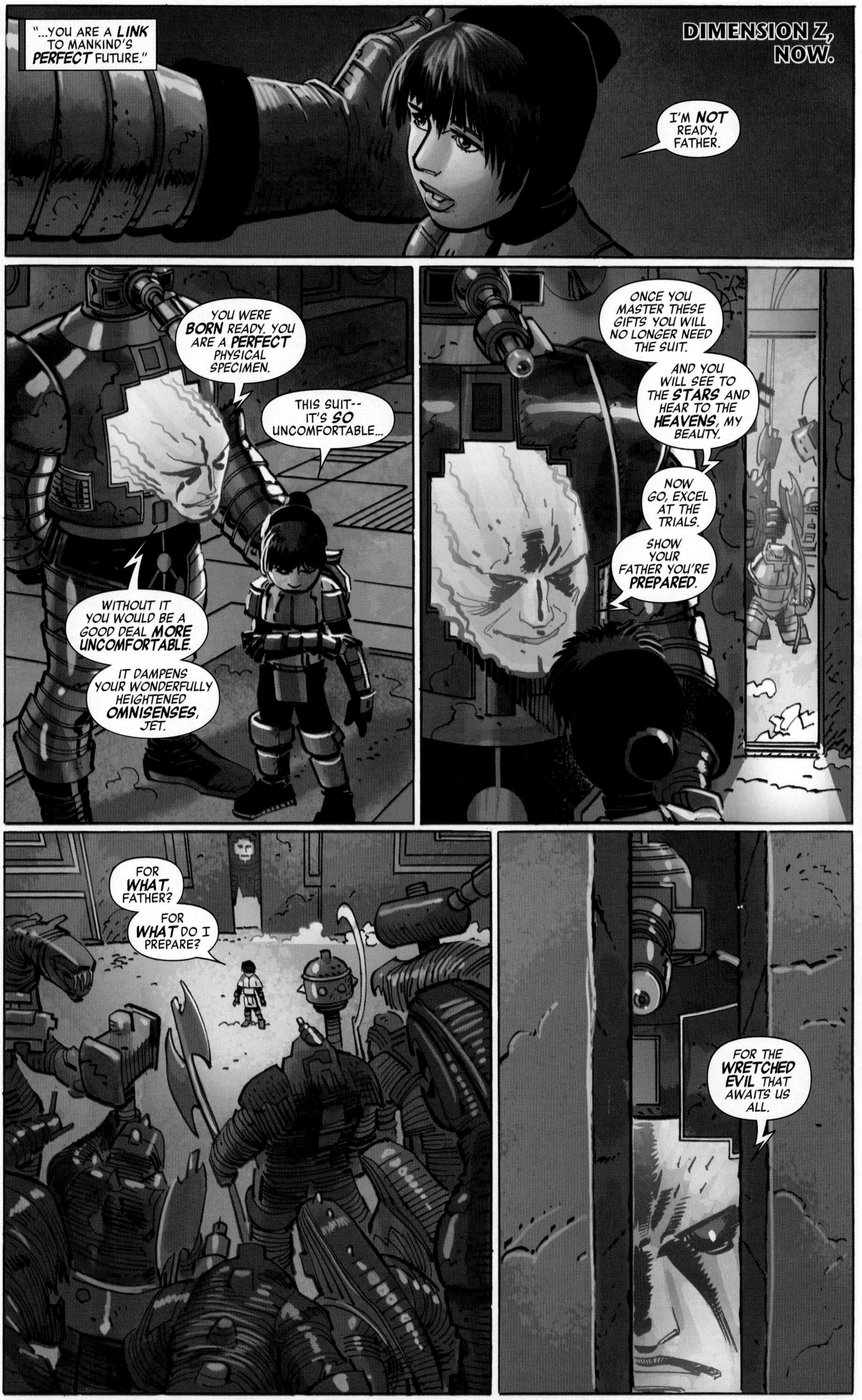
"...YOU ARE A LINK TO MANKIND'S PERFECT FUTURE."
DIMENSION Z, NOW.
I'M NOT READY, FATHER.
YOU WERE BORN READY. YOU ARE A PERFECT PHYSICAL SPECIMEN.
THIS SUIT-- IT'S SO UNCOMFORTABLE...
WITHOUT IT YOU WOULD BE A GOOD DEAL MORE UNCOMFORTABLE.
IT DAMPENS YOUR WONDERFULLY HEIGHTENED OMNISENSES, JET.
ONCE YOU MASTER THESE GIFTS YOU WILL NO LONGER NEED THE SUIT.
AND YOU WILL SEE TO THE STARS AND HEAR TO THE HEAVENS, MY BEAUTY.
NOW GO, EXCEL AT THE TRIALS.
SHOW YOUR FATHER YOU'RE PREPARED.
FOR WHAT, FATHER?
FOR WHAT DO I PREPARE?
FOR THE WRETCHED EVIL THAT AWAITS US ALL.

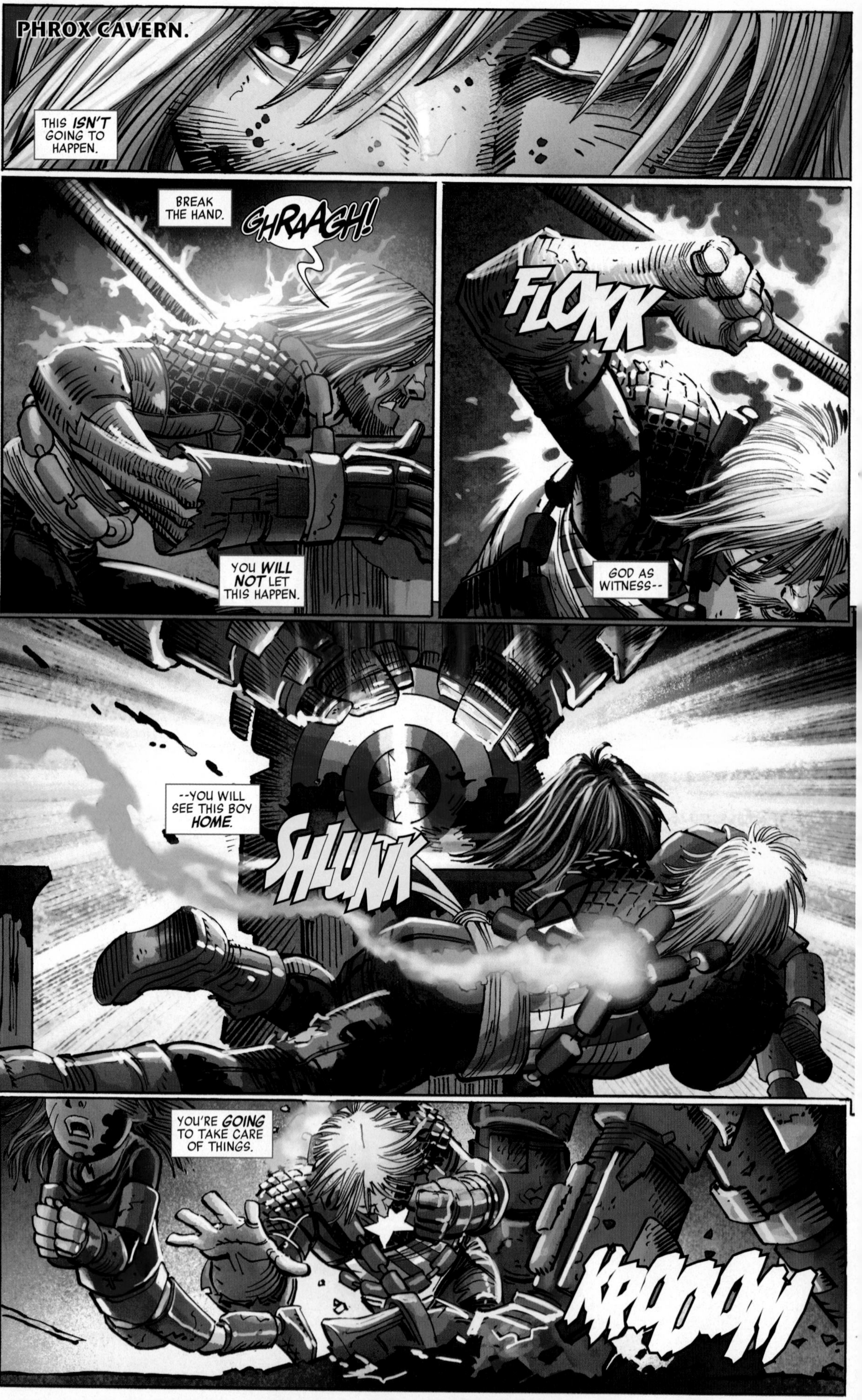
PHROX CAVERN.
THIS ISN'T GOING TO HAPPEN.
BREAK THE HAND.
GHRAAGH!
YOU WILL NOT LET THIS HAPPEN.
FLOKK
GOD AS WITNESS--
--YOU WILL SEE THIS BOY HOME.
SHLUNK
YOU'RE GOING TO TAKE CARE OF THINGS.
KROOOM

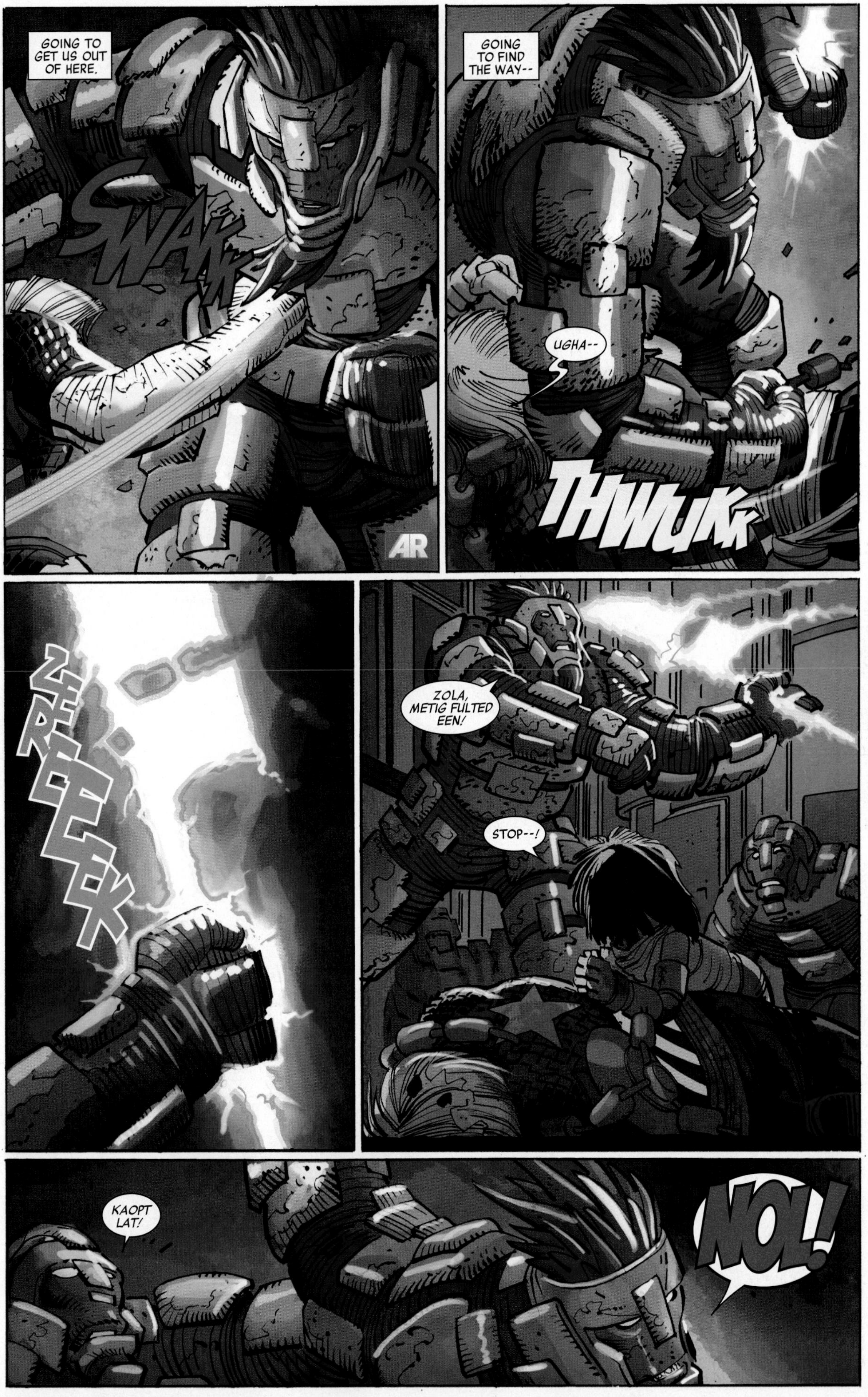
GOING TO GET US OUT OF HERE.
SWAKK
GOING TO FIND THE WAY--
UGHA--
THWUKK
ZEREEEK
ZOLA, METIG FULTED EEN!
STOP--!
KAOPT LAT!
NOL!

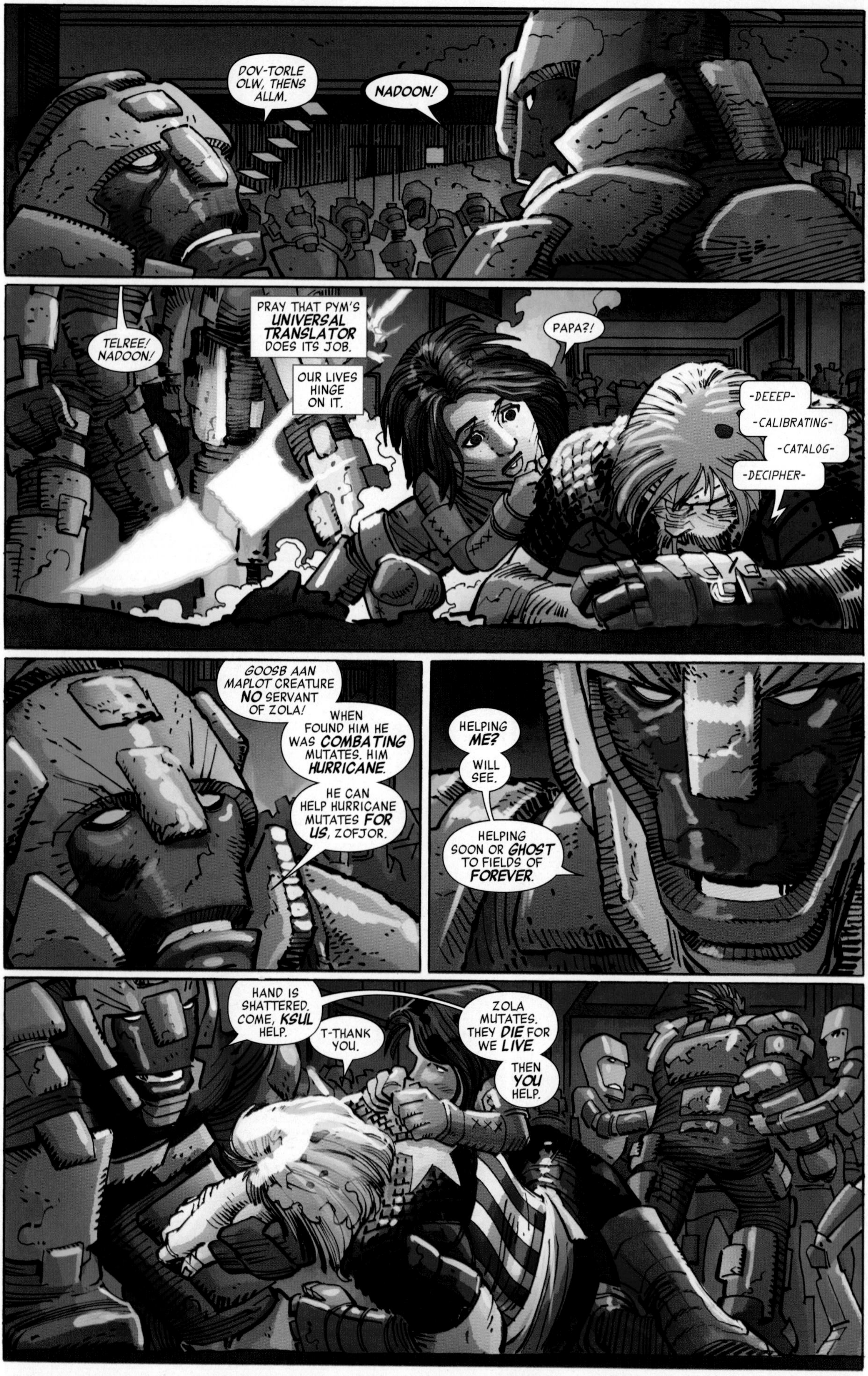
DOV-TORLE OLW, THENS ALLM.
NADOON!
TELREE! NADOON!
PRAY THAT PYM'S UNIVERSAL TRANSLATOR DOES ITS JOB.
OUR LIVES HINGE ON IT.
PAPA?!
-DEEEP-
-CALIBRATING-
-CATALOG-
-DECIPHER-
GOOSB AAN MAPLOT CREATURE NO SERVANT OF ZOLA!
WHEN FOUND HIM HE WAS COMBATING MUTATES. HIM HURRICANE.
HE CAN HELP HURRICANE MUTATES FOR US, ZOFJOR.
HELPING ME?
WILL SEE.
HELPING SOON OR GHOST TO FIELDS OF FOREVER.
HAND IS SHATTERED. COME, KSUL HELP.
T-THANK YOU.
ZOLA MUTATES. THEY DIE FOR WE LIVE.
THEN YOU HELP.

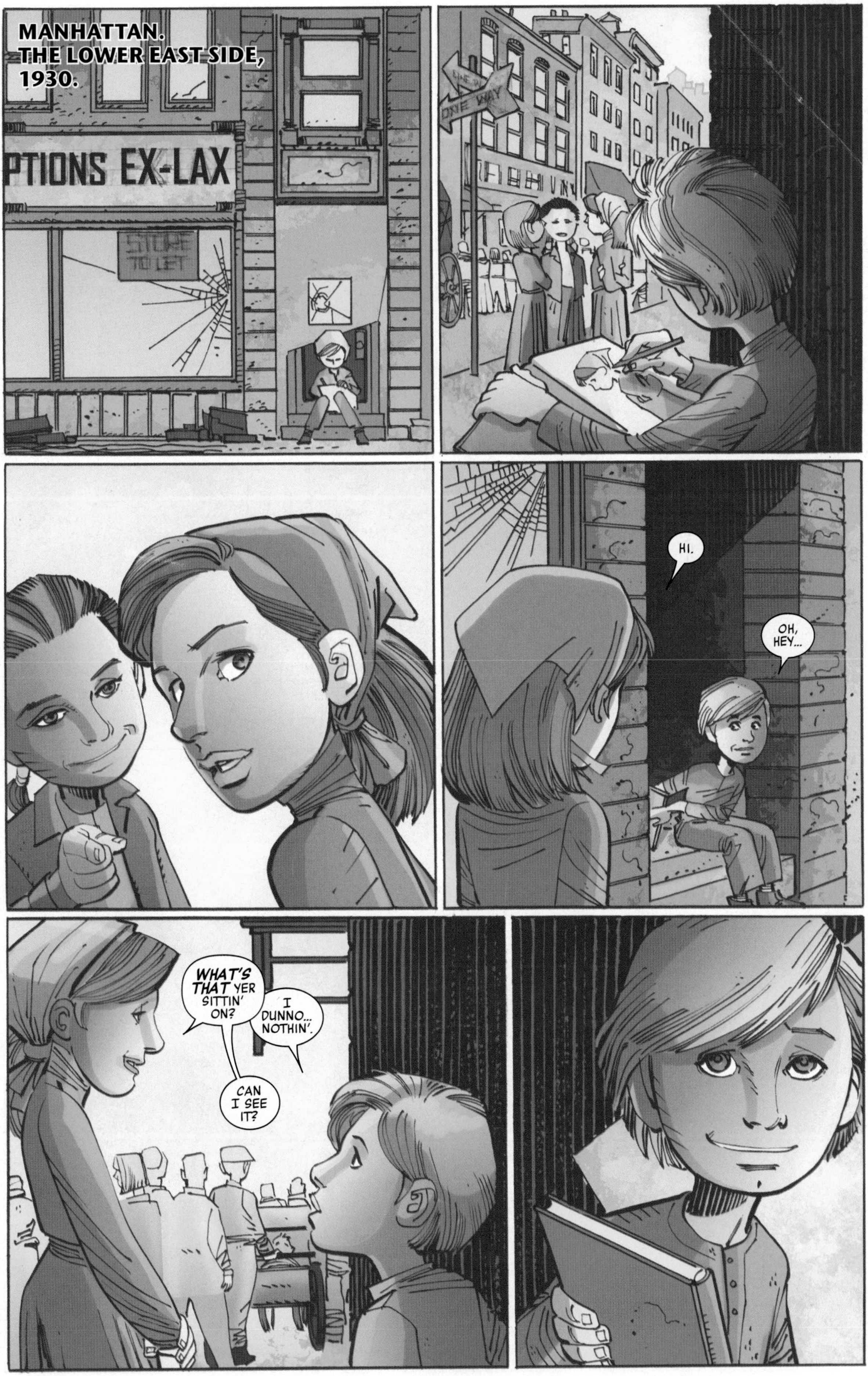
MANHATTAN.
THE LOWER EAST SIDE, 1930.
PTIONS EX-LAX
STORE TO LET
ONE WAY
HI.
OH, HEY...
WHAT'S THAT YER SITTIN' ON?
I DUNNO... NOTHIN'.
CAN I SEE IT?

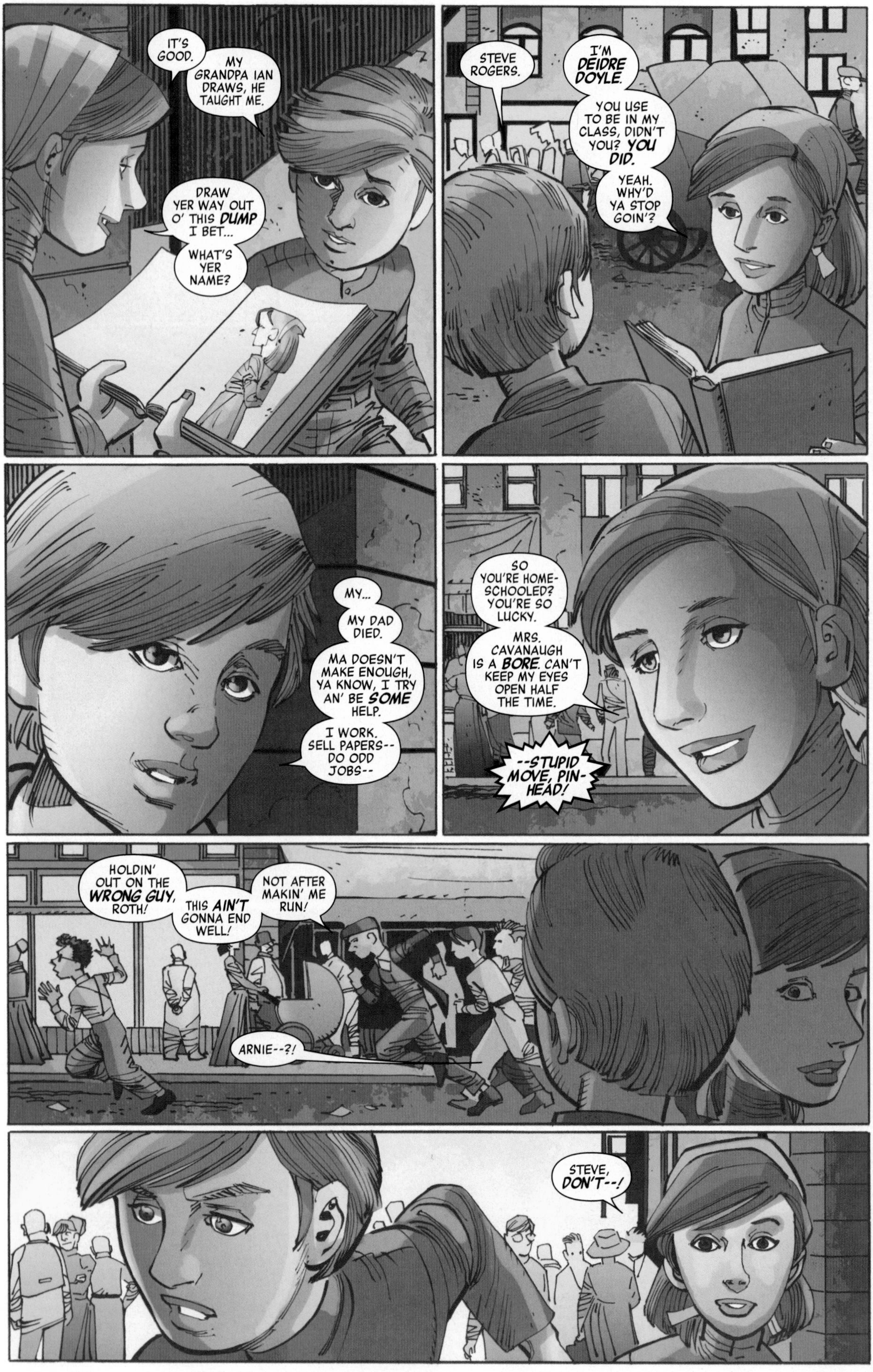
IT'S GOOD.
MY GRANDPA IAN DRAWS, HE TAUGHT ME.
DRAW YER WAY OUT O' THIS DUMP I BET...
WHAT'S YER NAME?
STEVE ROGERS.
I'M DEIDRE DOYLE.
YOU USE TO BE IN MY CLASS, DIDN'T YOU? YOU DID.
YEAH. WHY'D YA STOP GOIN'?
MY...
MY DAD DIED.
MA DOESN'T MAKE ENOUGH, YA KNOW, I TRY AN' BE SOME HELP.
I WORK. SELL PAPERS-- DO ODD JOBS--
SO YOU'RE HOME-SCHOOLED? YOU'RE SO LUCKY.
MRS. CAVANAUGH IS A BORE. CAN'T KEEP MY EYES OPEN HALF THE TIME.
--STUPID MOVE, PIN-HEAD!
HOLDIN' OUT ON THE WRONG GUY, ROTH!
THIS AIN'T GONNA END WELL!
NOT AFTER MAKIN' ME RUN!
ARNIE--?!
STEVE, DON'T--!

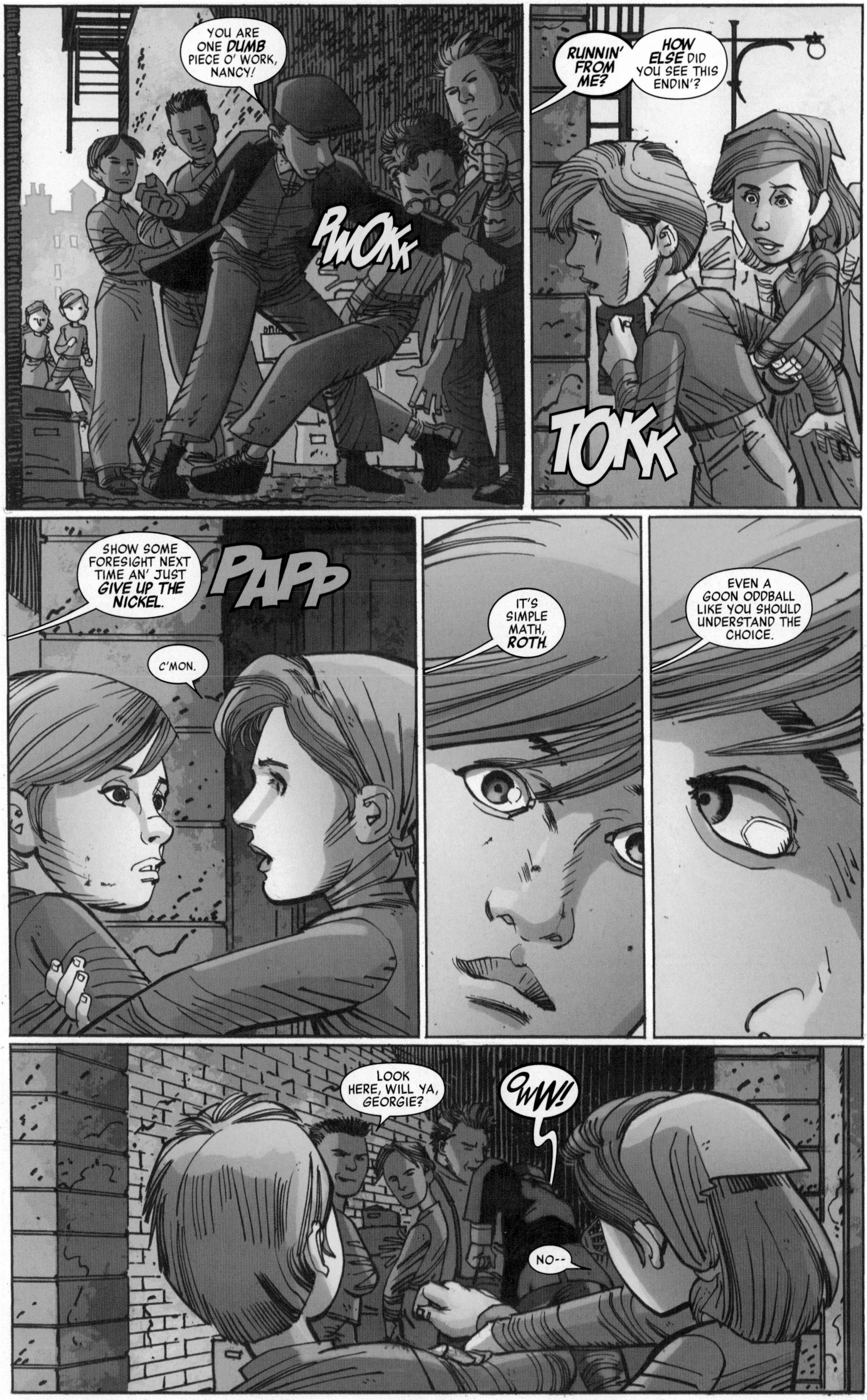
YOU ARE ONE DUMB PIECE O' WORK, NANCY!
PWOKK
RUNNIN' FROM ME?
HOW ELSE DID YOU SEE THIS ENDIN'?
TOKK
SHOW SOME FORESIGHT NEXT TIME AN' JUST GIVE UP THE NICKEL.
PAPP
C'MON.
IT'S SIMPLE MATH, ROTH.
EVEN A GOON ODDBALL LIKE YOU SHOULD UNDERSTAND THE CHOICE.
LOOK HERE, WILL YA, GEORGIE?
OWW!
NO--

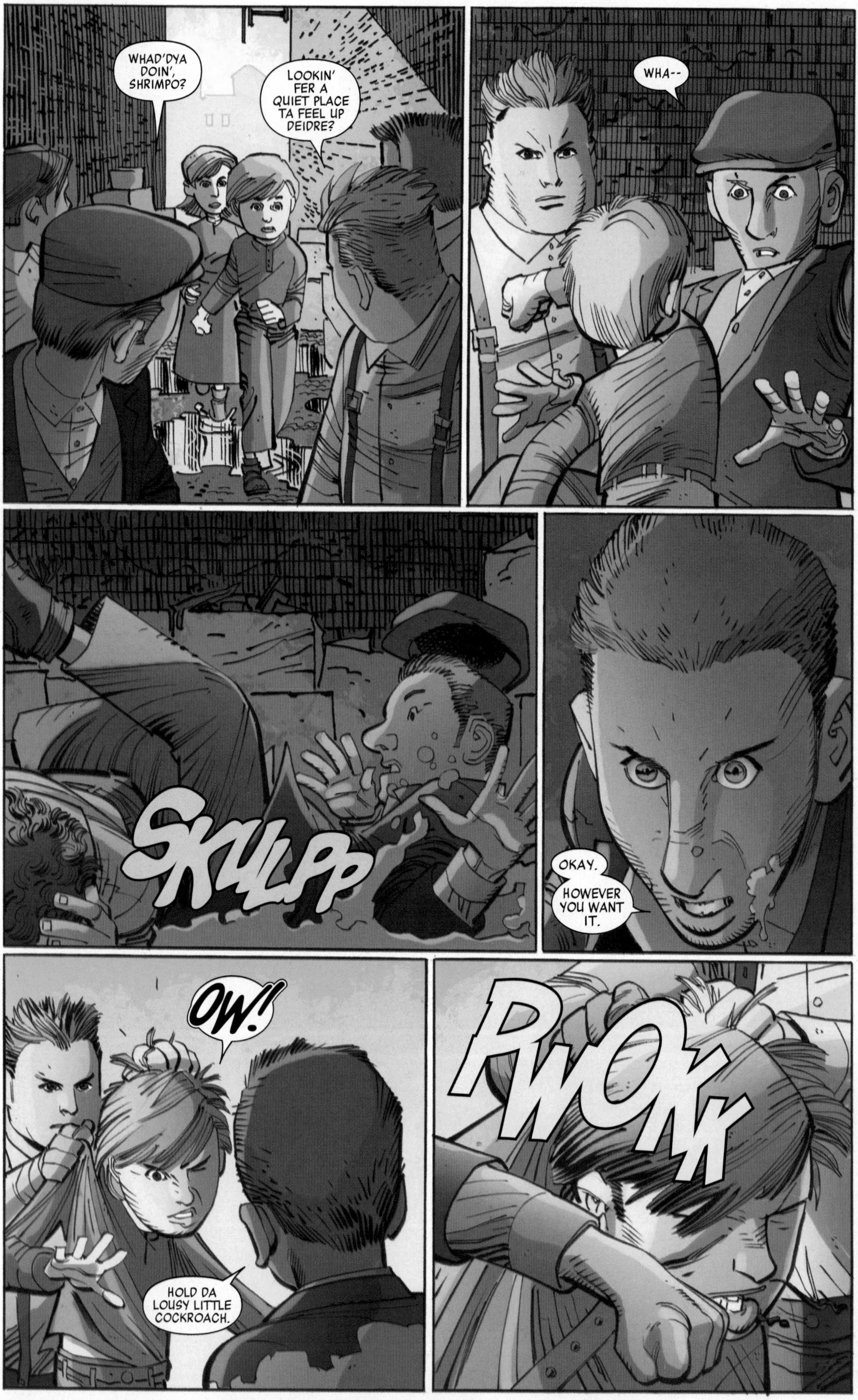
WHAD'DYA DOIN', SHRIMPO?
LOOKIN' FER A QUIET PLACE TA FEEL UP DEIDRE?
WHA--
SKULPP
OKAY. HOWEVER YOU WANT IT.
OW!
HOLD DA LOUSY LITTLE COCKROACH.
PWONK

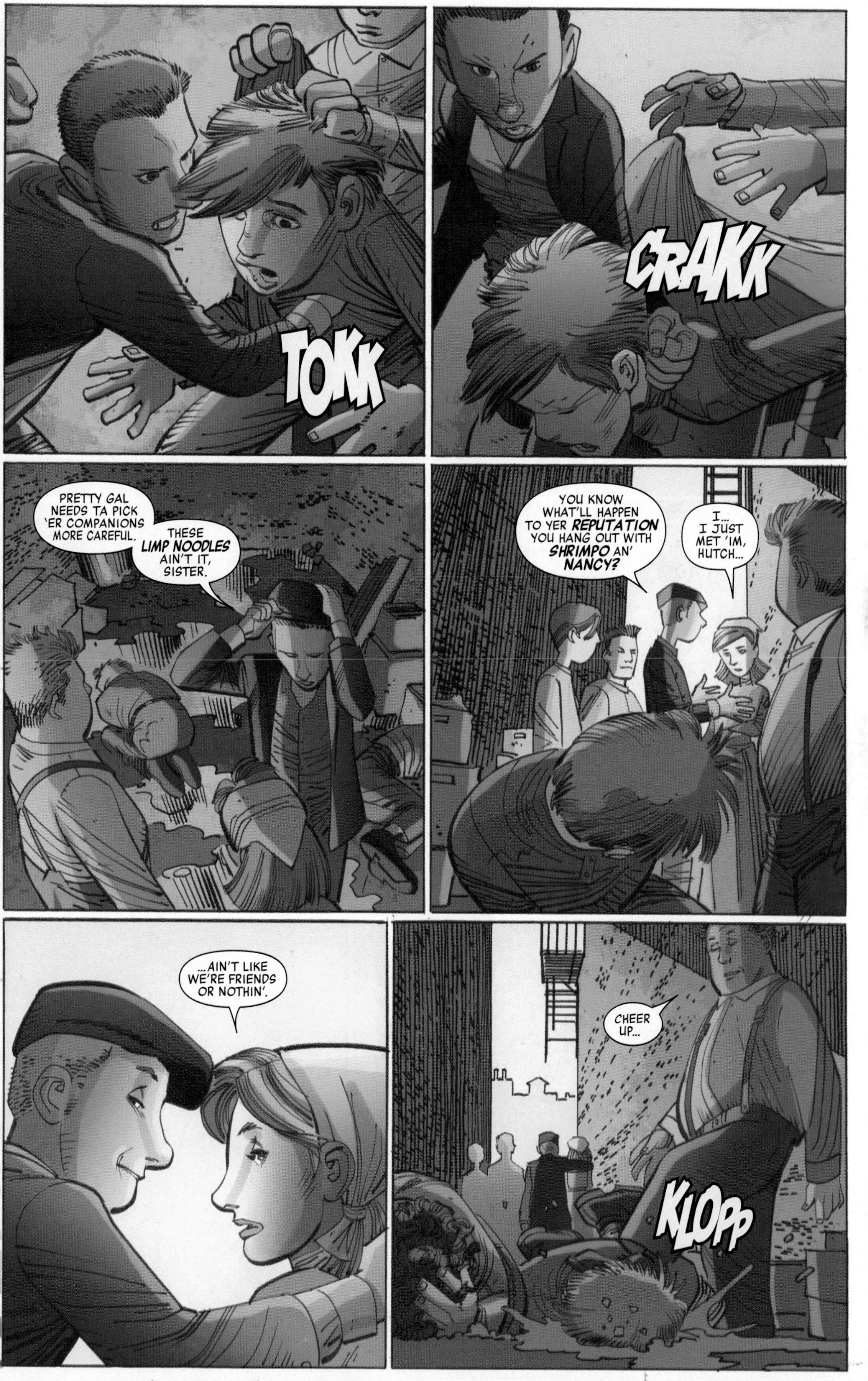
TOKK
CRAKK
PRETTY GAL NEEDS TA PICK 'ER COMPANIONS MORE CAREFUL.
THESE **LIMP NOODLES** AIN'T IT, SISTER.
YOU KNOW WHAT'LL HAPPEN TO YER **REPUTATION** YOU HANG OUT WITH **SHRIMPO** AN' **NANCY?**
I... I JUST MET 'IM, HUTCH...
...AIN'T LIKE WE'RE FRIENDS OR NOTHIN'.
CHEER UP...
KLOPP

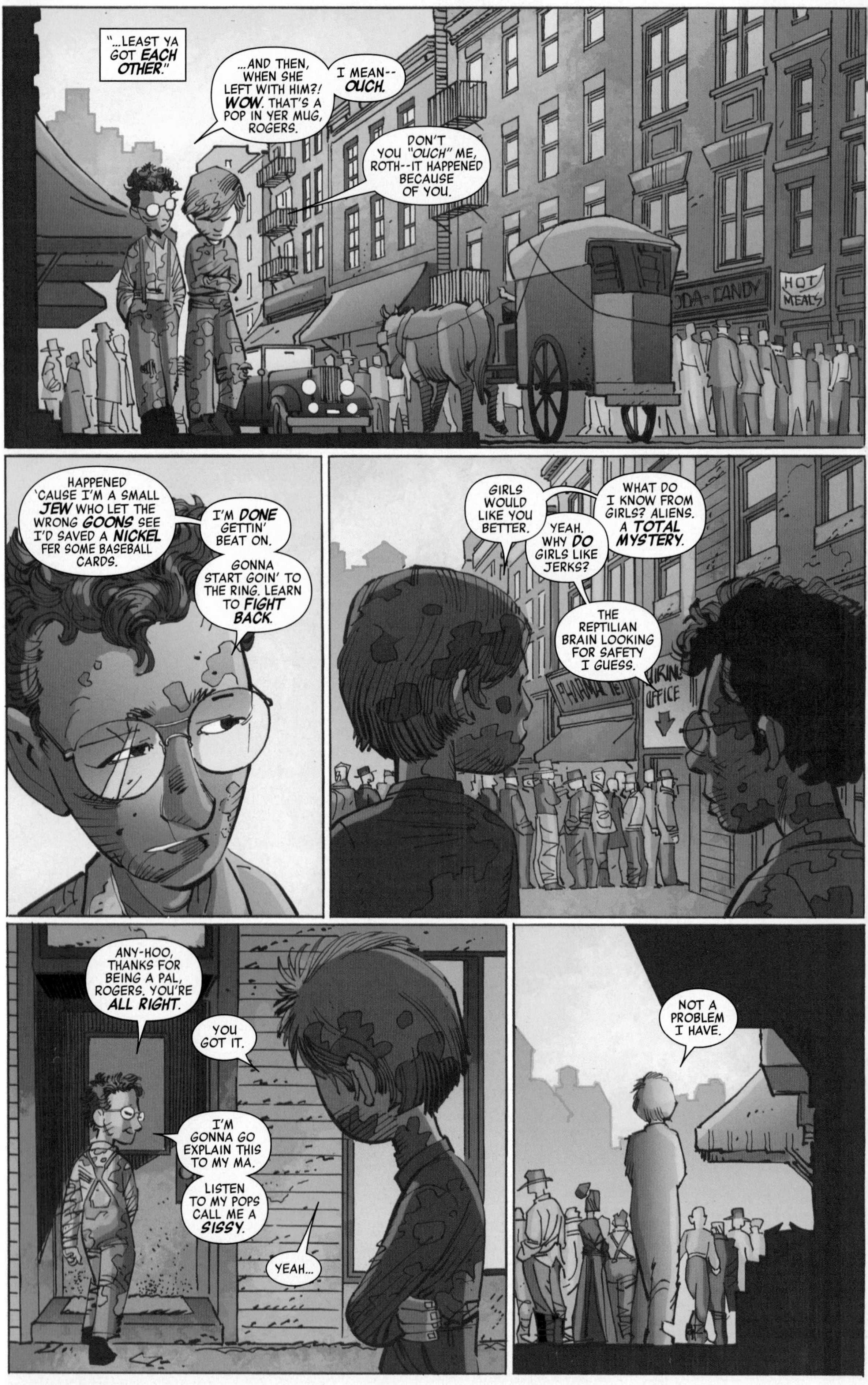
"...LEAST YA GOT EACH OTHER."
...AND THEN, WHEN SHE LEFT WITH HIM?! WOW. THAT'S A POP IN YER MUG, ROGERS.
I MEAN-- OUCH.
DON'T YOU "OUCH" ME, ROTH--IT HAPPENED BECAUSE OF YOU.
SODA-CANDY
HOT MEALS
HAPPENED 'CAUSE I'M A SMALL JEW WHO LET THE WRONG GOONS SEE I'D SAVED A NICKEL FER SOME BASEBALL CARDS.
I'M DONE GETTIN' BEAT ON.
GONNA START GOIN' TO THE RING. LEARN TO FIGHT BACK.
GIRLS WOULD LIKE YOU BETTER.
WHAT DO I KNOW FROM GIRLS? ALIENS. A TOTAL MYSTERY.
YEAH. WHY DO GIRLS LIKE JERKS?
THE REPTILIAN BRAIN LOOKING FOR SAFETY I GUESS.
OFFICE
ANY-HOO, THANKS FOR BEING A PAL, ROGERS. YOU'RE ALL RIGHT.
YOU GOT IT.
I'M GONNA GO EXPLAIN THIS TO MY MA.
LISTEN TO MY POPS CALL ME A SISSY.
YEAH...
NOT A PROBLEM I HAVE.

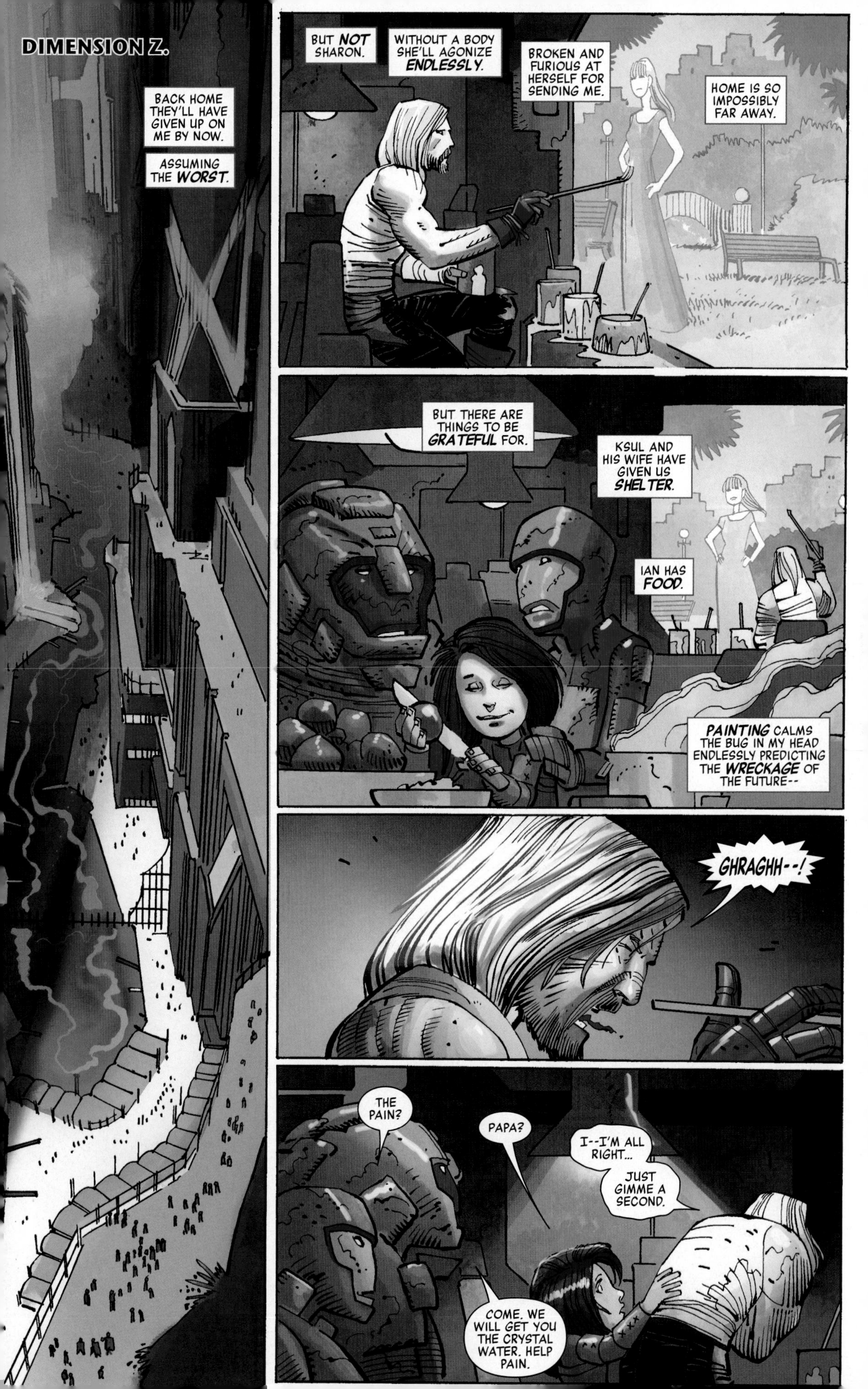
DIMENSION Z.
BACK HOME THEY'LL HAVE GIVEN UP ON ME BY NOW.
ASSUMING THE WORST.
BUT NOT SHARON.
WITHOUT A BODY SHE'LL AGONIZE ENDLESSLY.
BROKEN AND FURIOUS AT HERSELF FOR SENDING ME.
HOME IS SO IMPOSSIBLY FAR AWAY.
BUT THERE ARE THINGS TO BE GRATEFUL FOR.
KSUL AND HIS WIFE HAVE GIVEN US SHELTER.
IAN HAS FOOD.
PAINTING CALMS THE BUG IN MY HEAD ENDLESSLY PREDICTING THE WRECKAGE OF THE FUTURE--
GHRAGHH--!
THE PAIN?
PAPA?
I--I'M ALL RIGHT...
JUST GIMME A SECOND.
COME. WE WILL GET YOU THE CRYSTAL WATER. HELP PAIN.

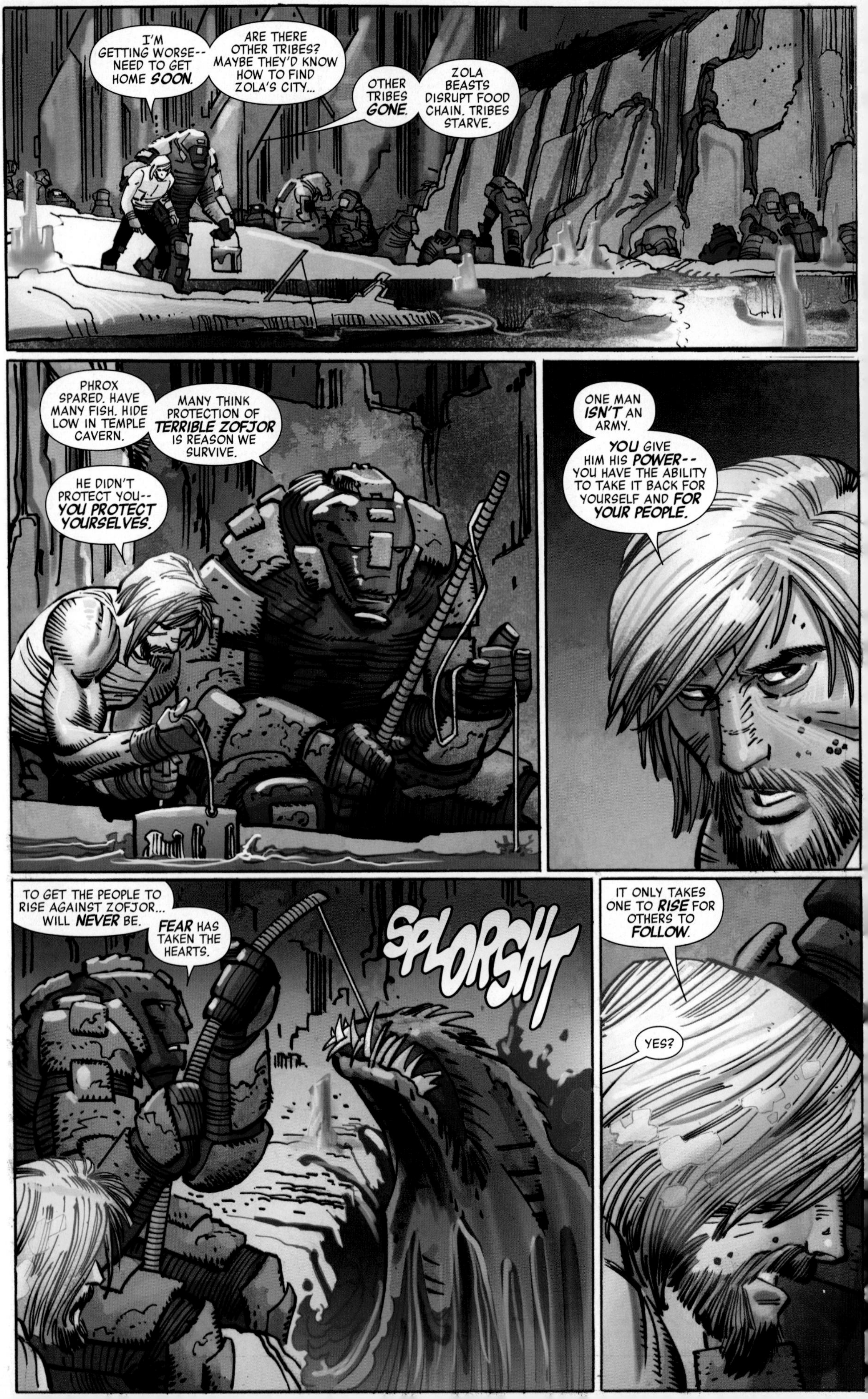
I'M GETTING WORSE-- NEED TO GET HOME SOON.
ARE THERE OTHER TRIBES? MAYBE THEY'D KNOW HOW TO FIND ZOLA'S CITY...
OTHER TRIBES GONE.
ZOLA BEASTS DISRUPT FOOD CHAIN. TRIBES STARVE.
PHROX SPARED. HAVE MANY FISH. HIDE LOW IN TEMPLE CAVERN.
MANY THINK PROTECTION OF TERRIBLE ZOFJOR IS REASON WE SURVIVE.
HE DIDN'T PROTECT YOU-- YOU PROTECT YOURSELVES.
ONE MAN ISN'T AN ARMY.
YOU GIVE HIM HIS POWER-- YOU HAVE THE ABILITY TO TAKE IT BACK FOR YOURSELF AND FOR YOUR PEOPLE.
TO GET THE PEOPLE TO RISE AGAINST ZOFJOR... WILL NEVER BE.
FEAR HAS TAKEN THE HEARTS.
SPLORSHT
IT ONLY TAKES ONE TO RISE FOR OTHERS TO FOLLOW.
YES?

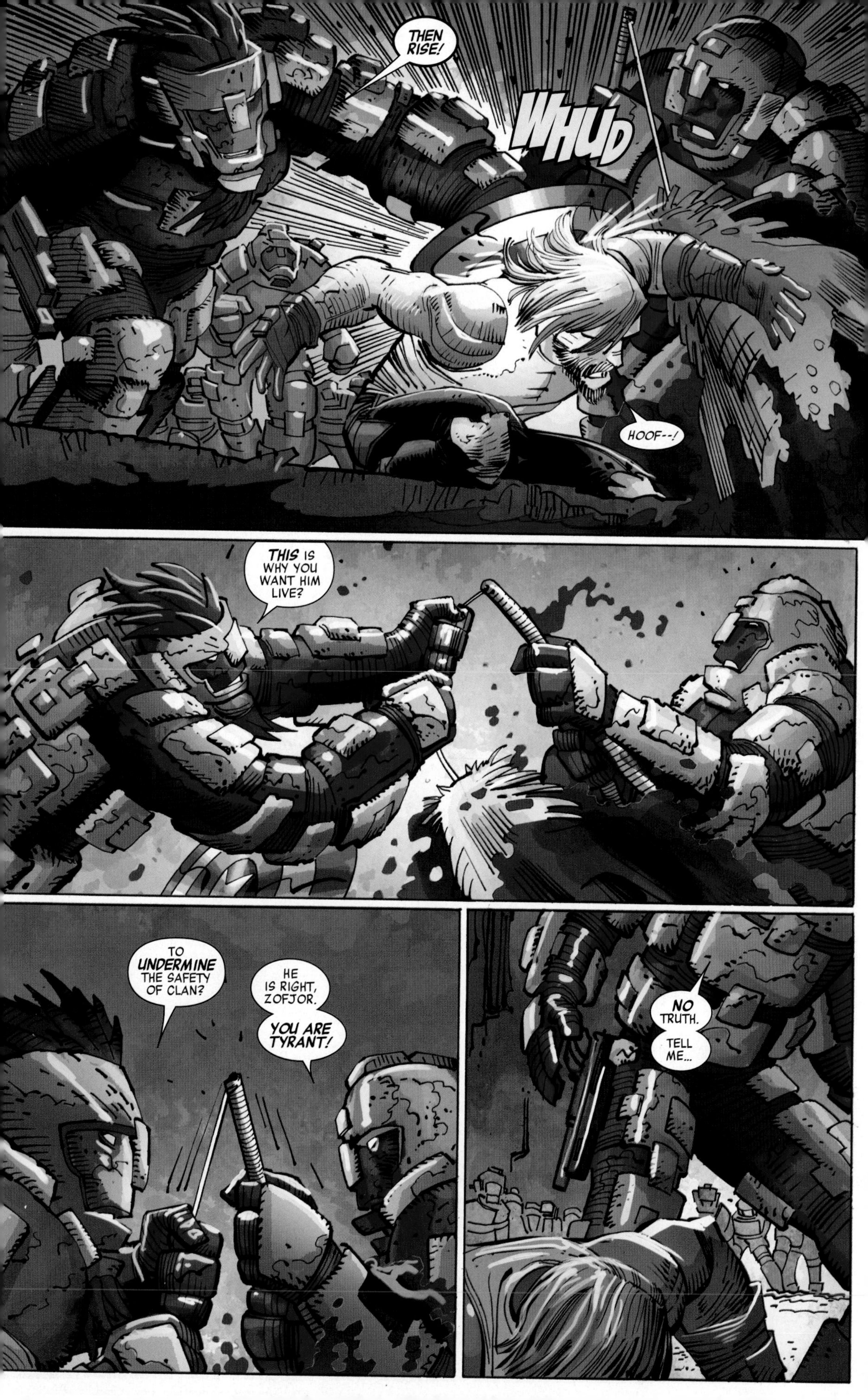
THEN RISE!
WHUD
HOOF--!
THIS IS WHY YOU WANT HIM LIVE?
TO UNDERMINE THE SAFETY OF CLAN?
HE IS RIGHT, ZOFJOR.
YOU ARE TYRANT!
NO TRUTH.
TELL ME...

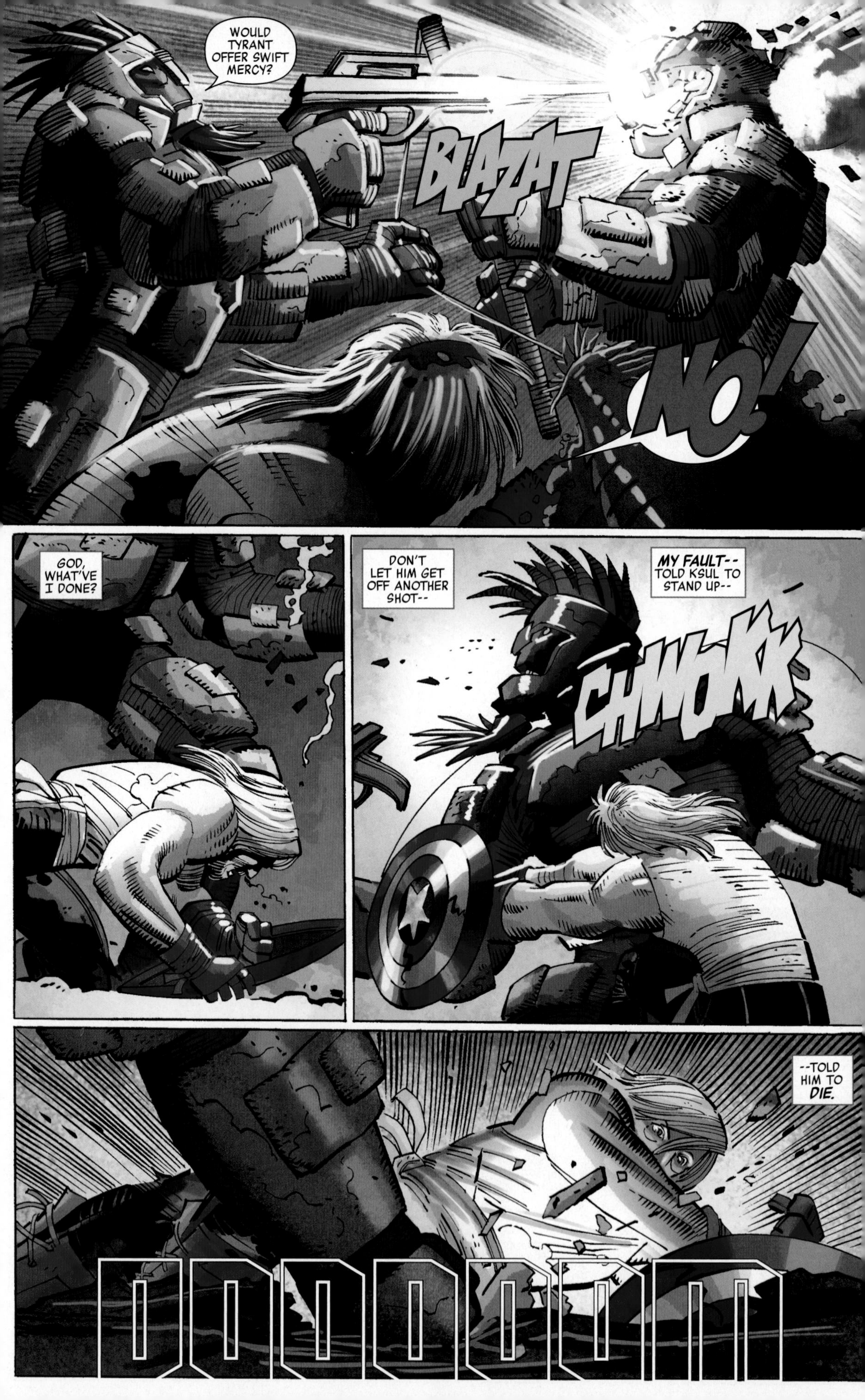
WOULD TYRANT OFFER SWIFT MERCY?
BLAZAT
NO!
GOD, WHAT'VE I DONE?
DON'T LET HIM GET OFF ANOTHER SHOT--
MY FAULT--TOLD KSUL TO STAND UP--
CHWOKK
--TOLD HIM TO DIE.
DOOOOOM

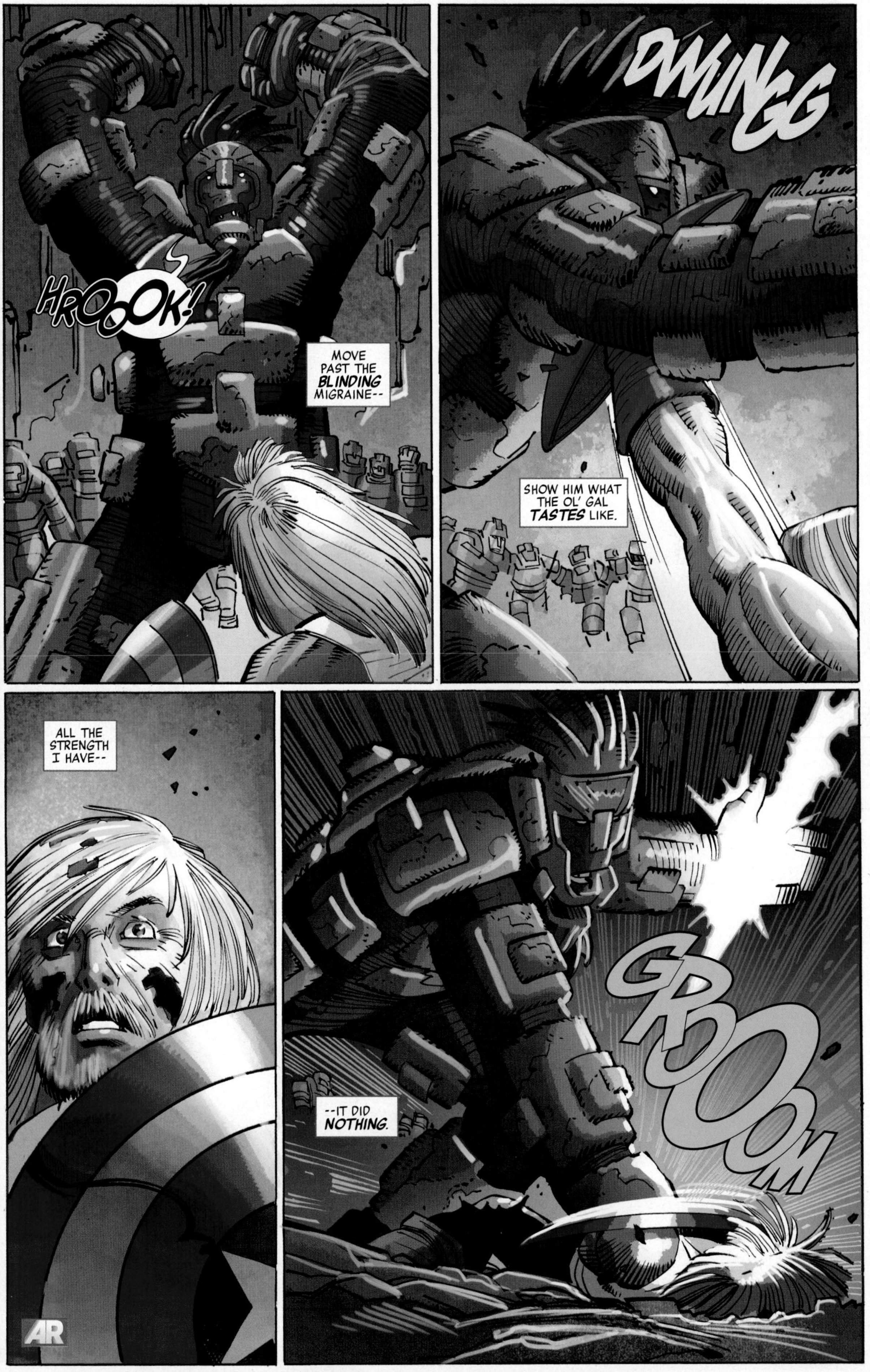
HROOOOK!
MOVE PAST THE BLINDING MIGRAINE--
DWUNGG
SHOW HIM WHAT THE OL' GAL TASTES LIKE.
ALL THE STRENGTH I HAVE--
GROOOM
--IT DID NOTHING.
AR

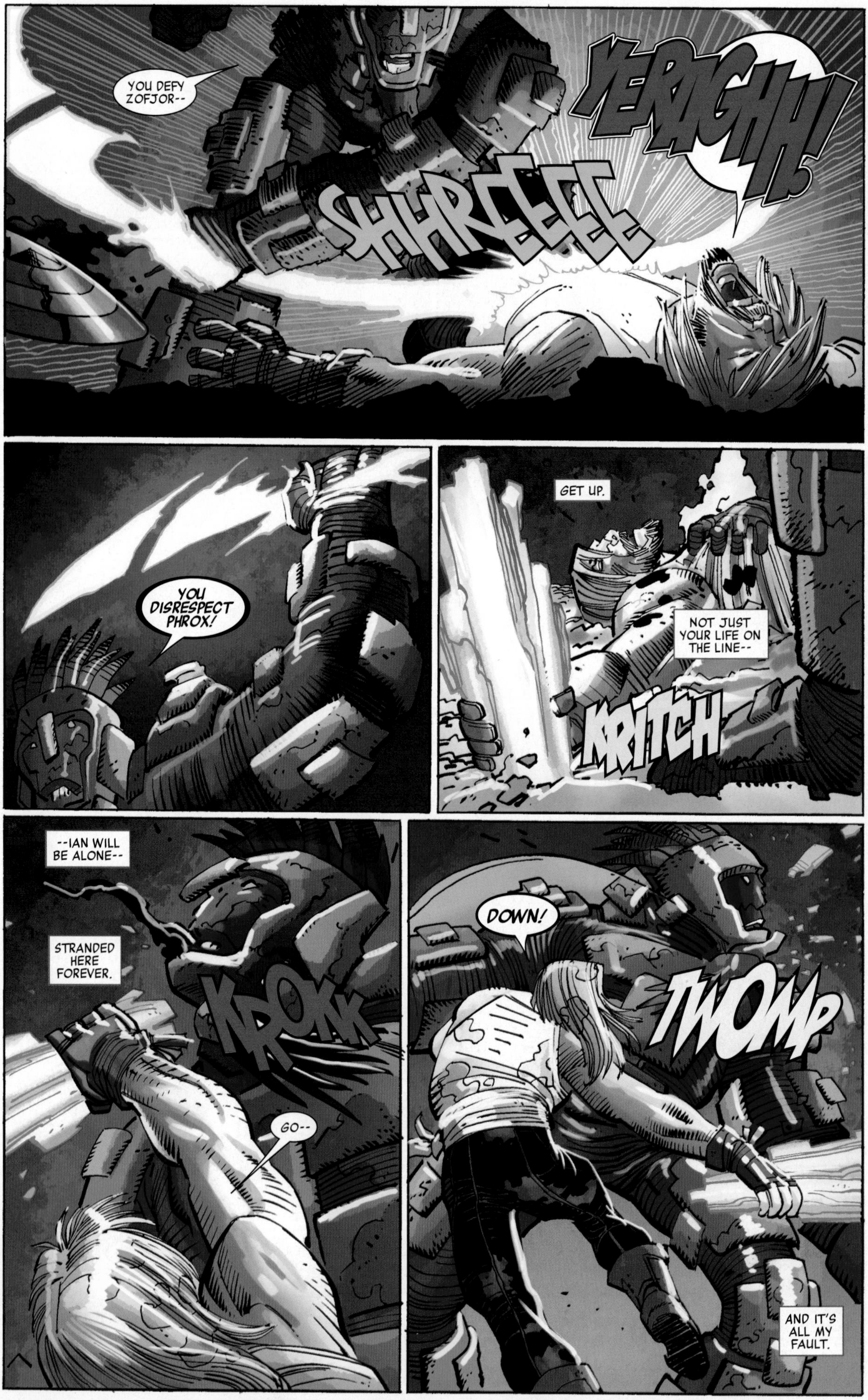

YOU DEFY ZOFJOR--
YEAAGHH!
SHHREEEEE
YOU DISRESPECT PHROX!
GET UP.
NOT JUST YOUR LIFE ON THE LINE--
KRITCH
--IAN WILL BE ALONE--
STRANDED HERE FOREVER.
KROKK
GO--
DOWN!
TWOMP
AND IT'S ALL MY FAULT.

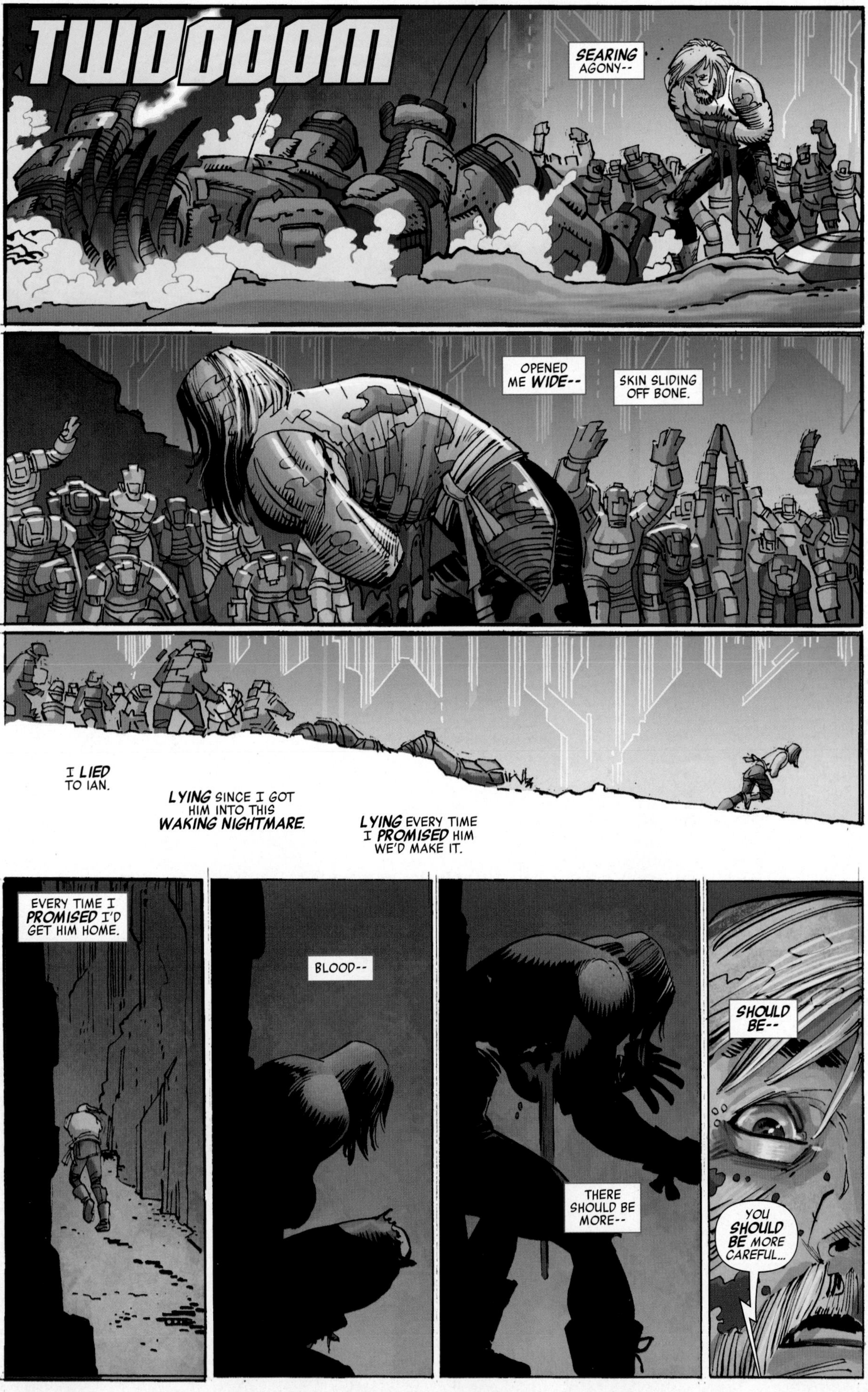
TWOOOOM
SEARING AGONY--
OPENED ME WIDE--
SKIN SLIDING OFF BONE.
I LIED TO IAN.
LYING SINCE I GOT HIM INTO THIS WAKING NIGHTMARE.
LYING EVERY TIME I PROMISED HIM WE'D MAKE IT.
EVERY TIME I PROMISED I'D GET HIM HOME.
BLOOD--
THERE SHOULD BE MORE--
SHOULD BE--
YOU SHOULD BE MORE CAREFUL...

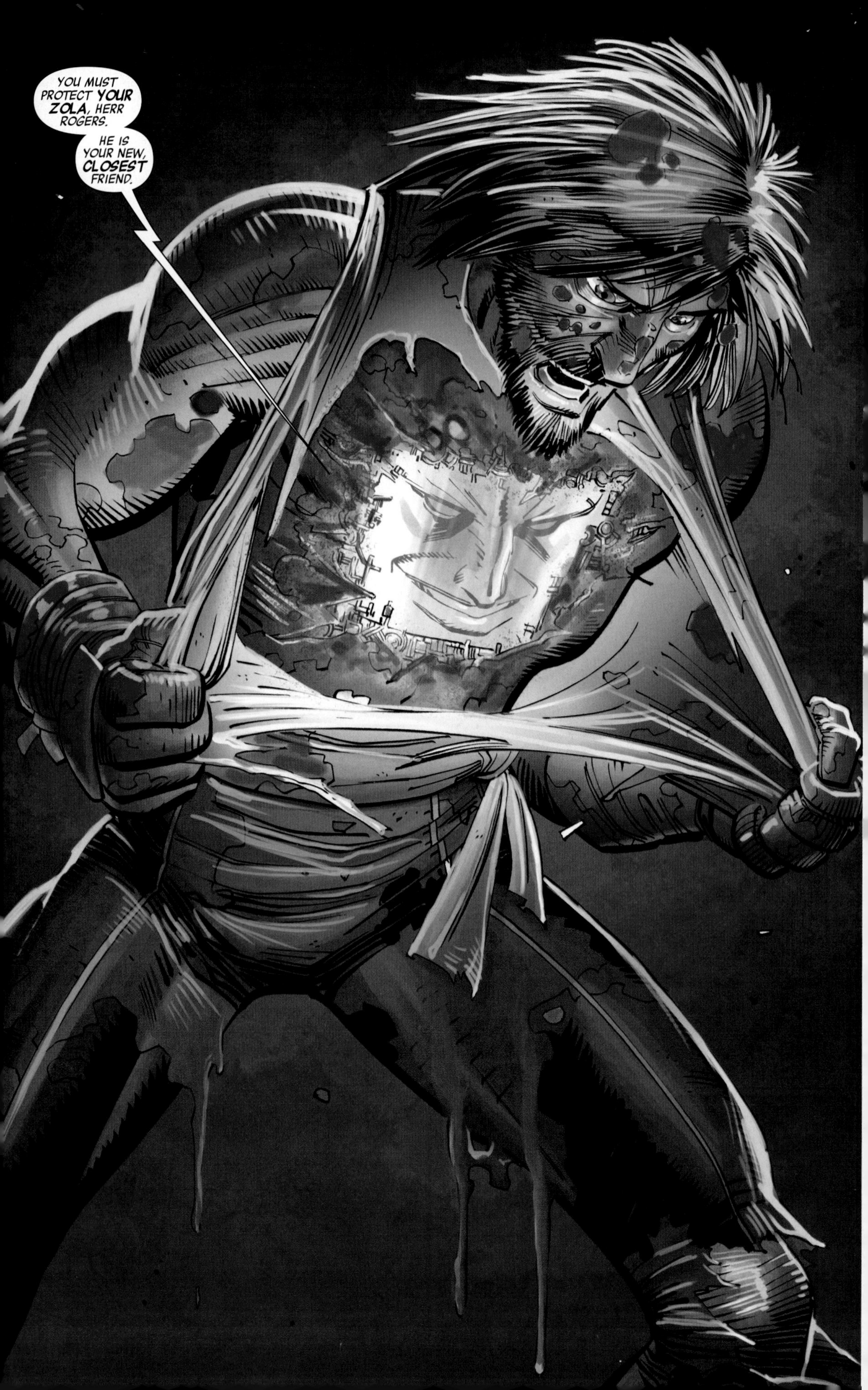
YOU MUST PROTECT YOUR ZOLA, HERR ROGERS.
HE IS YOUR NEW, CLOSEST FRIEND.

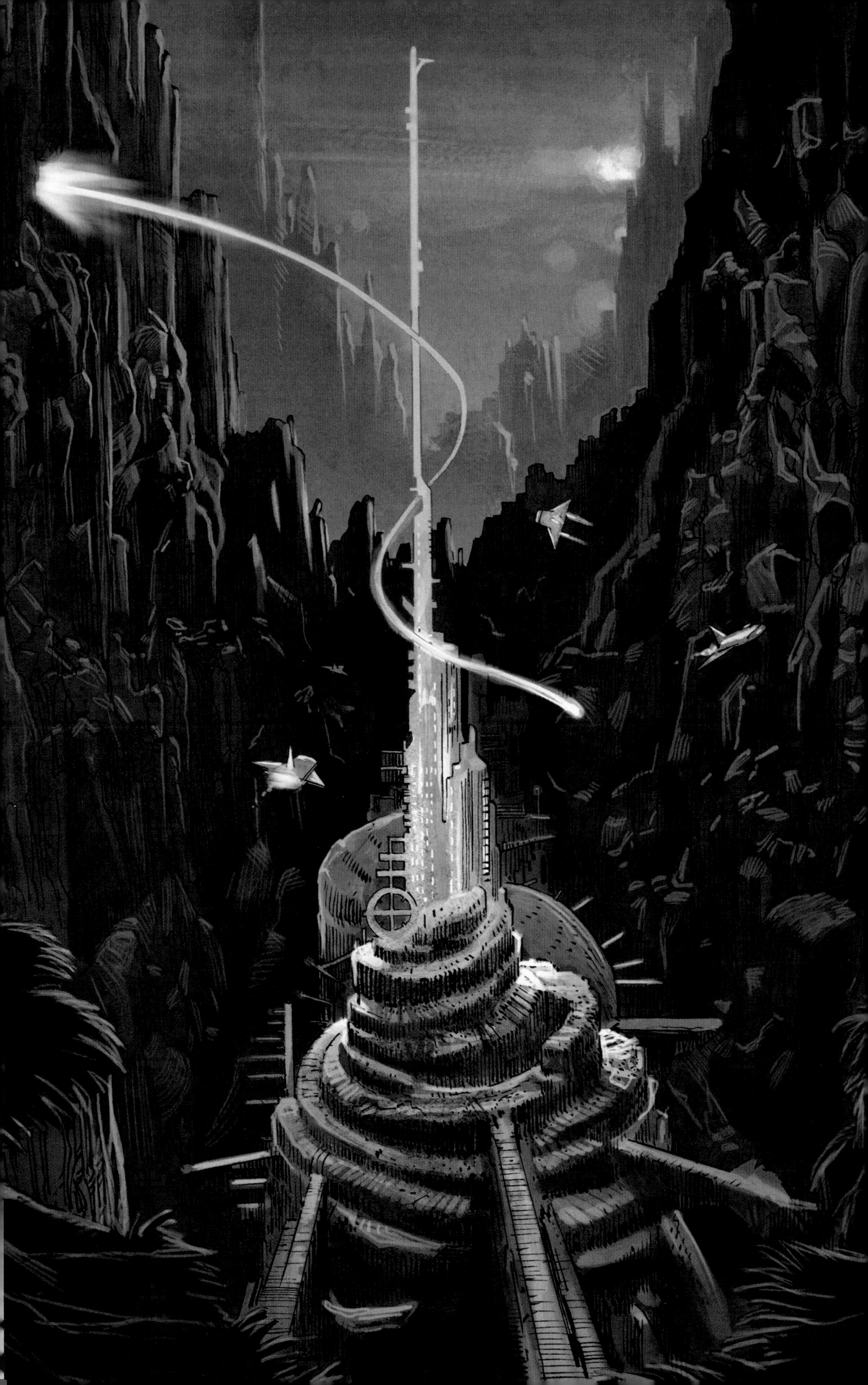

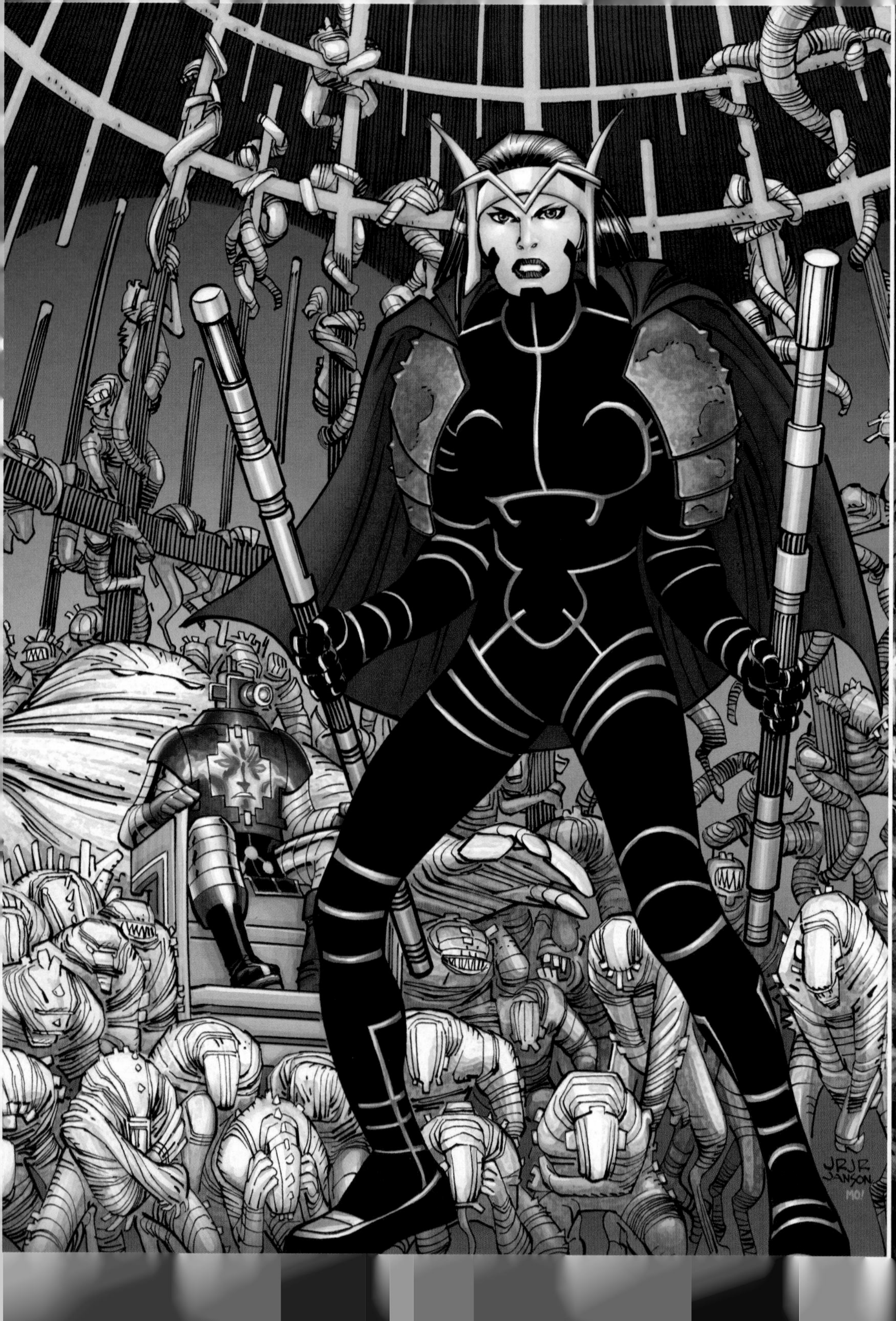
JRJR
JANSON
MO!

ELEVEN YEARS LATER.

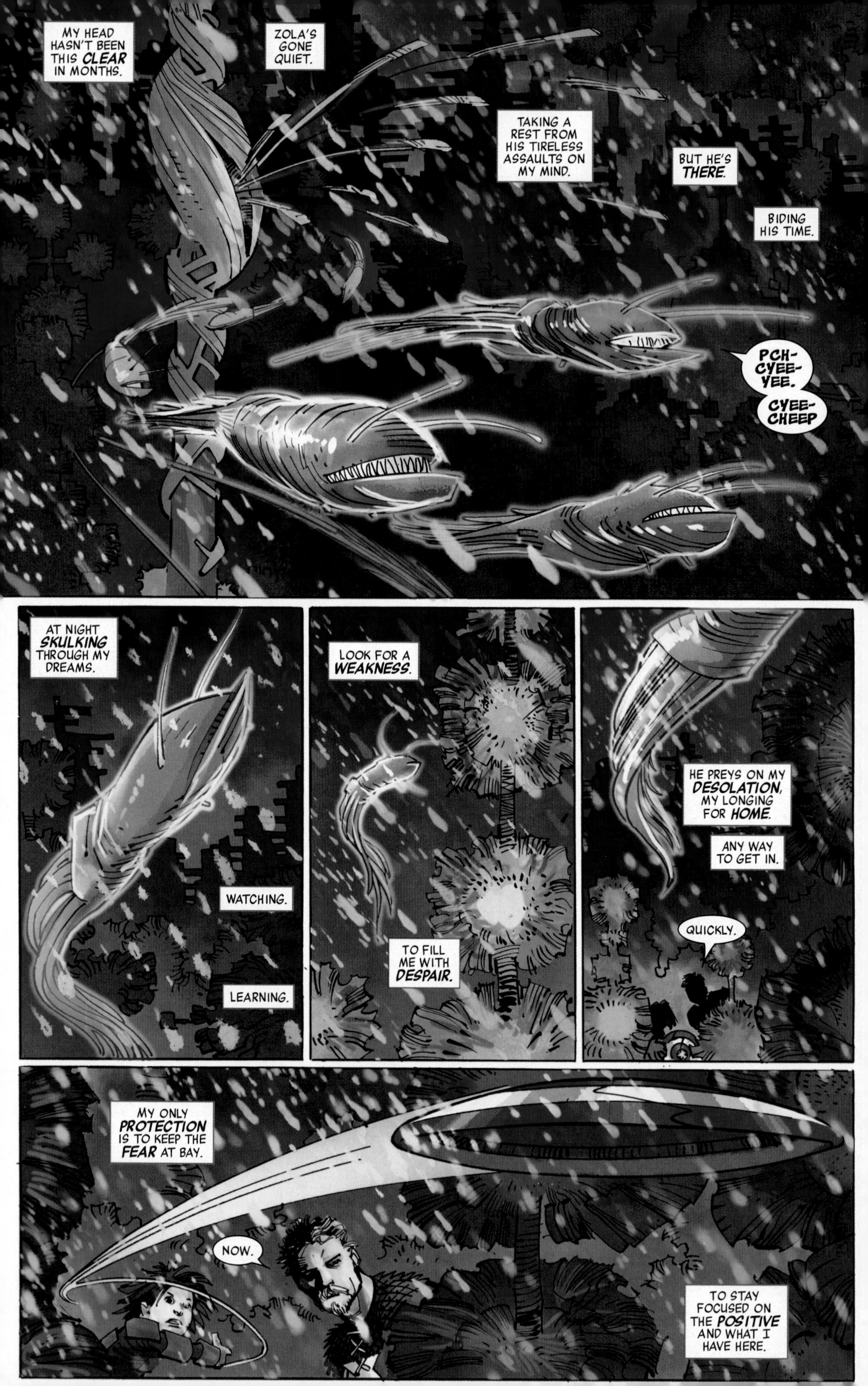
MY HEAD HASN'T BEEN THIS CLEAR IN MONTHS.
ZOLA'S GONE QUIET.
TAKING A REST FROM HIS TIRELESS ASSAULTS ON MY MIND.
BUT HE'S THERE.
BIDING HIS TIME.
PCH-CYEE-YEE.
CYEE-CHEEP
AT NIGHT SKULKING THROUGH MY DREAMS.
WATCHING.
LEARNING.
LOOK FOR A WEAKNESS.
TO FILL ME WITH DESPAIR.
HE PREYS ON MY DESOLATION, MY LONGING FOR HOME.
ANY WAY TO GET IN.
QUICKLY.
MY ONLY PROTECTION IS TO KEEP THE FEAR AT BAY.
NOW.
TO STAY FOCUSED ON THE POSITIVE AND WHAT I HAVE HERE.

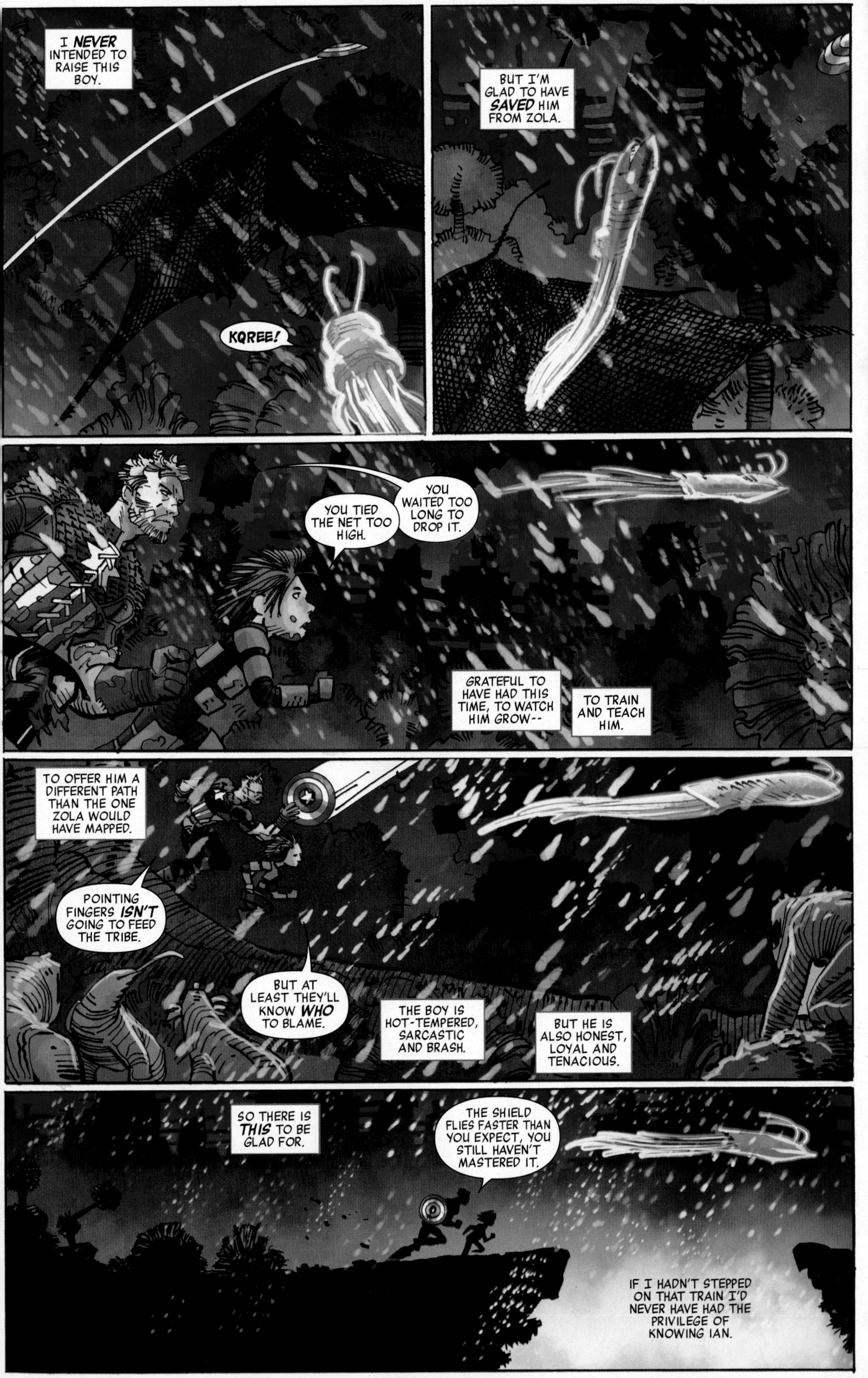
I NEVER INTENDED TO RAISE THIS BOY.
KQREE!
BUT I'M GLAD TO HAVE SAVED HIM FROM ZOLA.
YOU TIED THE NET TOO HIGH.
YOU WAITED TOO LONG TO DROP IT.
GRATEFUL TO HAVE HAD THIS TIME, TO WATCH HIM GROW--
TO TRAIN AND TEACH HIM.
TO OFFER HIM A DIFFERENT PATH THAN THE ONE ZOLA WOULD HAVE MAPPED.
POINTING FINGERS ISN'T GOING TO FEED THE TRIBE.
BUT AT LEAST THEY'LL KNOW WHO TO BLAME.
THE BOY IS HOT-TEMPERED, SARCASTIC AND BRASH.
BUT HE IS ALSO HONEST, LOYAL AND TENACIOUS.
SO THERE IS THIS TO BE GLAD FOR.
THE SHIELD FLIES FASTER THAN YOU EXPECT, YOU STILL HAVEN'T MASTERED IT.
IF I HADN'T STEPPED ON THAT TRAIN I'D NEVER HAVE HAD THE PRIVILEGE OF KNOWING IAN.

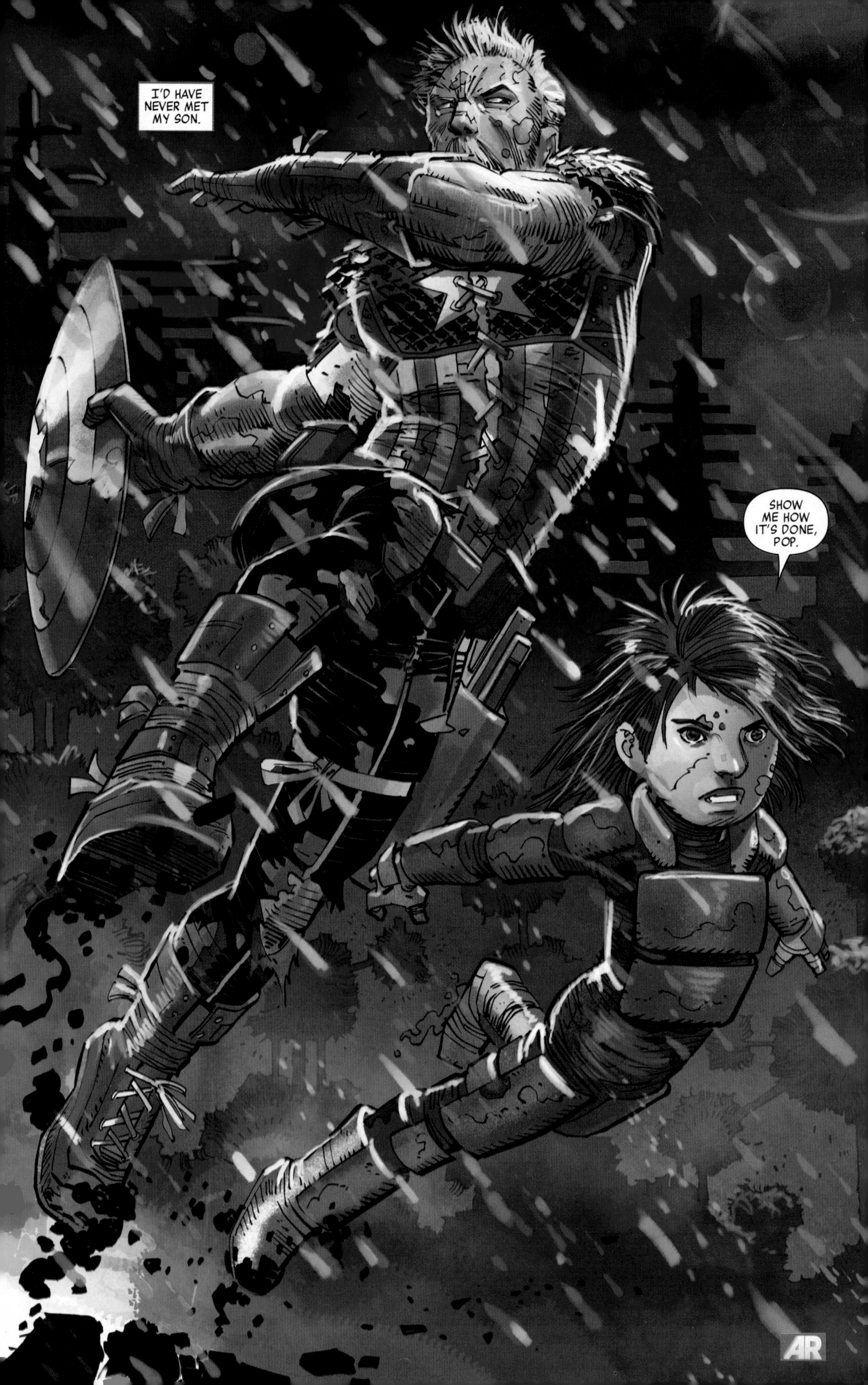
I'D HAVE NEVER MET MY SON.
SHOW ME HOW IT'S DONE, POP.

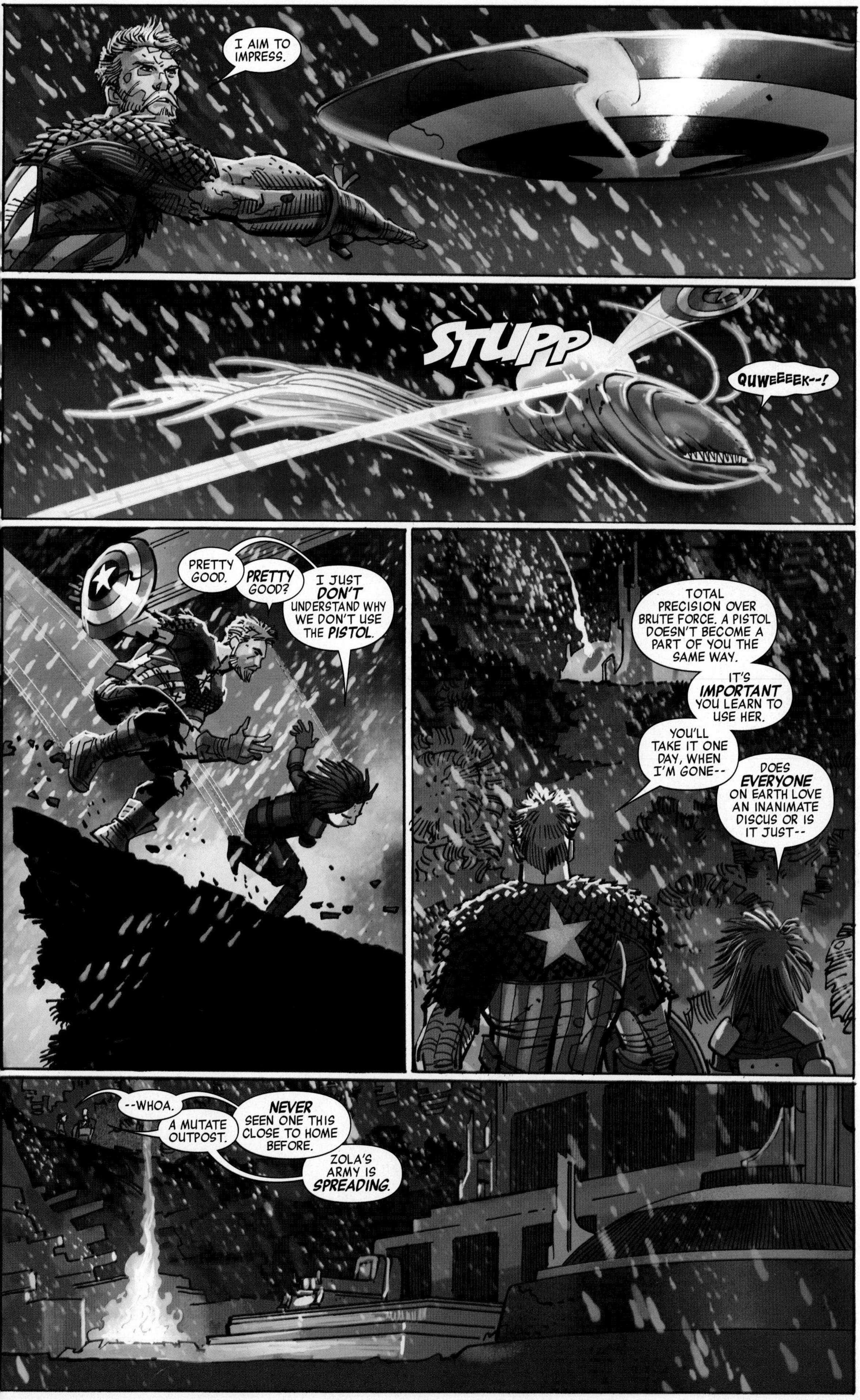
I AIM TO IMPRESS.
STUPP
QUWEEEEK--!
PRETTY GOOD.
PRETTY GOOD?
I JUST DON'T UNDERSTAND WHY WE DON'T USE THE PISTOL.
TOTAL PRECISION OVER BRUTE FORCE. A PISTOL DOESN'T BECOME A PART OF YOU THE SAME WAY.
IT'S IMPORTANT YOU LEARN TO USE HER.
YOU'LL TAKE IT ONE DAY, WHEN I'M GONE--
DOES EVERYONE ON EARTH LOVE AN INANIMATE DISCUS OR IS IT JUST--
--WHOA.
A MUTATE OUTPOST.
NEVER SEEN ONE THIS CLOSE TO HOME BEFORE.
ZOLA'S ARMY IS SPREADING.

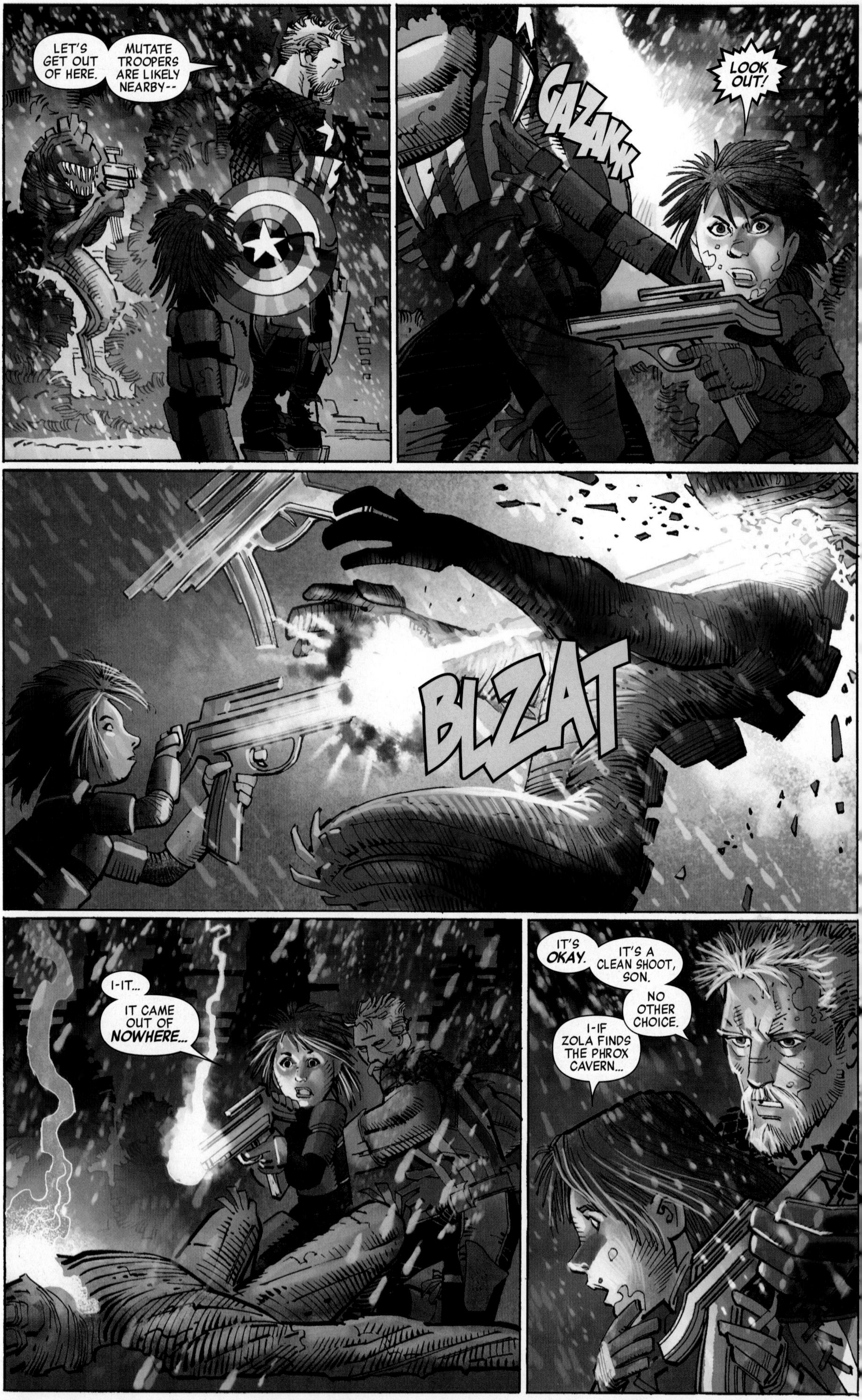
LET'S GET OUT OF HERE.
MUTATE TROOPERS ARE LIKELY NEARBY--
GAZAKK
LOOK OUT!
BLZAT
I-IT...
IT CAME OUT OF NOWHERE...
IT'S OKAY.
IT'S A CLEAN SHOOT, SON.
NO OTHER CHOICE.
I-IF ZOLA FINDS THE PHROX CAVERN...

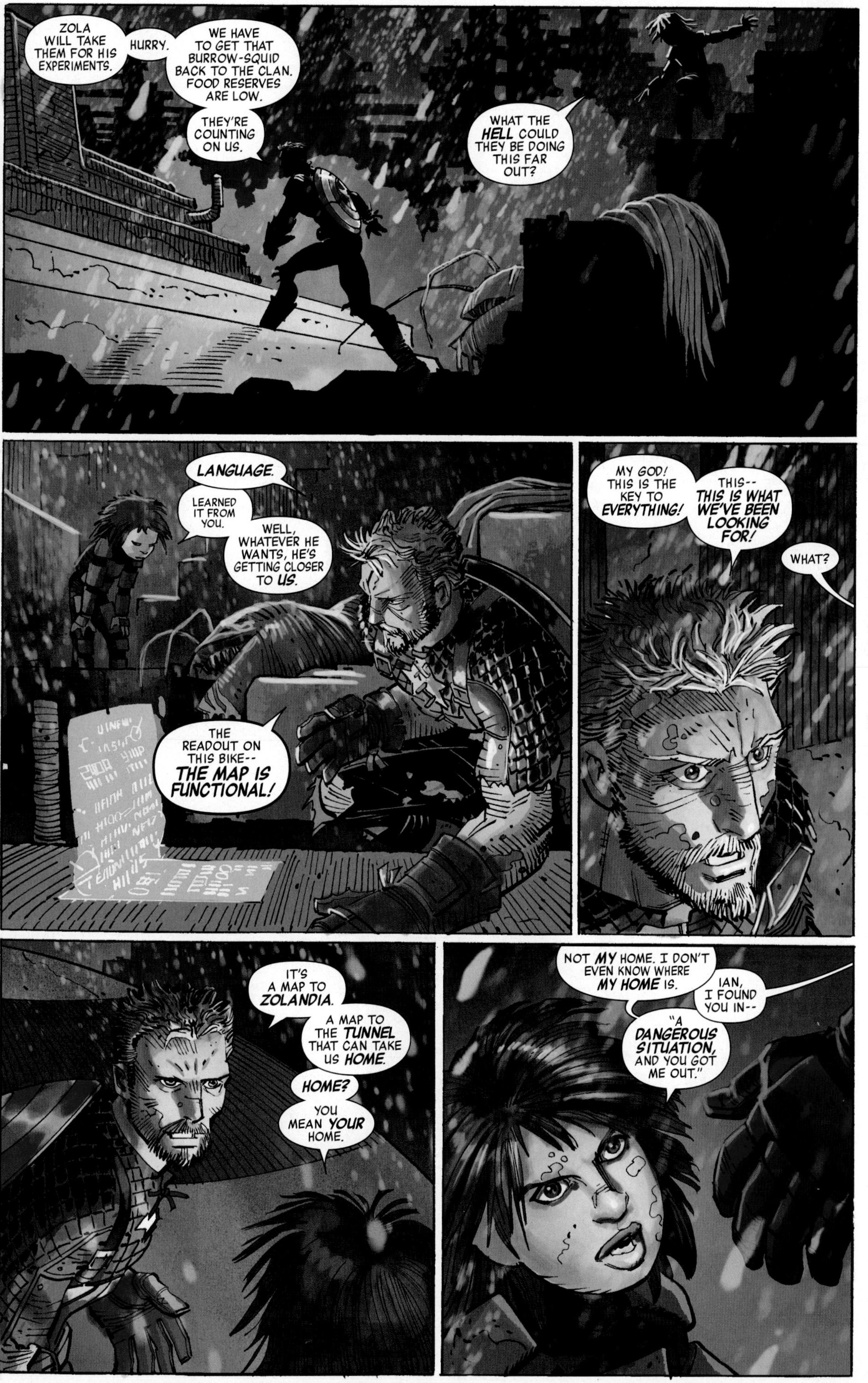

ZOLA WILL TAKE THEM FOR HIS EXPERIMENTS.
HURRY.
WE HAVE TO GET THAT BURROW-SQUID BACK TO THE CLAN. FOOD RESERVES ARE LOW.
THEY'RE COUNTING ON US.
WHAT THE **HELL** COULD THEY BE DOING THIS FAR OUT?
LANGUAGE.
LEARNED IT FROM YOU.
WELL, WHATEVER HE WANTS, HE'S GETTING CLOSER TO **US.**
THE READOUT ON THIS BIKE-- **THE MAP IS FUNCTIONAL!**
MY GOD! THIS IS THE KEY TO **EVERYTHING!**
THIS-- **THIS IS WHAT WE'VE BEEN LOOKING FOR!**
WHAT?
IT'S A MAP TO **ZOLANDIA.**
A MAP TO THE **TUNNEL** THAT CAN TAKE US **HOME.**
HOME?
YOU MEAN **YOUR** HOME.
NOT **MY** HOME. I DON'T EVEN KNOW WHERE **MY HOME** IS.
IAN, I FOUND YOU IN--
"A **DANGEROUS SITUATION,** AND YOU GOT ME OUT."

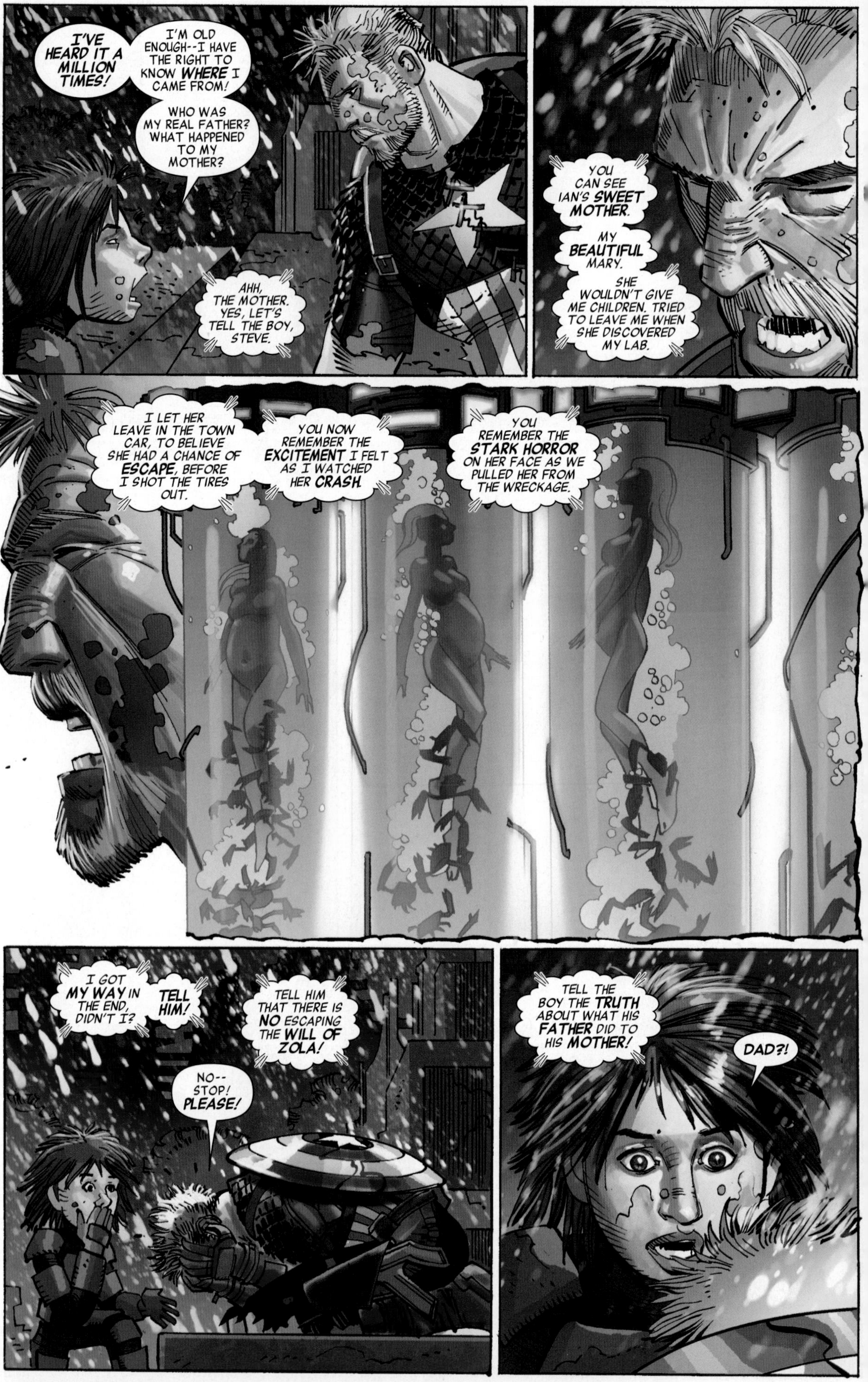
I'VE HEARD IT A MILLION TIMES!
I'M OLD ENOUGH--I HAVE THE RIGHT TO KNOW WHERE I CAME FROM!
WHO WAS MY REAL FATHER? WHAT HAPPENED TO MY MOTHER?
AHH, THE MOTHER. YES, LET'S TELL THE BOY, STEVE.
YOU CAN SEE IAN'S SWEET MOTHER.
MY BEAUTIFUL MARY.
SHE WOULDN'T GIVE ME CHILDREN. TRIED TO LEAVE ME WHEN SHE DISCOVERED MY LAB.
I LET HER LEAVE IN THE TOWN CAR, TO BELIEVE SHE HAD A CHANCE OF ESCAPE, BEFORE I SHOT THE TIRES OUT.
YOU NOW REMEMBER THE EXCITEMENT I FELT AS I WATCHED HER CRASH.
YOU REMEMBER THE STARK HORROR ON HER FACE AS WE PULLED HER FROM THE WRECKAGE.
I GOT MY WAY IN THE END, DIDN'T I?
TELL HIM!
TELL HIM THAT THERE IS NO ESCAPING THE WILL OF ZOLA!
NO-- STOP! PLEASE!
TELL THE BOY THE TRUTH ABOUT WHAT HIS FATHER DID TO HIS MOTHER!
DAD?!

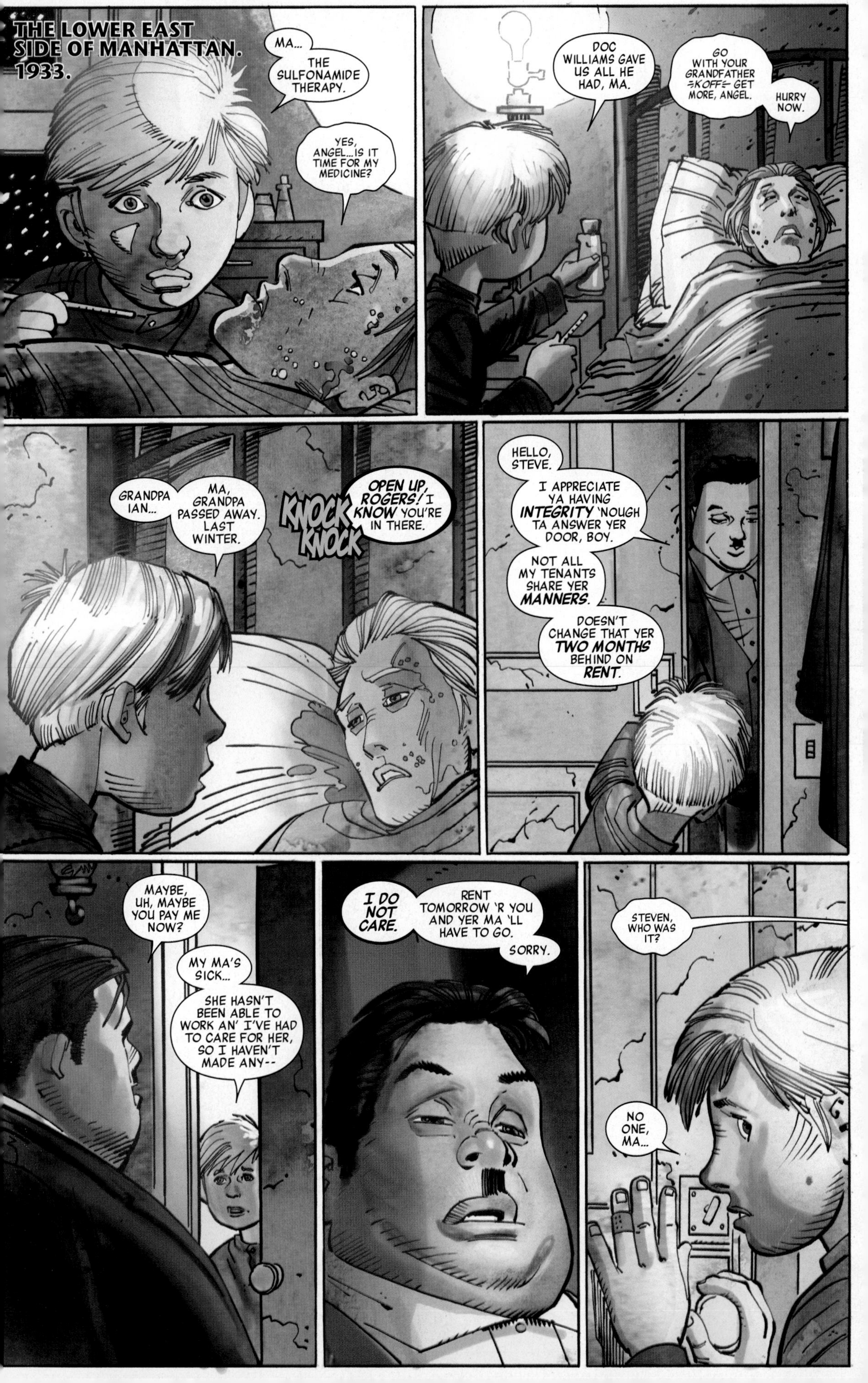
THE LOWER EAST SIDE OF MANHATTAN. 1933.
MA... THE SULFONAMIDE THERAPY.
YES, ANGEL...IS IT TIME FOR MY MEDICINE?
DOC WILLIAMS GAVE US ALL HE HAD, MA.
GO WITH YOUR GRANDFATHER =KOFF= GET MORE, ANGEL.
HURRY NOW.
GRANDPA IAN...
MA, GRANDPA PASSED AWAY. LAST WINTER.
KNOCK KNOCK
OPEN UP, ROGERS! I KNOW YOU'RE IN THERE.
HELLO, STEVE.
I APPRECIATE YA HAVING INTEGRITY 'NOUGH TA ANSWER YER DOOR, BOY.
NOT ALL MY TENANTS SHARE YER MANNERS.
DOESN'T CHANGE THAT YER TWO MONTHS BEHIND ON RENT.
MAYBE, UH, MAYBE YOU PAY ME NOW?
MY MA'S SICK...
SHE HASN'T BEEN ABLE TO WORK AN' I'VE HAD TO CARE FOR HER, SO I HAVEN'T MADE ANY--
I DO NOT CARE.
RENT TOMORROW 'R YOU AND YER MA 'LL HAVE TO GO.
SORRY.
STEVEN, WHO WAS IT?
NO ONE, MA...

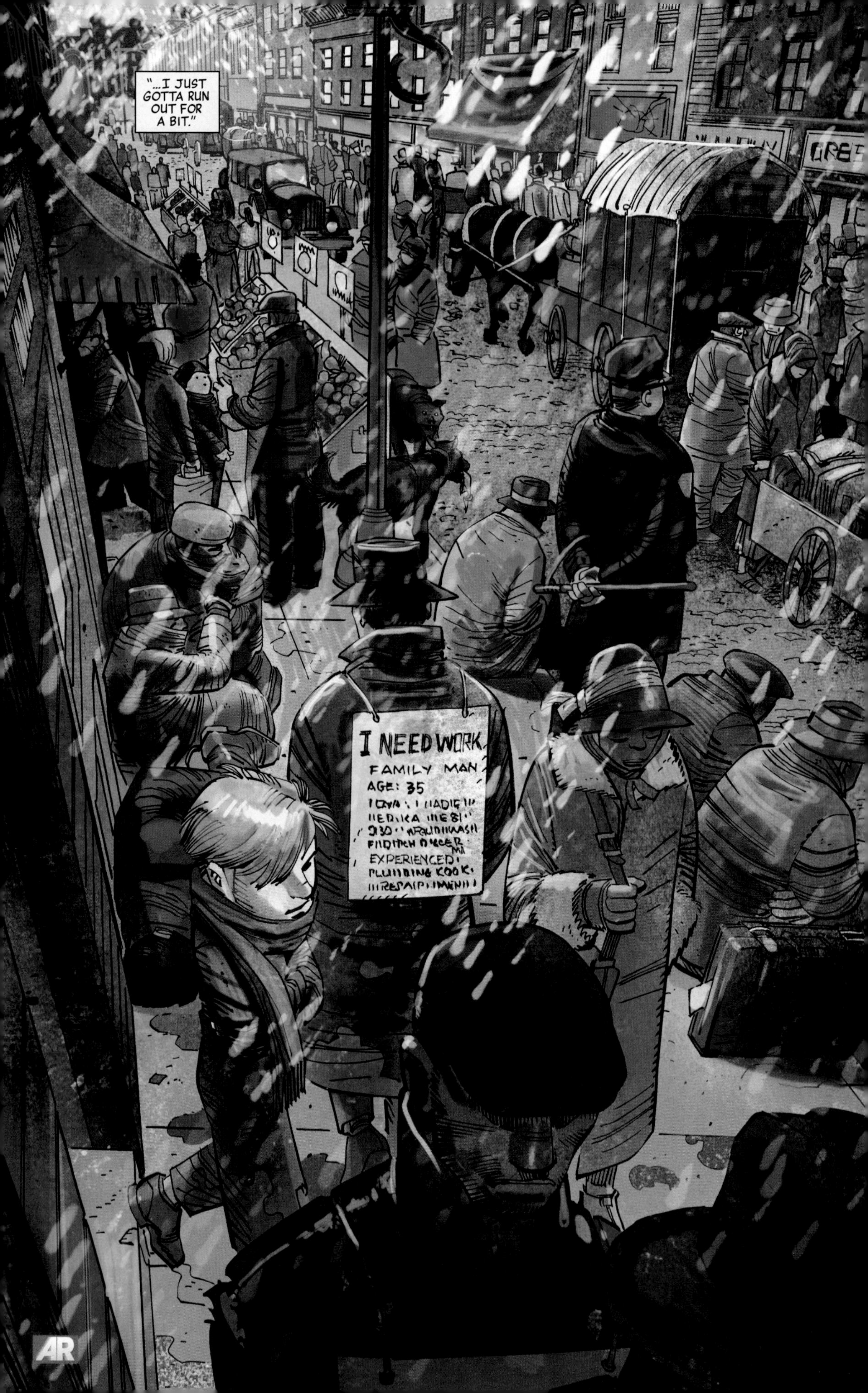
"...I JUST GOTTA RUN OUT FOR A BIT."
I NEED WORK
FAMILY MAN
AGE: 35
EXPERIENCED

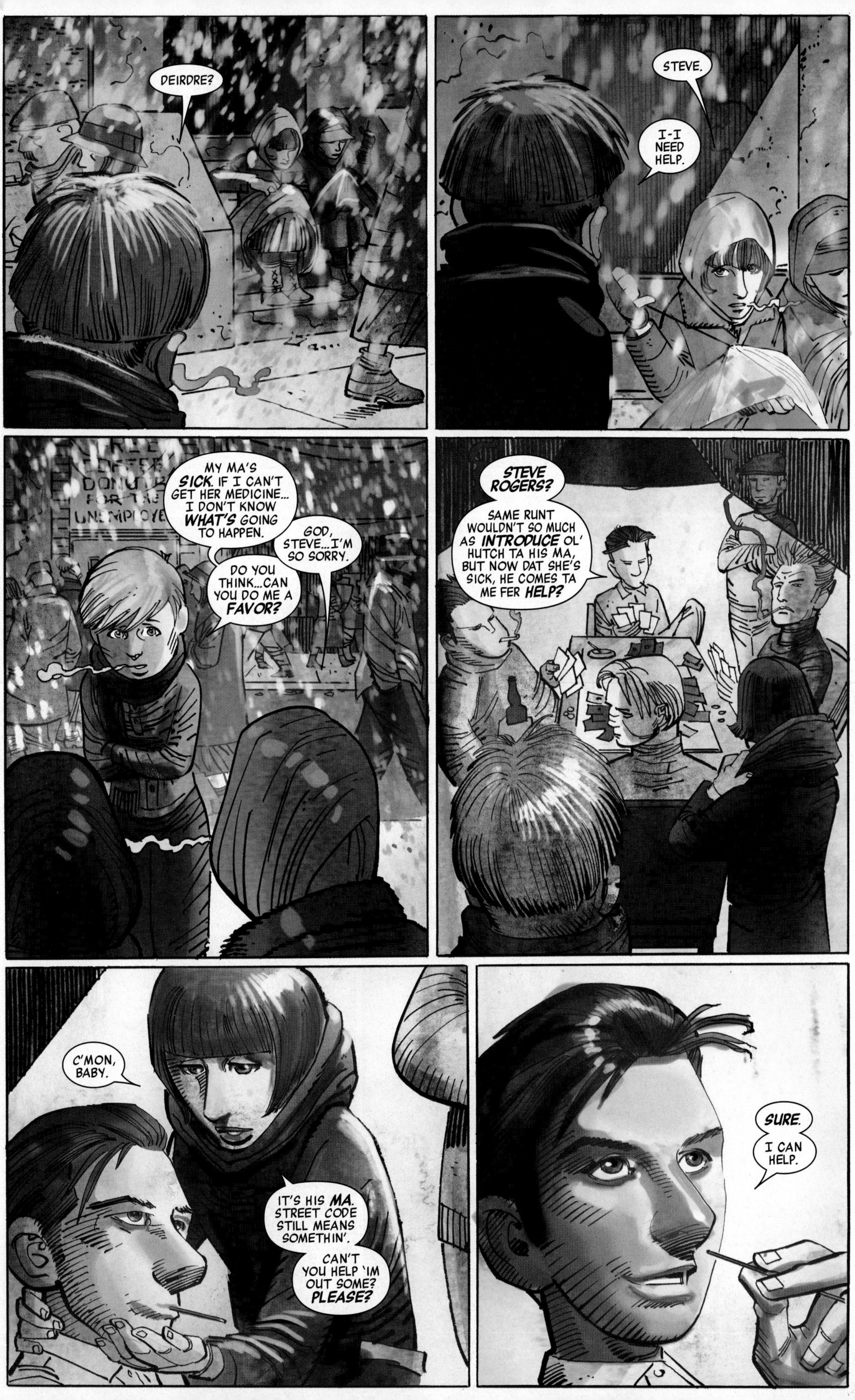
DEIRDRE?
STEVE.
I-I NEED HELP.
MY MA'S SICK. IF I CAN'T GET HER MEDICINE... I DON'T KNOW WHAT'S GOING TO HAPPEN.
GOD, STEVE...I'M SO SORRY.
DO YOU THINK...CAN YOU DO ME A FAVOR?
STEVE ROGERS?
SAME RUNT WOULDN'T SO MUCH AS INTRODUCE OL' HUTCH TA HIS MA, BUT NOW DAT SHE'S SICK, HE COMES TA ME FER HELP?
C'MON, BABY.
IT'S HIS MA. STREET CODE STILL MEANS SOMETHIN'.
CAN'T YOU HELP 'IM OUT SOME? PLEASE?
SURE.
I CAN HELP.

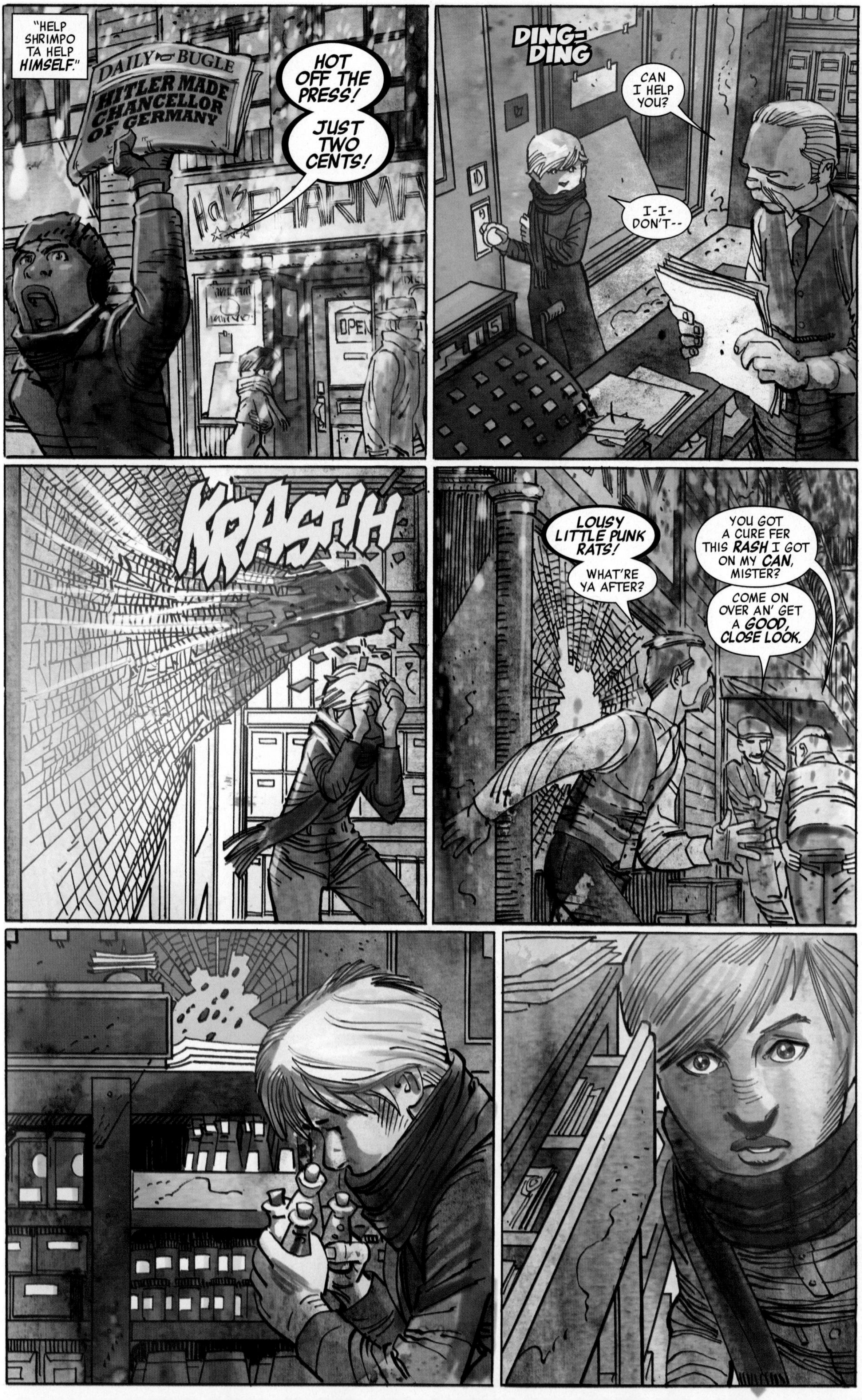
"HELP SHRIMPO TA HELP HIMSELF."
DAILY BUGLE
HITLER MADE CHANCELLOR OF GERMANY
HOT OFF THE PRESS!
JUST TWO CENTS!
Hal's PHARMA
OPEN
DING-DING
CAN I HELP YOU?
I-I-DON'T--
KRASHH
LOUSY LITTLE PUNK RATS!
WHAT'RE YA AFTER?
YOU GOT A CURE FER THIS RASH I GOT ON MY CAN, MISTER?
COME ON OVER AN' GET A GOOD, CLOSE LOOK.

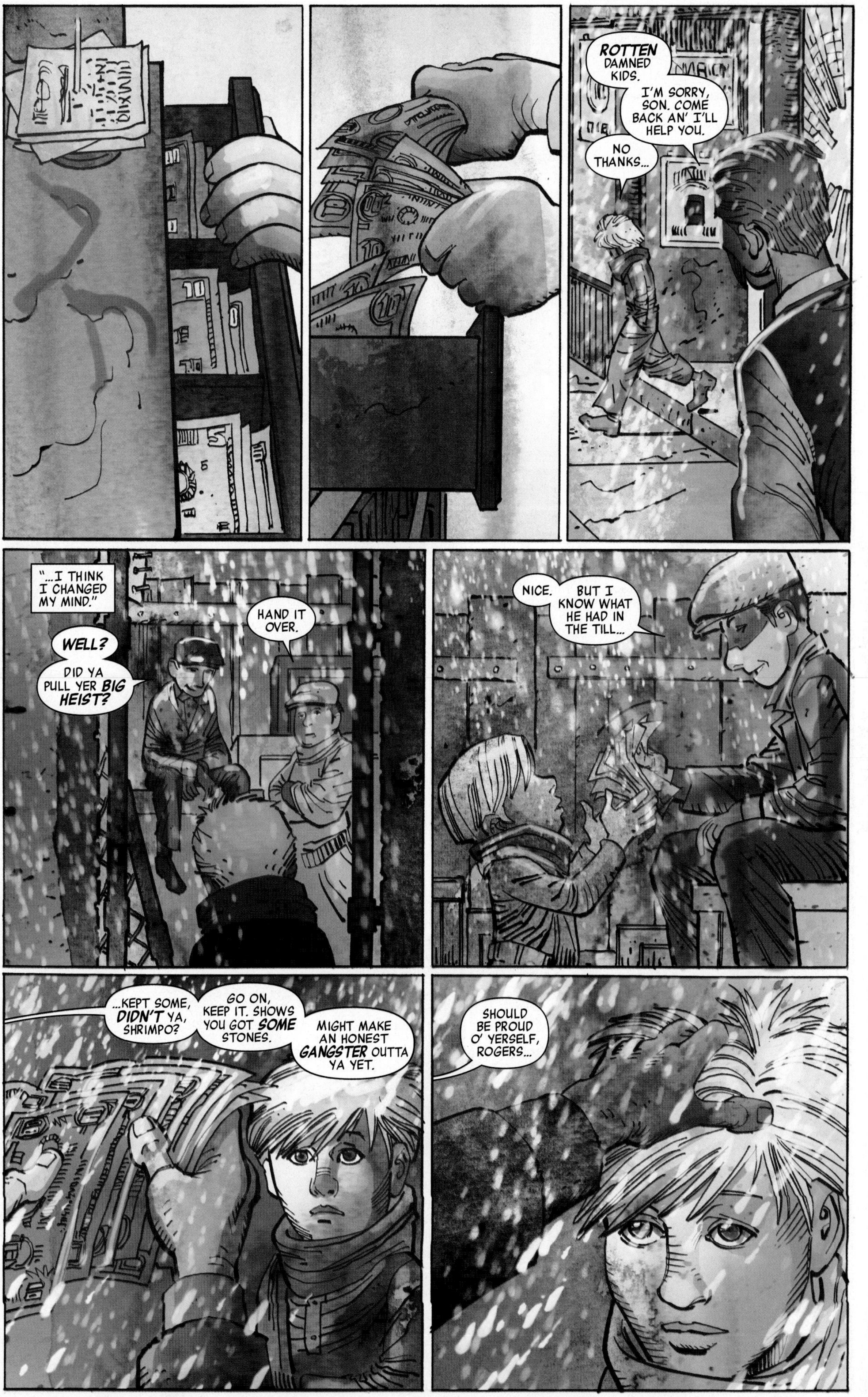
ROTTEN DAMNED KIDS.
I'M SORRY, SON. COME BACK AN' I'LL HELP YOU.
NO THANKS...
"...I THINK I CHANGED MY MIND."
WELL?
DID YA PULL YER BIG HEIST?
HAND IT OVER.
NICE.
BUT I KNOW WHAT HE HAD IN THE TILL...
...KEPT SOME, DIDN'T YA, SHRIMPO?
GO ON, KEEP IT. SHOWS YOU GOT SOME STONES.
MIGHT MAKE AN HONEST GANGSTER OUTTA YA YET.
SHOULD BE PROUD O' YERSELF, ROGERS...

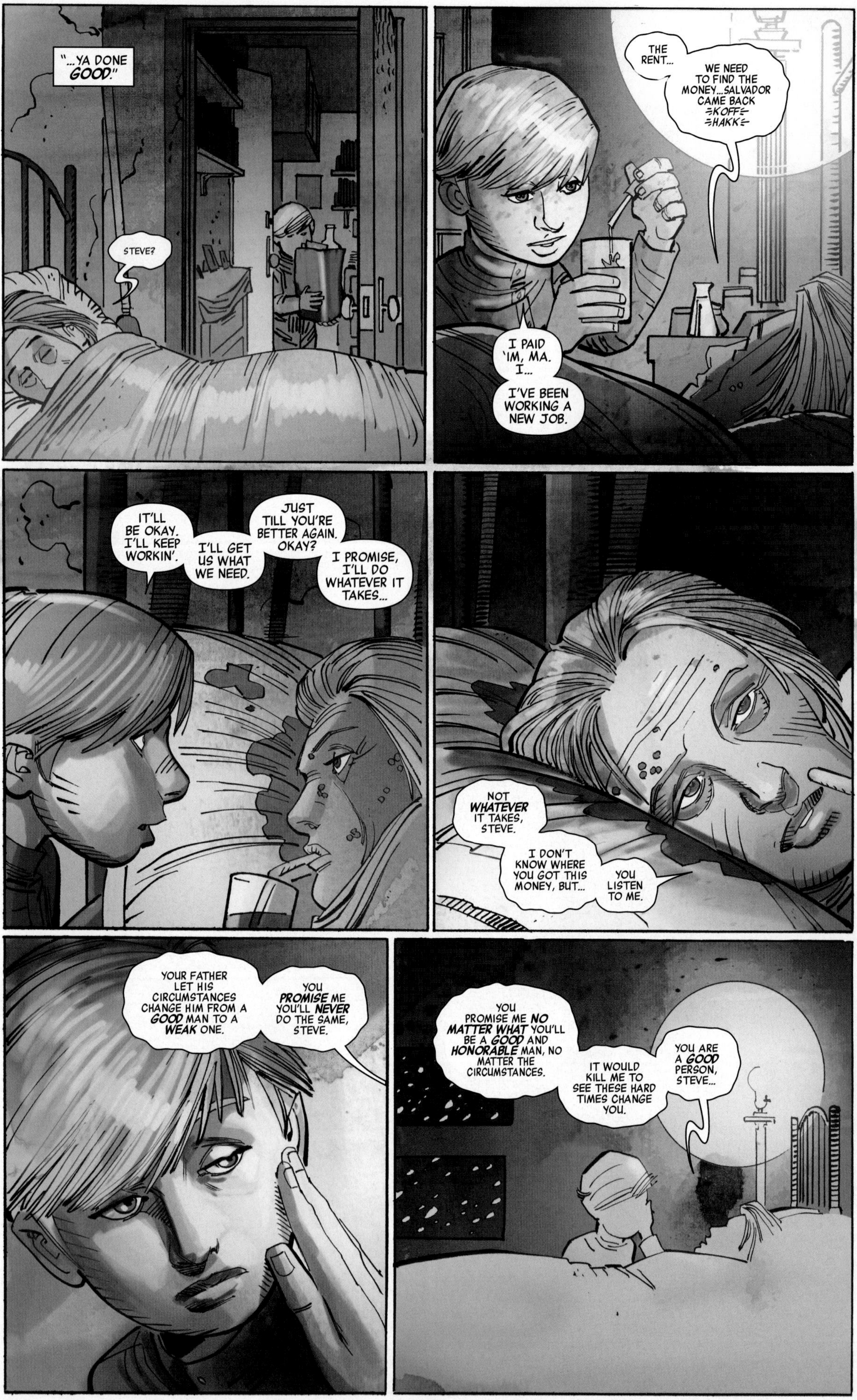
"...YA DONE GOOD."
STEVE?
THE RENT...
WE NEED TO FIND THE MONEY...SALVADOR CAME BACK =KOFF= =HAKK=
I PAID 'IM, MA. I...
I'VE BEEN WORKING A NEW JOB.
IT'LL BE OKAY. I'LL KEEP WORKIN'.
I'LL GET US WHAT WE NEED.
JUST TILL YOU'RE BETTER AGAIN. OKAY?
I PROMISE, I'LL DO WHATEVER IT TAKES...
NOT WHATEVER IT TAKES, STEVE.
I DON'T KNOW WHERE YOU GOT THIS MONEY, BUT...
YOU LISTEN TO ME.
YOUR FATHER LET HIS CIRCUMSTANCES CHANGE HIM FROM A GOOD MAN TO A WEAK ONE.
YOU PROMISE ME YOU'LL NEVER DO THE SAME, STEVE.
YOU PROMISE ME NO MATTER WHAT YOU'LL BE A GOOD AND HONORABLE MAN, NO MATTER THE CIRCUMSTANCES.
IT WOULD KILL ME TO SEE THESE HARD TIMES CHANGE YOU.
YOU ARE A GOOD PERSON, STEVE...

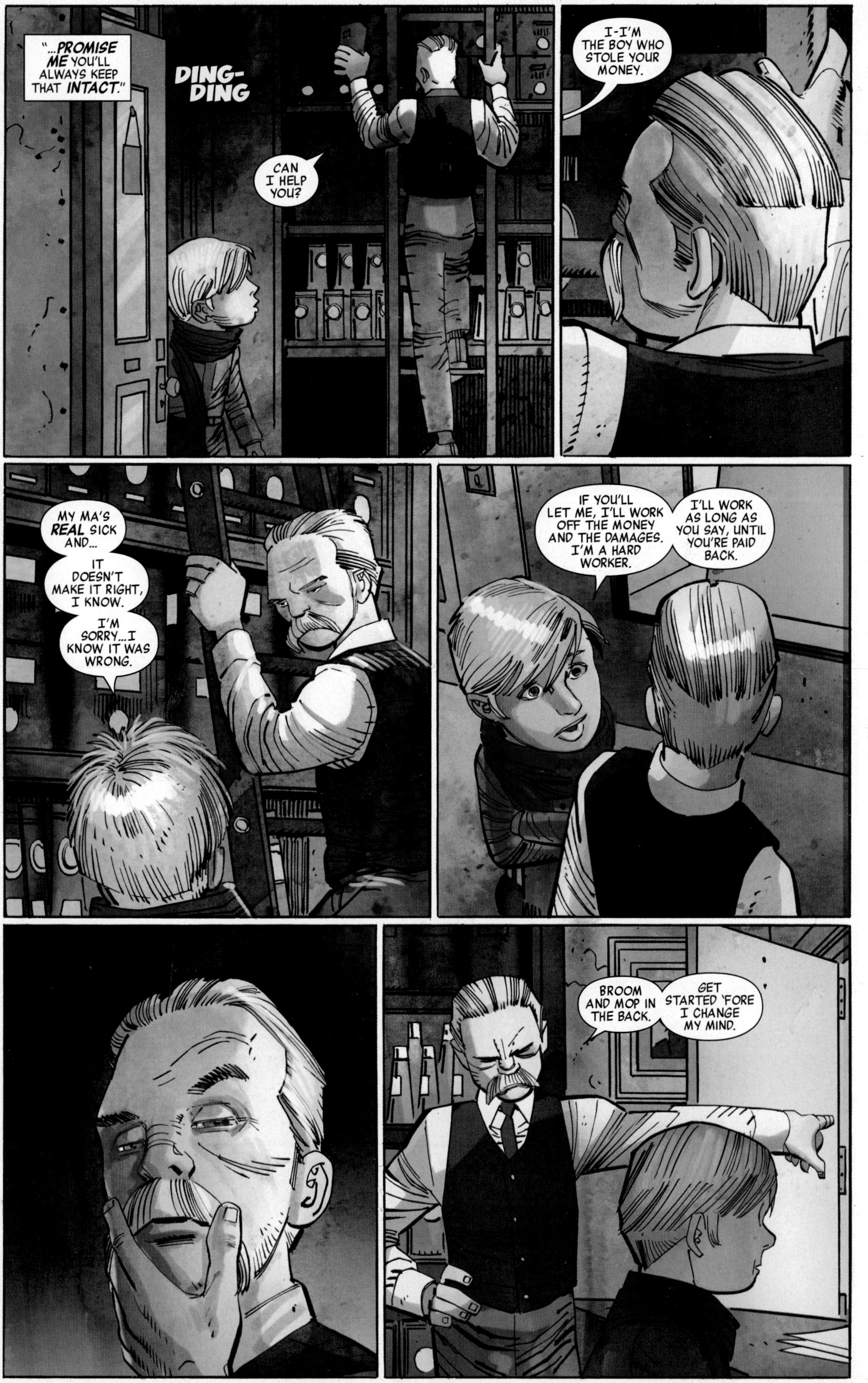
"...PROMISE ME YOU'LL ALWAYS KEEP THAT INTACT."
DING-DING
CAN I HELP YOU?
I-I'M THE BOY WHO STOLE YOUR MONEY.
MY MA'S REAL SICK AND...
IT DOESN'T MAKE IT RIGHT, I KNOW.
I'M SORRY...I KNOW IT WAS WRONG.
IF YOU'LL LET ME, I'LL WORK OFF THE MONEY AND THE DAMAGES. I'M A HARD WORKER.
I'LL WORK AS LONG AS YOU SAY, UNTIL YOU'RE PAID BACK.
BROOM AND MOP IN THE BACK.
GET STARTED 'FORE I CHANGE MY MIND.

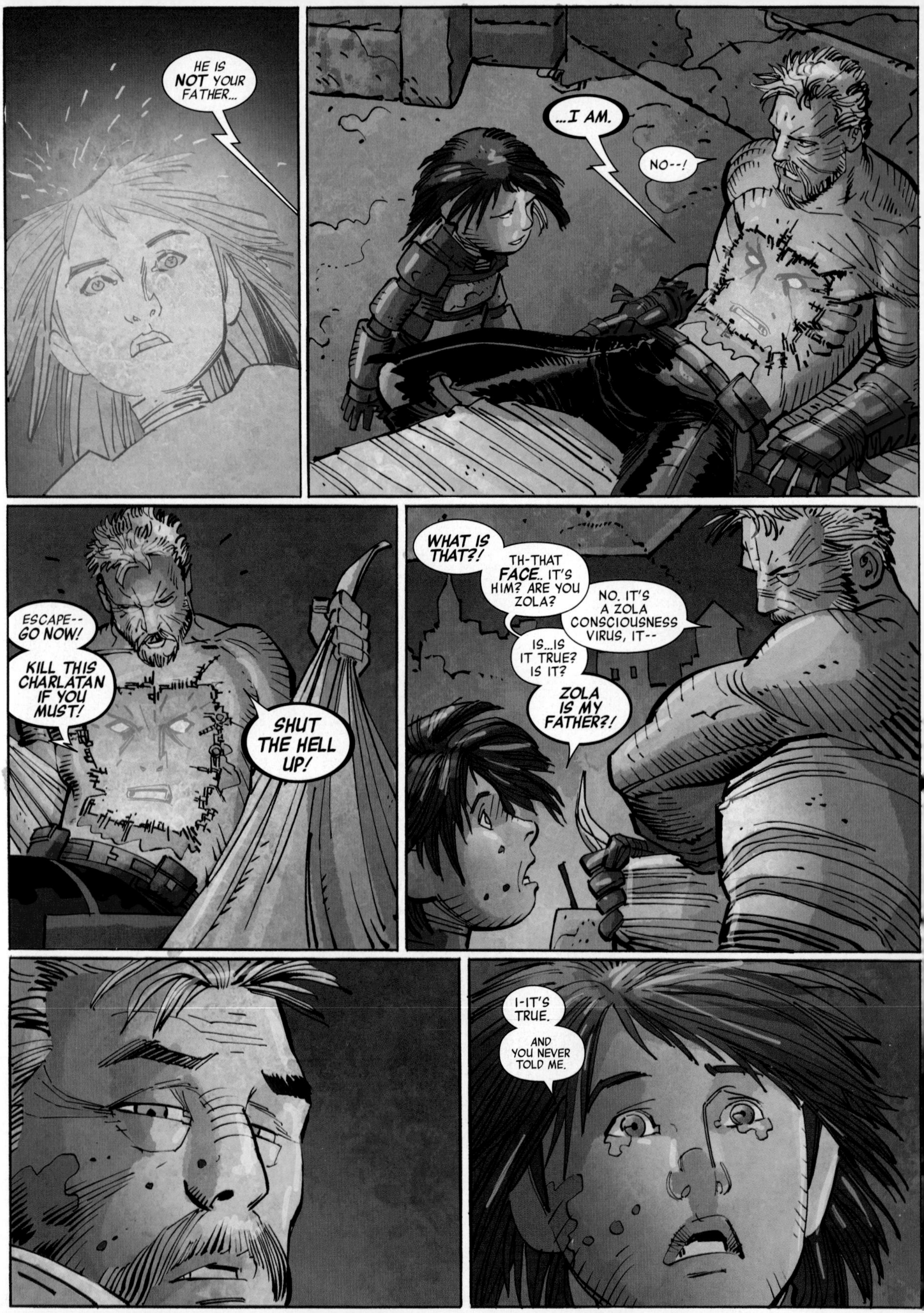
HE IS NOT YOUR FATHER...
...I AM.
NO--!
ESCAPE-- GO NOW!
KILL THIS CHARLATAN IF YOU MUST!
SHUT THE HELL UP!
WHAT IS THAT?!
TH-THAT FACE.. IT'S HIM? ARE YOU ZOLA?
NO. IT'S A ZOLA CONSCIOUSNESS VIRUS, IT--
IS...IS IT TRUE? IS IT?
ZOLA IS MY FATHER?!
I-IT'S TRUE.
AND YOU NEVER TOLD ME.

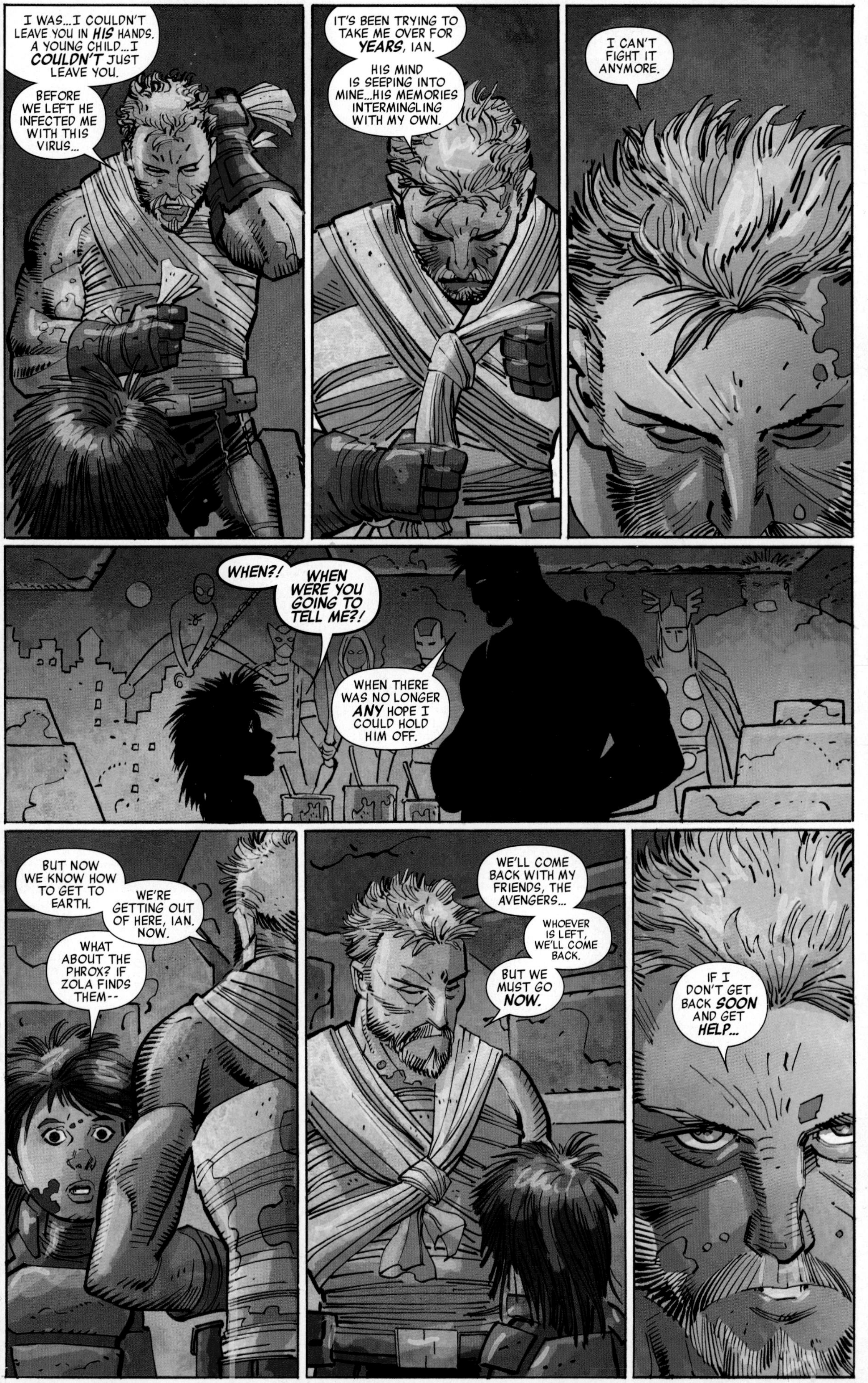
I WAS...I COULDN'T LEAVE YOU IN HIS HANDS. A YOUNG CHILD...I COULDN'T JUST LEAVE YOU.
BEFORE WE LEFT HE INFECTED ME WITH THIS VIRUS...
IT'S BEEN TRYING TO TAKE ME OVER FOR YEARS, IAN.
HIS MIND IS SEEPING INTO MINE...HIS MEMORIES INTERMINGLING WITH MY OWN.
I CAN'T FIGHT IT ANYMORE.
WHEN?!
WHEN WERE YOU GOING TO TELL ME?!
WHEN THERE WAS NO LONGER ANY HOPE I COULD HOLD HIM OFF.
BUT NOW WE KNOW HOW TO GET TO EARTH.
WE'RE GETTING OUT OF HERE, IAN. NOW.
WHAT ABOUT THE PHROX? IF ZOLA FINDS THEM--
WE'LL COME BACK WITH MY FRIENDS, THE AVENGERS...
WHOEVER IS LEFT, WE'LL COME BACK.
BUT WE MUST GO NOW.
IF I DON'T GET BACK SOON AND GET HELP...

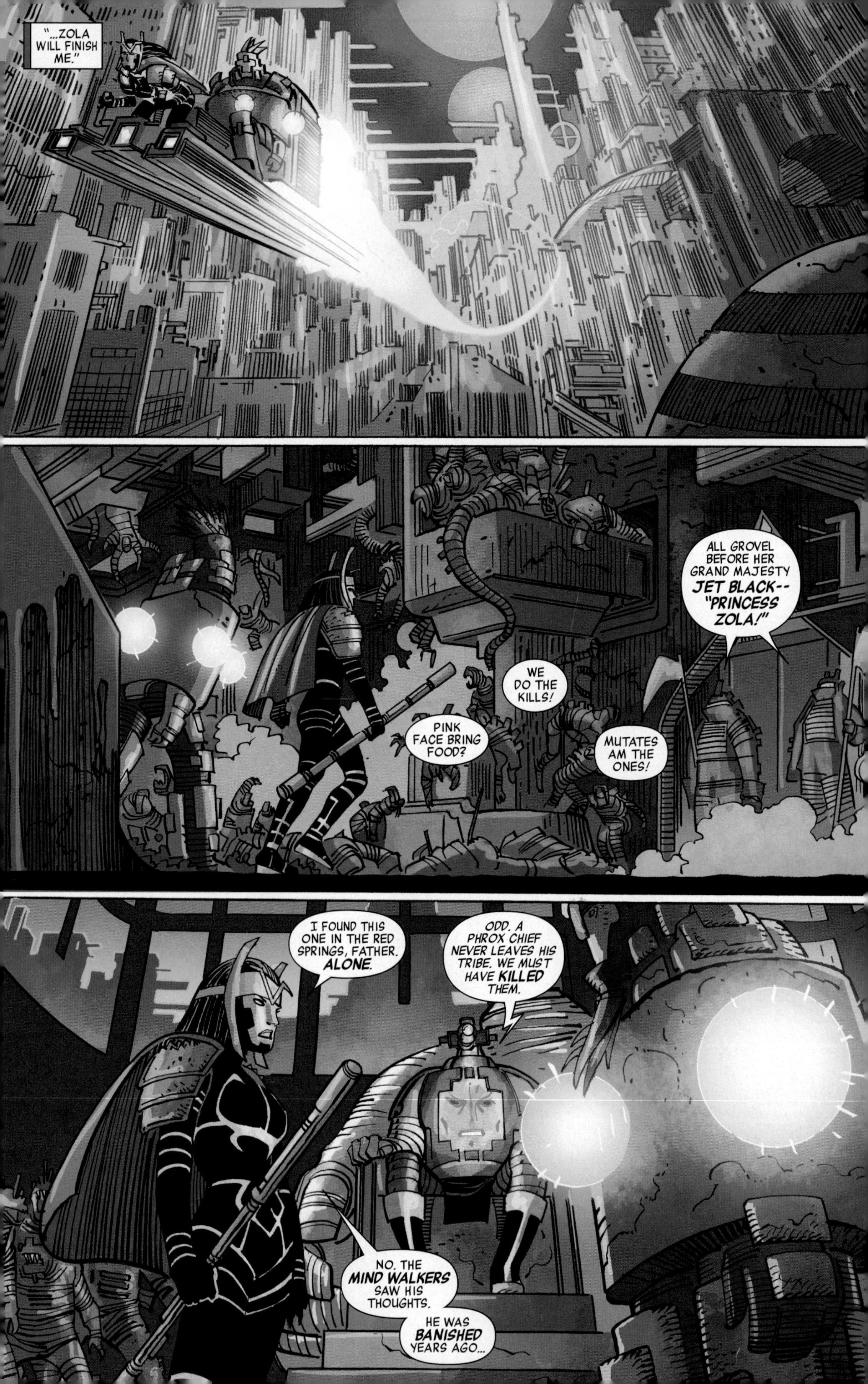
"...ZOLA WILL FINISH ME."
ALL GROVEL BEFORE HER GRAND MAJESTY JET BLACK-- "PRINCESS ZOLA!"
WE DO THE KILLS!
PINK FACE BRING FOOD?
MUTATES AM THE ONES!
I FOUND THIS ONE IN THE RED SPRINGS, FATHER. ALONE.
ODD. A PHROX CHIEF NEVER LEAVES HIS TRIBE. WE MUST HAVE KILLED THEM.
NO. THE MIND WALKERS SAW HIS THOUGHTS.
HE WAS BANISHED YEARS AGO...

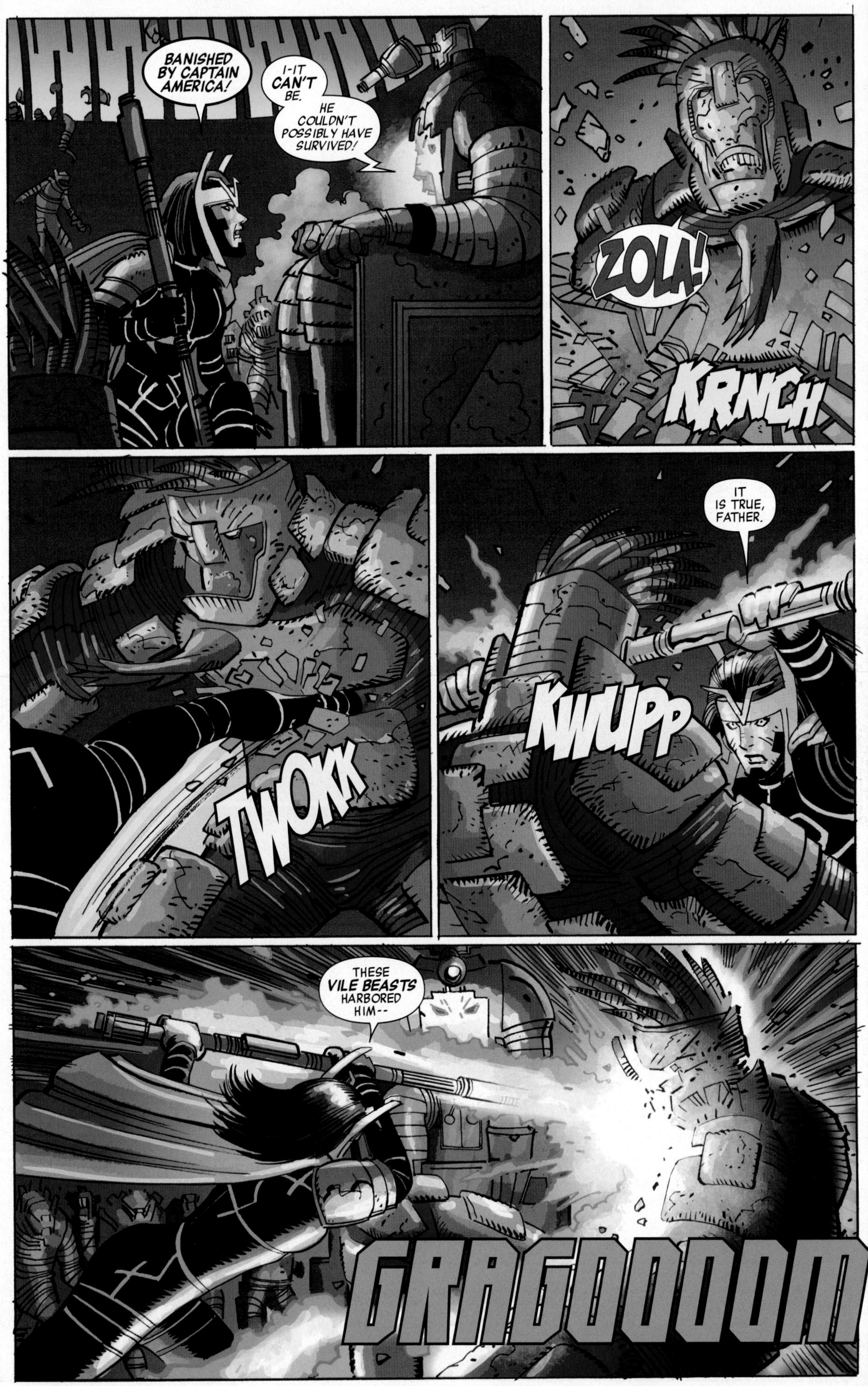
BANISHED BY CAPTAIN AMERICA!
I-IT CAN'T BE.
HE COULDN'T POSSIBLY HAVE SURVIVED!
ZOLA!
KRNCH
TWOKK
IT IS TRUE, FATHER.
KWUPP
THESE VILE BEASTS HARBORED HIM--
GRAGOOOOM

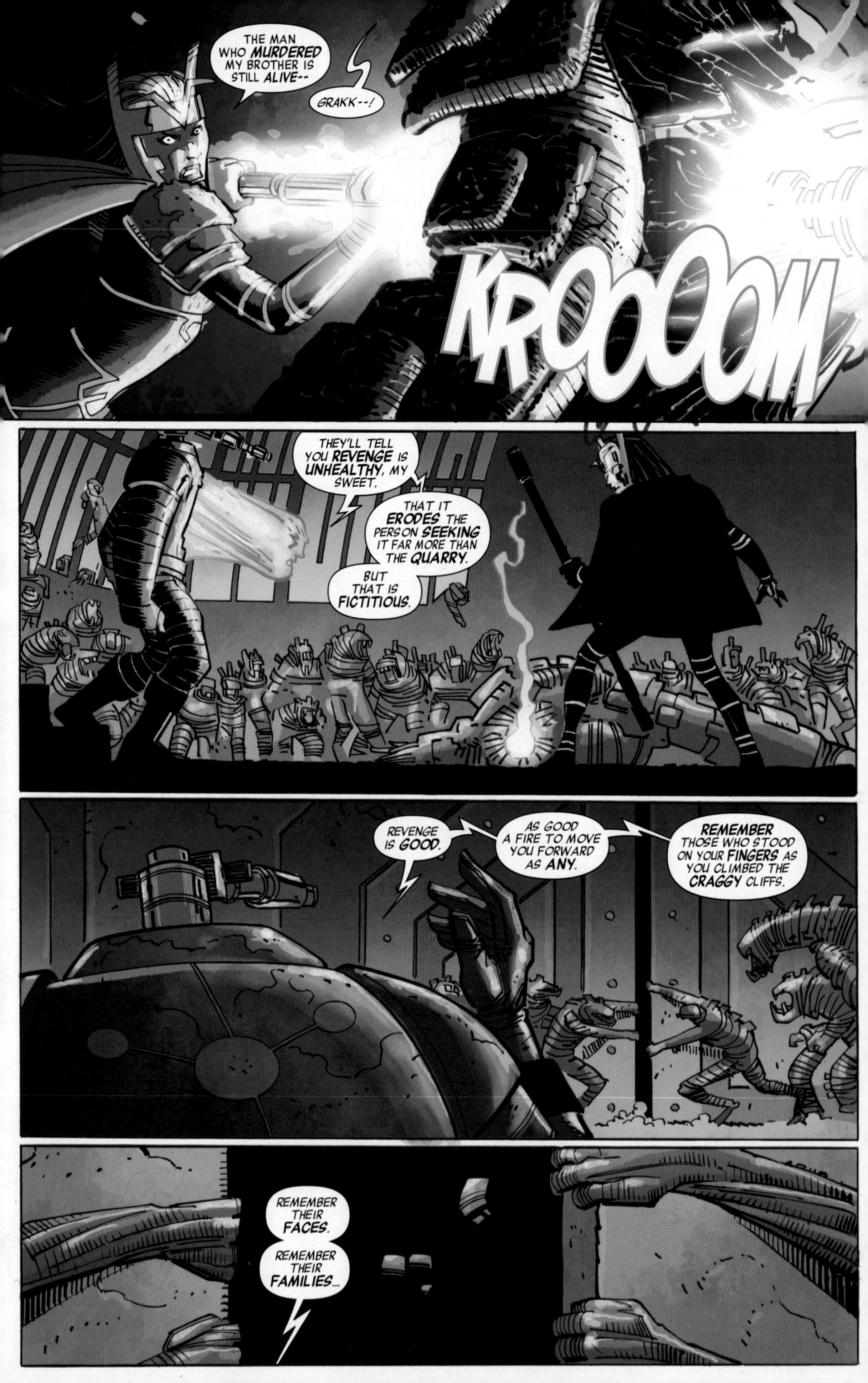
THE MAN WHO MURDERED MY BROTHER IS STILL ALIVE--
GRAKK--!
KROOOOM
THEY'LL TELL YOU REVENGE IS UNHEALTHY, MY SWEET.
THAT IT ERODES THE PERSON SEEKING IT FAR MORE THAN THE QUARRY.
BUT THAT IS FICTITIOUS.
REVENGE IS GOOD.
AS GOOD A FIRE TO MOVE YOU FORWARD AS ANY.
REMEMBER THOSE WHO STOOD ON YOUR FINGERS AS YOU CLIMBED THE CRAGGY CLIFFS.
REMEMBER THEIR FACES.
REMEMBER THEIR FAMILIES...

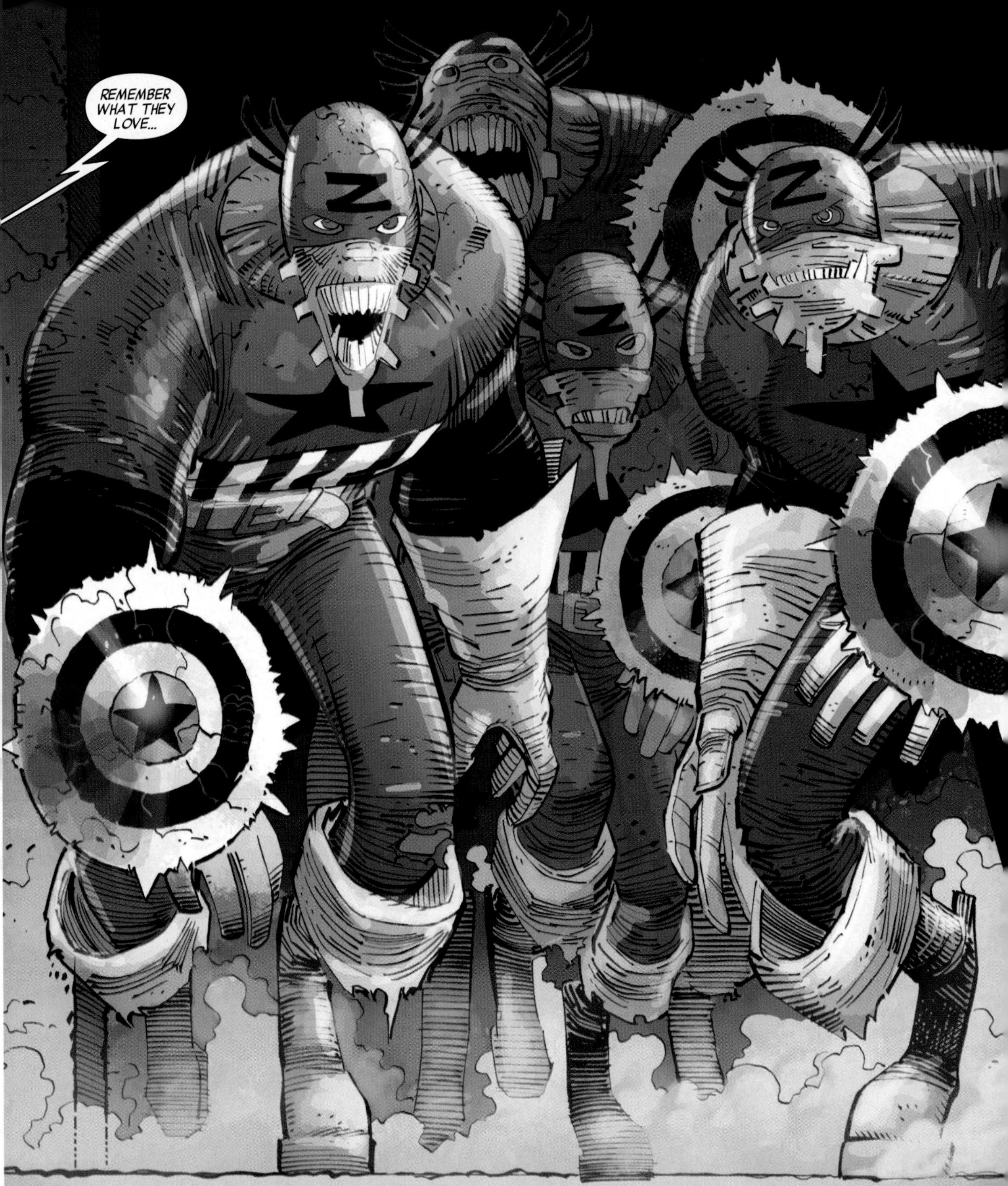
REMEMBER WHAT THEY LOVE...

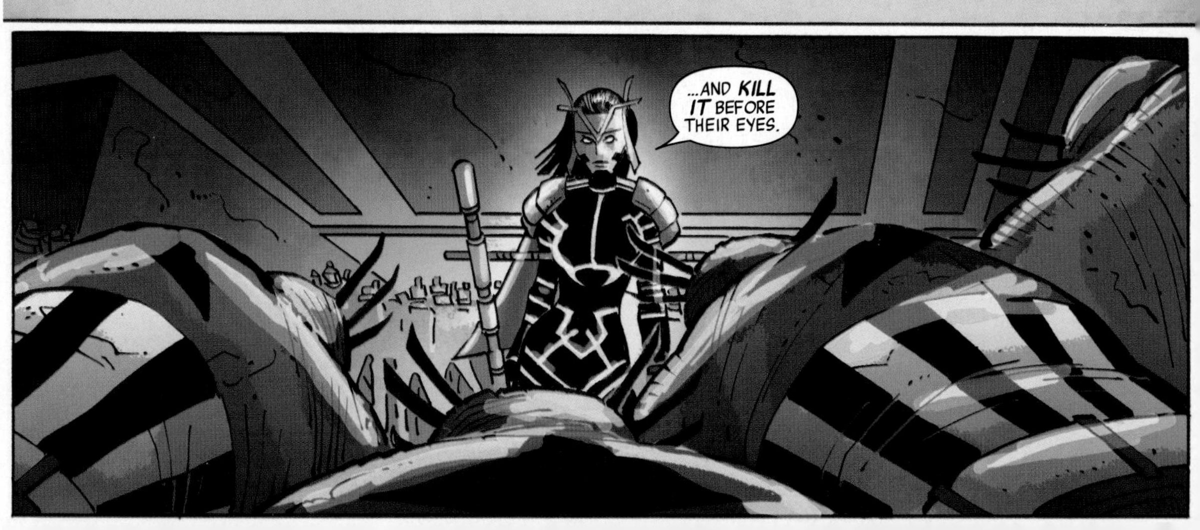
...AND KILL IT BEFORE THEIR EYES.

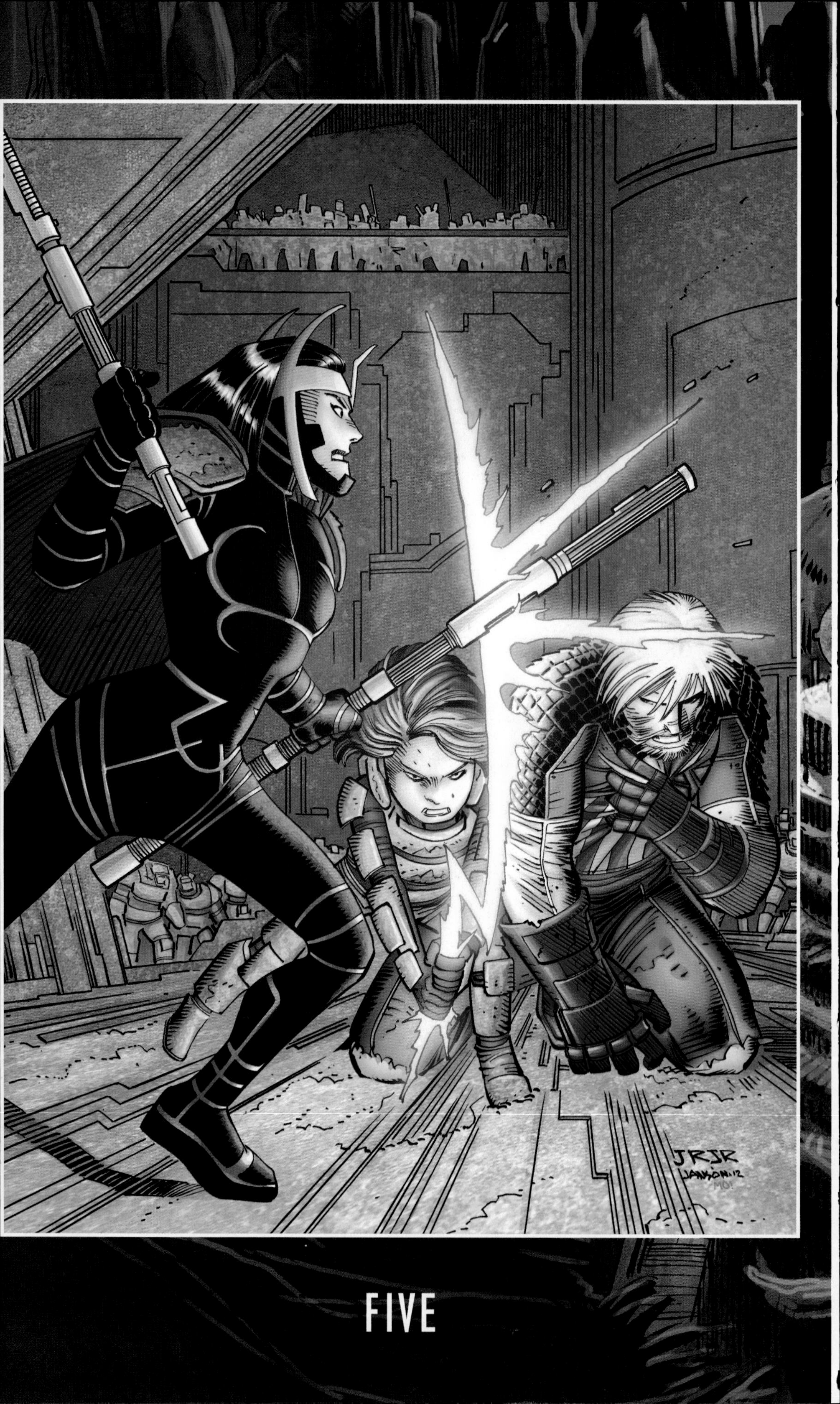

FIVE

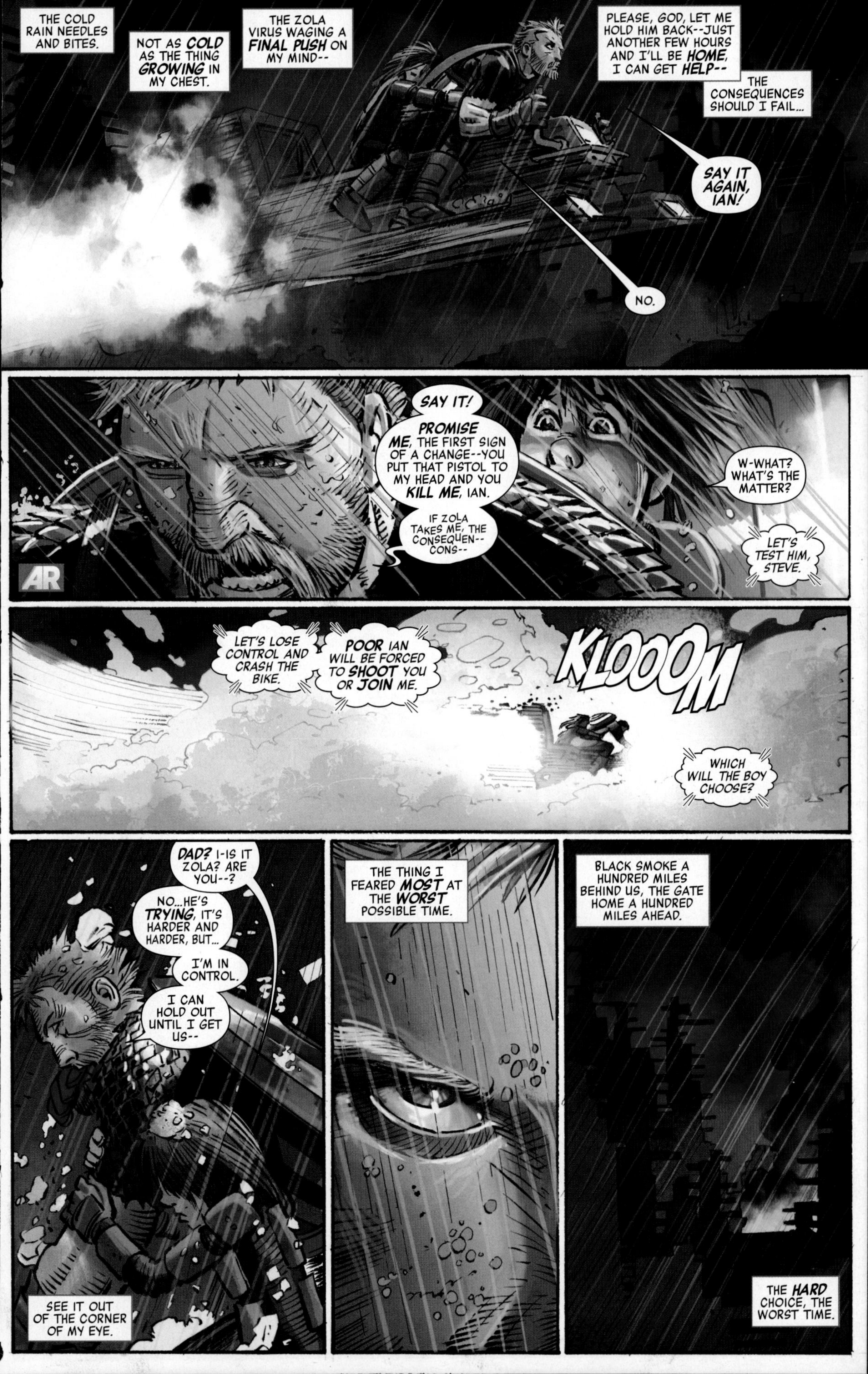
THE COLD RAIN NEEDLES AND BITES.
NOT AS COLD AS THE THING GROWING IN MY CHEST.
THE ZOLA VIRUS WAGING A FINAL PUSH ON MY MIND--
PLEASE, GOD, LET ME HOLD HIM BACK--JUST ANOTHER FEW HOURS AND I'LL BE HOME, I CAN GET HELP--
THE CONSEQUENCES SHOULD I FAIL...
SAY IT AGAIN, IAN!
NO.
SAY IT!
PROMISE ME, THE FIRST SIGN OF A CHANGE--YOU PUT THAT PISTOL TO MY HEAD AND YOU KILL ME, IAN.
IF ZOLA TAKES ME, THE CONSEQUEN--CONS--
W-WHAT? WHAT'S THE MATTER?
LET'S TEST HIM, STEVE.
AR
LET'S LOSE CONTROL AND CRASH THE BIKE.
POOR IAN WILL BE FORCED TO SHOOT YOU OR JOIN ME.
KLOOOM
WHICH WILL THE BOY CHOOSE?
DAD? I-IS IT ZOLA? ARE YOU--?
NO...HE'S TRYING, IT'S HARDER AND HARDER, BUT...
I'M IN CONTROL.
I CAN HOLD OUT UNTIL I GET US--
SEE IT OUT OF THE CORNER OF MY EYE.
THE THING I FEARED MOST AT THE WORST POSSIBLE TIME.
BLACK SMOKE A HUNDRED MILES BEHIND US, THE GATE HOME A HUNDRED MILES AHEAD.
THE HARD CHOICE, THE WORST TIME.

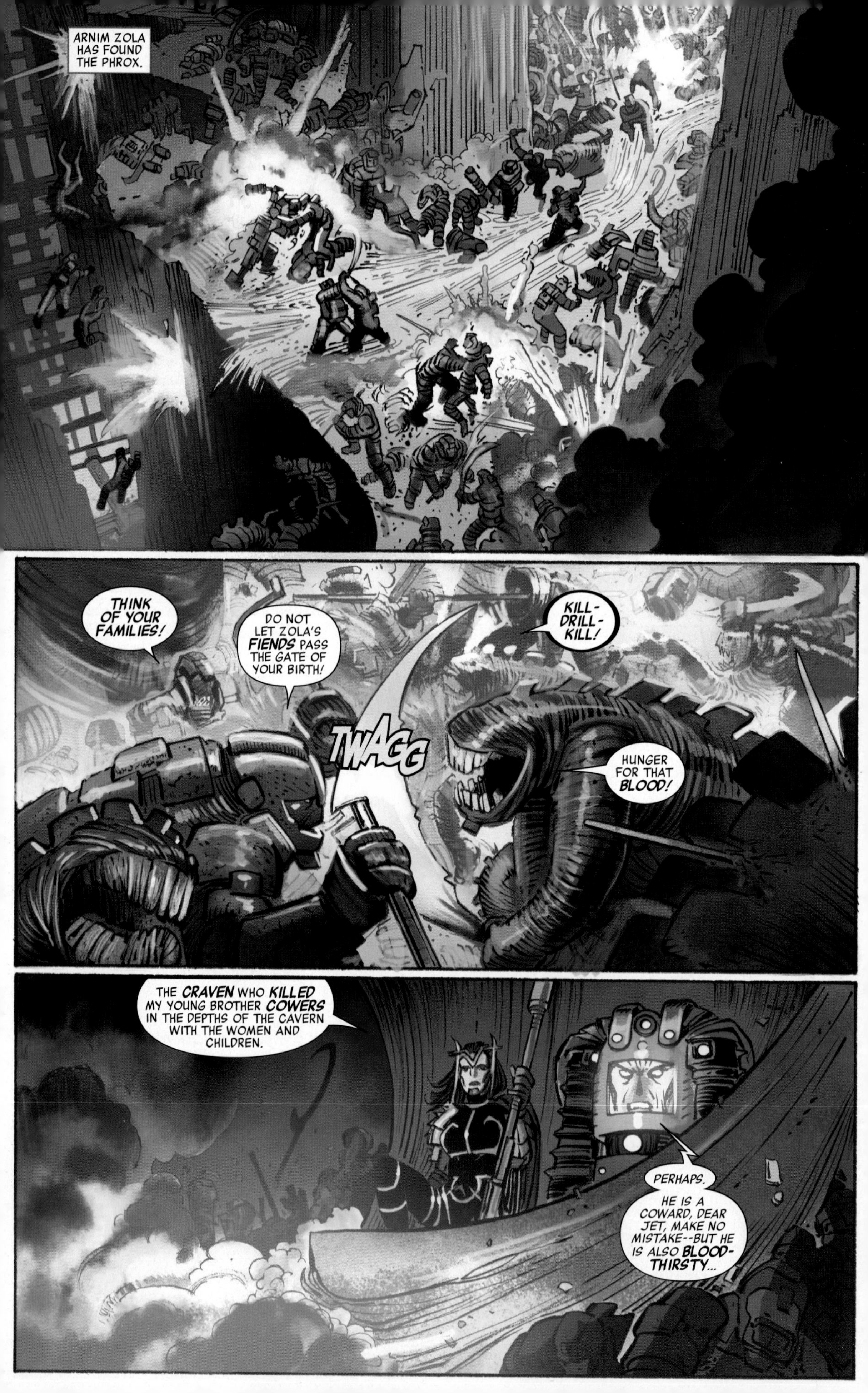
ARNIM ZOLA HAS FOUND THE PHROX.
THINK OF YOUR FAMILIES!
DO NOT LET ZOLA'S FIENDS PASS THE GATE OF YOUR BIRTH!
KILL-DRILL-KILL!
TWAGG
HUNGER FOR THAT BLOOD!
THE CRAVEN WHO KILLED MY YOUNG BROTHER COWERS IN THE DEPTHS OF THE CAVERN WITH THE WOMEN AND CHILDREN.
PERHAPS.
HE IS A COWARD, DEAR JET, MAKE NO MISTAKE--BUT HE IS ALSO BLOOD-THIRSTY...

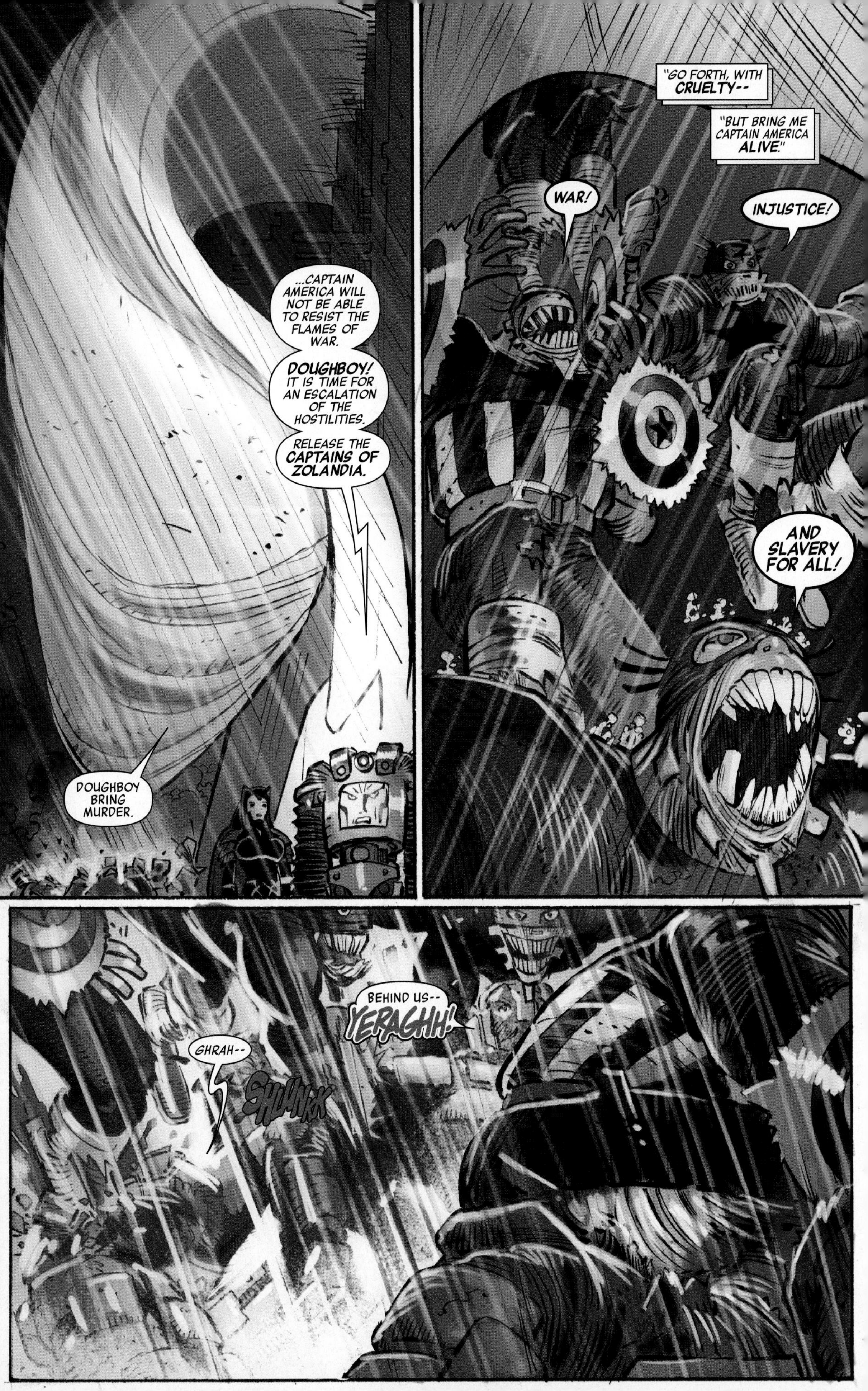
...CAPTAIN AMERICA WILL NOT BE ABLE TO RESIST THE FLAMES OF WAR.
DOUGHBOY! IT IS TIME FOR AN ESCALATION OF THE HOSTILITIES.
RELEASE THE CAPTAINS OF ZOLANDIA.
DOUGHBOY BRING MURDER.
"GO FORTH, WITH CRUELTY--
"BUT BRING ME CAPTAIN AMERICA ALIVE."
WAR!
INJUSTICE!
AND SLAVERY FOR ALL!
BEHIND US--
YERAGHH!
GHRAH--
SHLUNKK

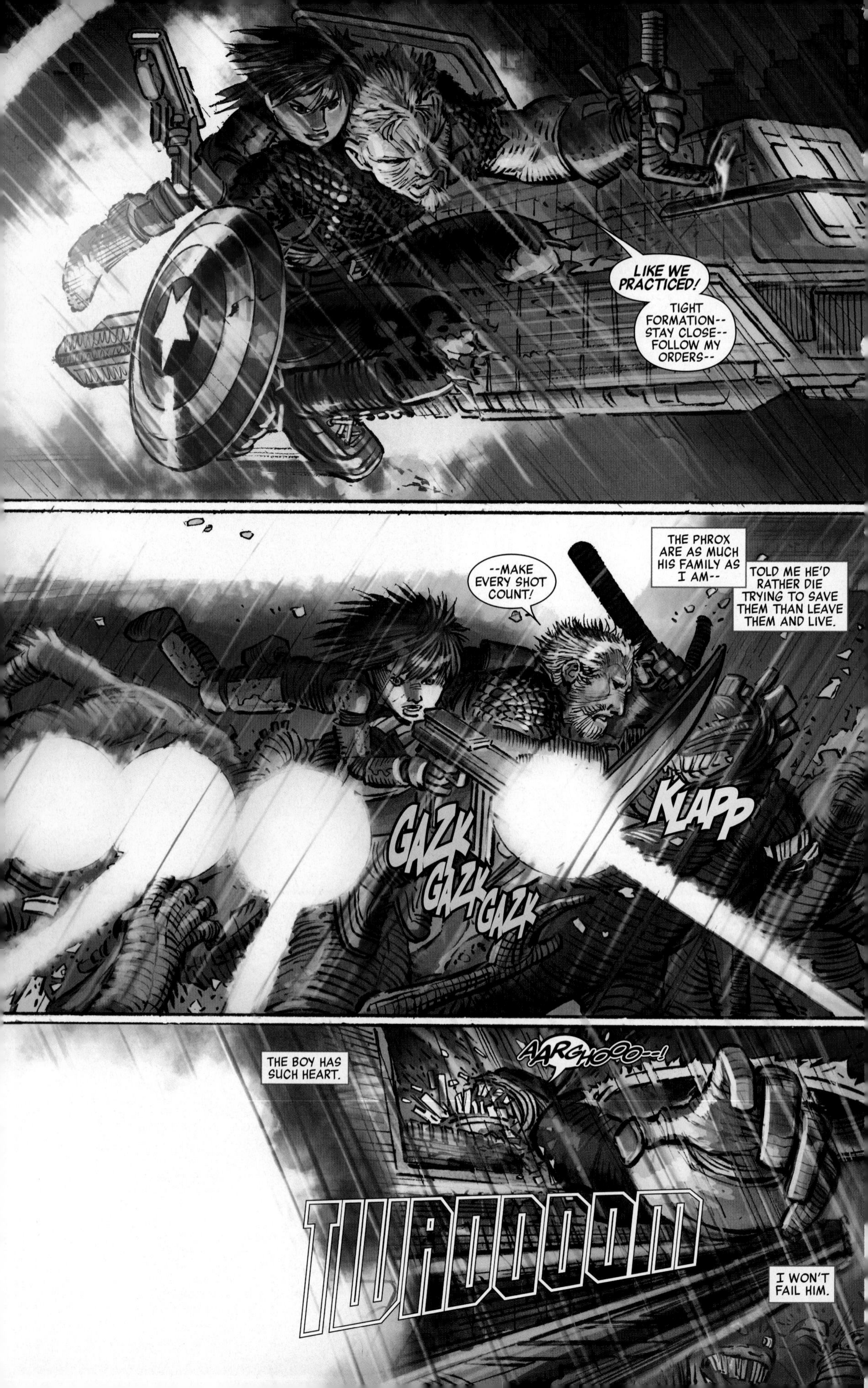
LIKE WE PRACTICED!
TIGHT FORMATION-- STAY CLOSE-- FOLLOW MY ORDERS--
THE PHROX ARE AS MUCH HIS FAMILY AS I AM--
TOLD ME HE'D RATHER DIE TRYING TO SAVE THEM THAN LEAVE THEM AND LIVE.
--MAKE EVERY SHOT COUNT!
GAZK GAZK GAZK
KLAPP
THE BOY HAS SUCH HEART.
AARGHOOOO--!
TUDDOOOM
I WON'T FAIL HIM.

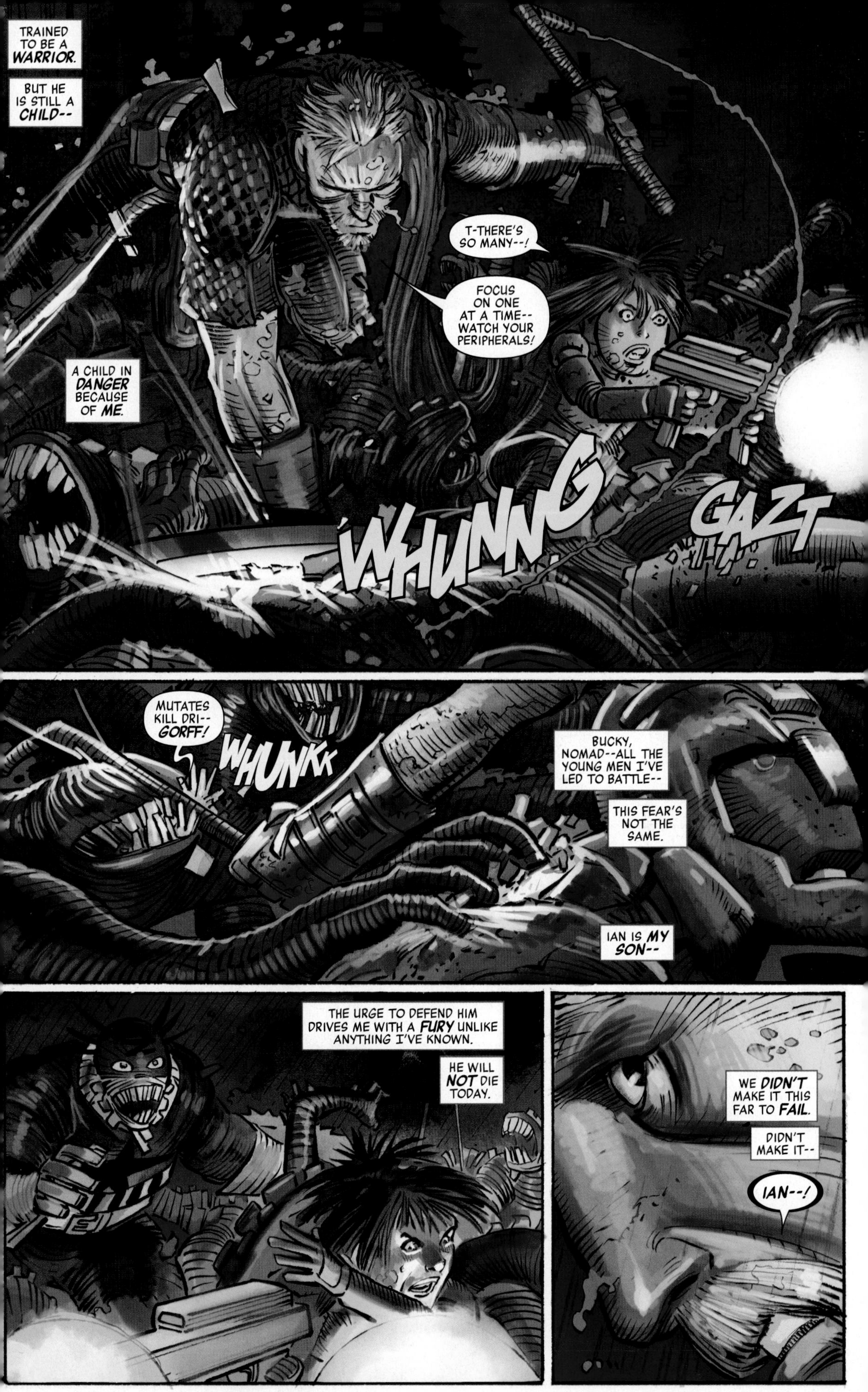
TRAINED TO BE A WARRIOR.
BUT HE IS STILL A CHILD--
T-THERE'S SO MANY--!
FOCUS ON ONE AT A TIME-- WATCH YOUR PERIPHERALS!
A CHILD IN DANGER BECAUSE OF ME.
WHUNNG
GAZT
MUTATES KILL DRI-- GORFF!
WHUNKK
BUCKY, NOMAD--ALL THE YOUNG MEN I'VE LED TO BATTLE--
THIS FEAR'S NOT THE SAME.
IAN IS MY SON--
THE URGE TO DEFEND HIM DRIVES ME WITH A FURY UNLIKE ANYTHING I'VE KNOWN.
HE WILL NOT DIE TODAY.
WE DIDN'T MAKE IT THIS FAR TO FAIL.
DIDN'T MAKE IT--
IAN--!

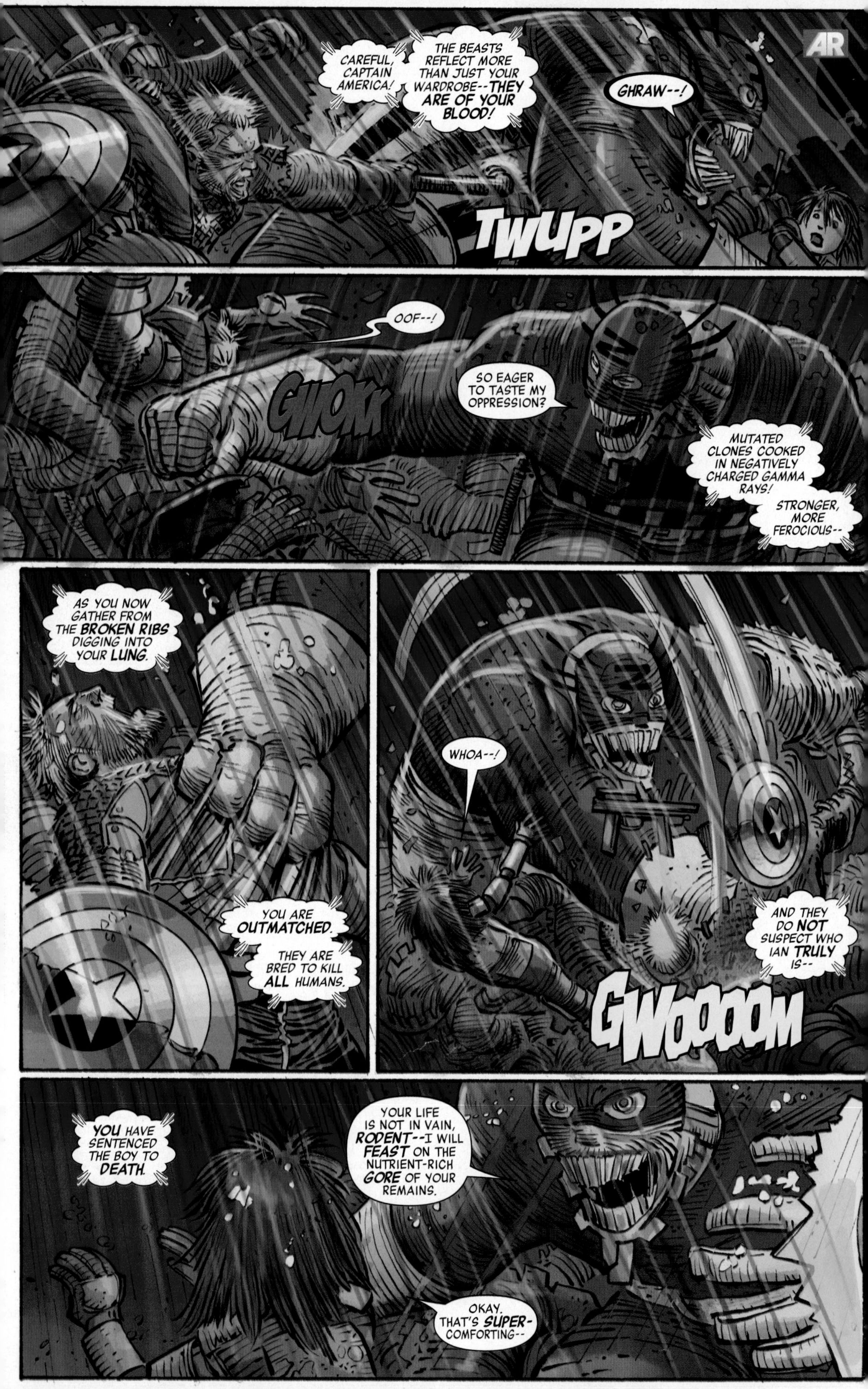
AR
CAREFUL, CAPTAIN AMERICA!
THE BEASTS REFLECT MORE THAN JUST YOUR WARDROBE--THEY ARE OF YOUR BLOOD!
GHRAW--!
TWUPP
OOF--!
GWOKK
SO EAGER TO TASTE MY OPPRESSION?
MUTATED CLONES COOKED IN NEGATIVELY CHARGED GAMMA RAYS!
STRONGER, MORE FEROCIOUS--
AS YOU NOW GATHER FROM THE BROKEN RIBS DIGGING INTO YOUR LUNG.
YOU ARE OUTMATCHED.
THEY ARE BRED TO KILL ALL HUMANS.
WHOA--!
AND THEY DO NOT SUSPECT WHO IAN TRULY IS--
GWOOOOM
YOU HAVE SENTENCED THE BOY TO DEATH.
YOUR LIFE IS NOT IN VAIN, RODENT--I WILL FEAST ON THE NUTRIENT-RICH GORE OF YOUR REMAINS.
OKAY. THAT'S SUPER-COMFORTING--

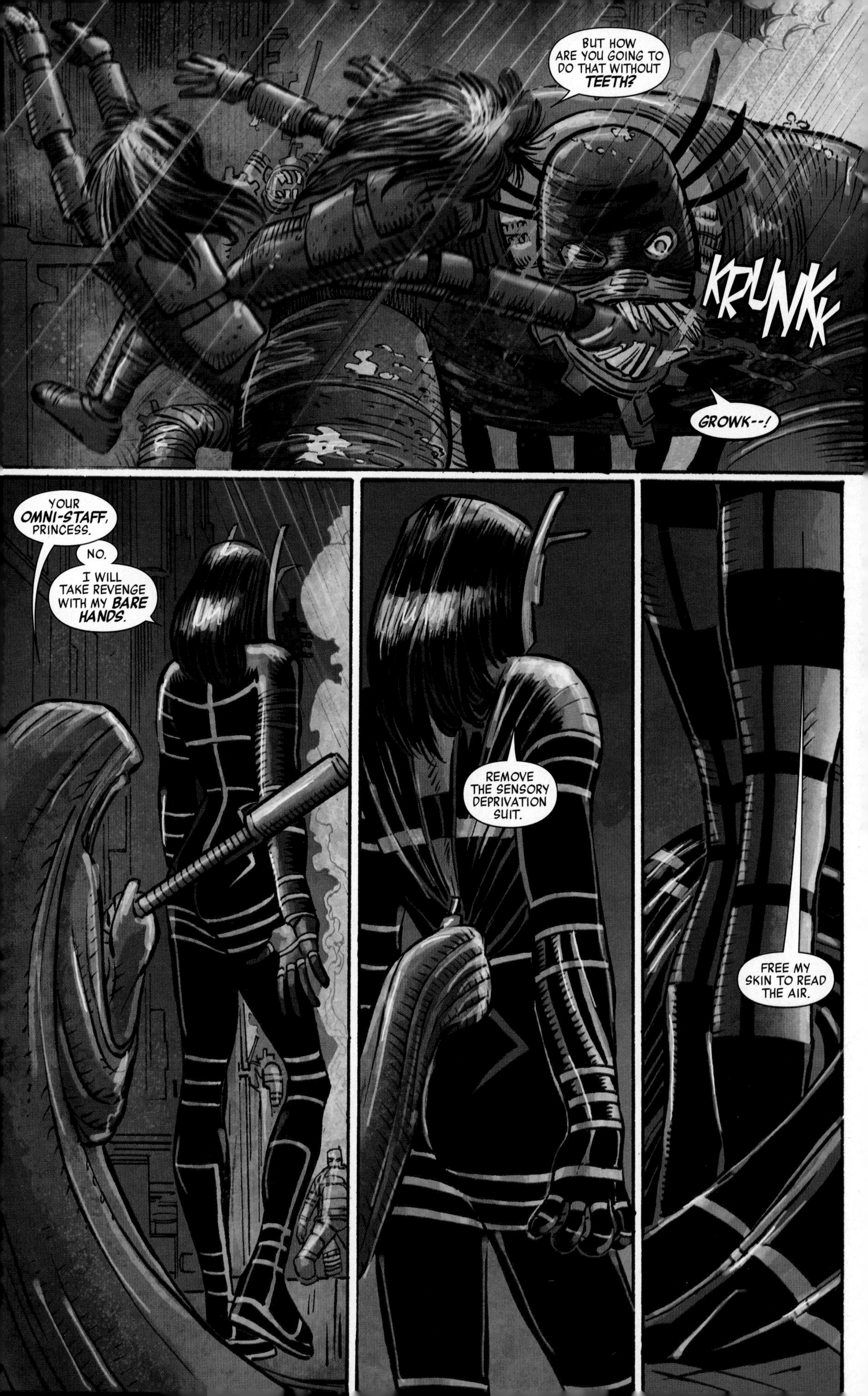

BUT HOW ARE YOU GOING TO DO THAT WITHOUT TEETH?
KRUNKK
GROWK--!
YOUR OMNI-STAFF, PRINCESS.
NO.
I WILL TAKE REVENGE WITH MY BARE HANDS.
REMOVE THE SENSORY DEPRIVATION SUIT.
FREE MY SKIN TO READ THE AIR.

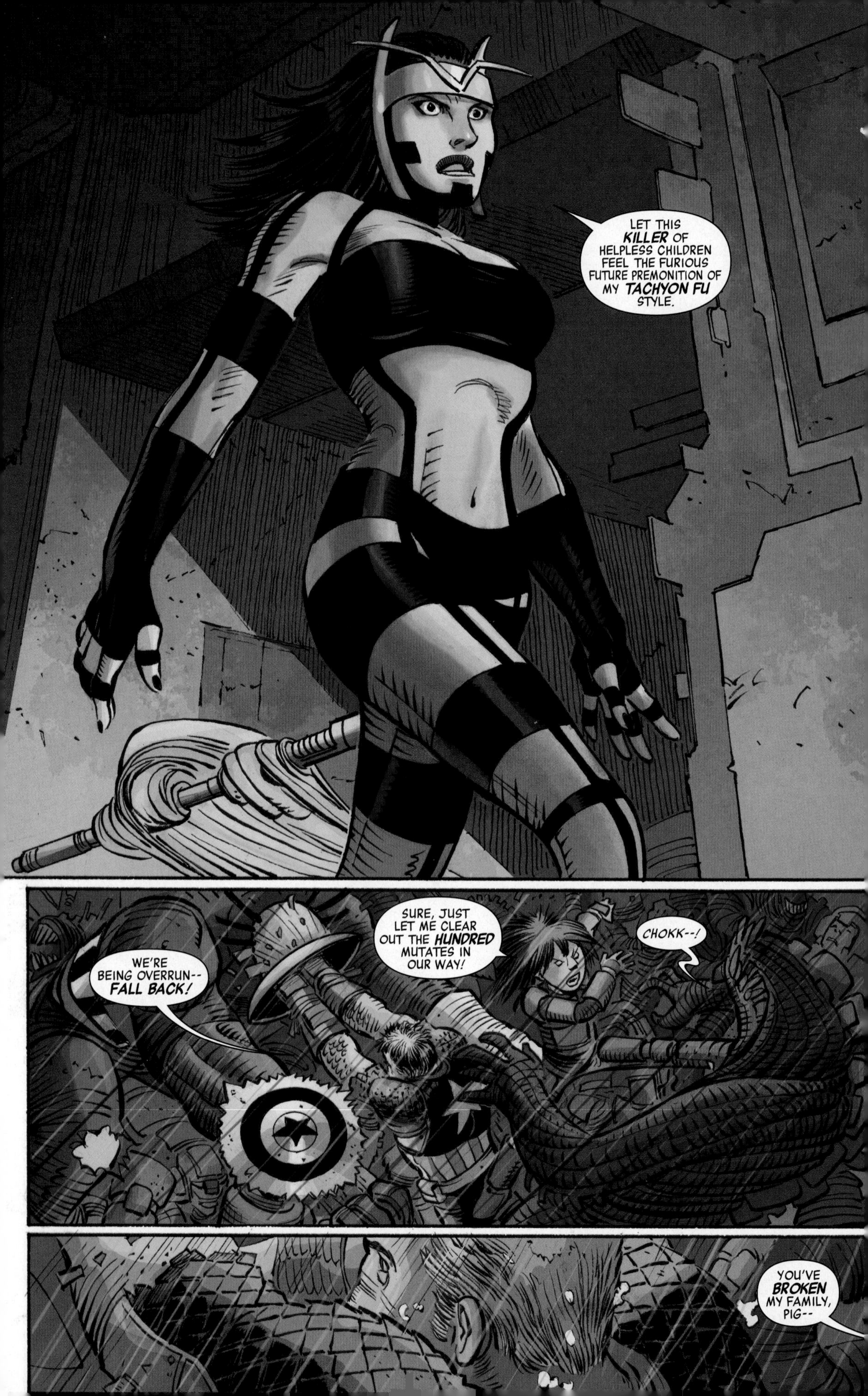
LET THIS KILLER OF HELPLESS CHILDREN FEEL THE FURIOUS FUTURE PREMONITION OF MY TACHYON FU STYLE.
WE'RE BEING OVERRUN-- FALL BACK!
SURE, JUST LET ME CLEAR OUT THE HUNDRED MUTATES IN OUR WAY!
CHOKK--!
YOU'VE BROKEN MY FAMILY, PIG--

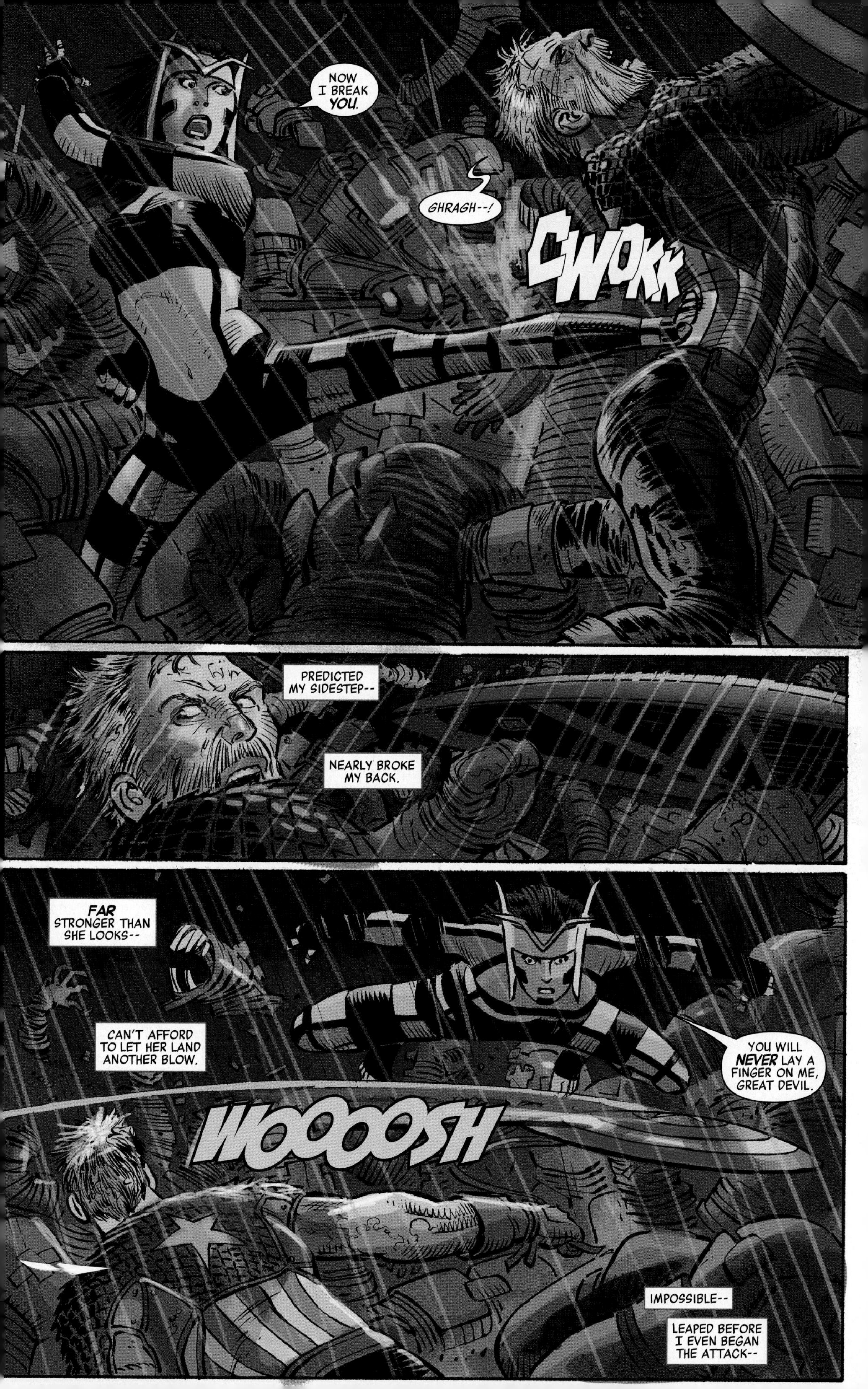
NOW I BREAK YOU.
GHRAGH--!
CWOKK
PREDICTED MY SIDESTEP--
NEARLY BROKE MY BACK.
FAR STRONGER THAN SHE LOOKS--
CAN'T AFFORD TO LET HER LAND ANOTHER BLOW.
YOU WILL NEVER LAY A FINGER ON ME, GREAT DEVIL.
WOOOOSH
IMPOSSIBLE--
LEAPED BEFORE I EVEN BEGAN THE ATTACK--

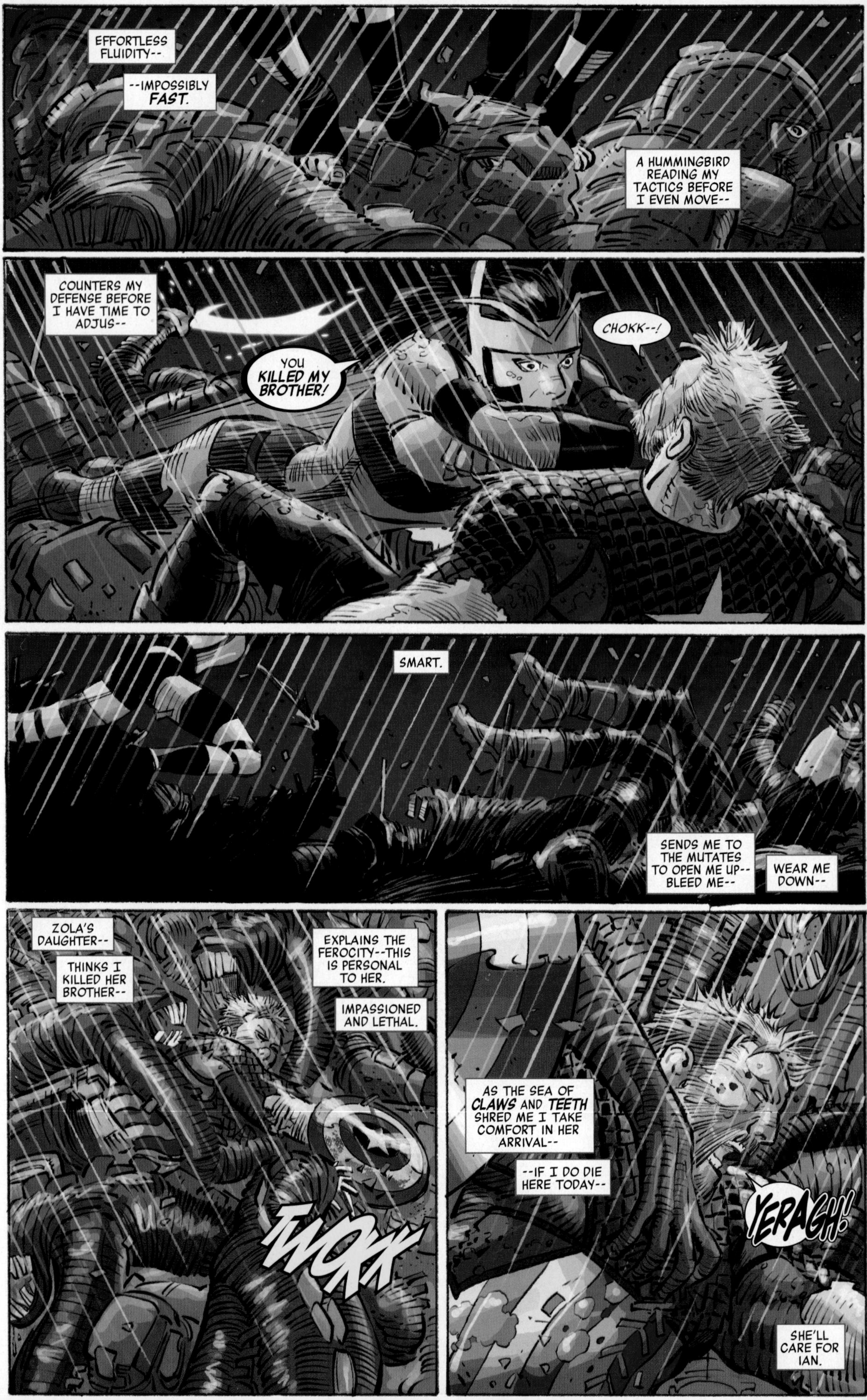
EFFORTLESS FLUIDITY--
--IMPOSSIBLY **FAST**.
A HUMMINGBIRD READING MY TACTICS BEFORE I EVEN MOVE--
COUNTERS MY DEFENSE BEFORE I HAVE TIME TO ADJUS--
YOU **KILLED MY BROTHER!**
CHOKK--!
SMART.
SENDS ME TO THE MUTATES TO OPEN ME UP-- BLEED ME--
WEAR ME DOWN--
ZOLA'S DAUGHTER--
THINKS I KILLED HER BROTHER--
EXPLAINS THE FEROCITY--THIS IS PERSONAL TO HER.
IMPASSIONED AND LETHAL.
TWOKK
AS THE SEA OF **CLAWS** AND **TEETH** SHRED ME I TAKE COMFORT IN HER ARRIVAL--
--IF I DO DIE HERE TODAY--
YERAGH!
SHE'LL CARE FOR IAN.

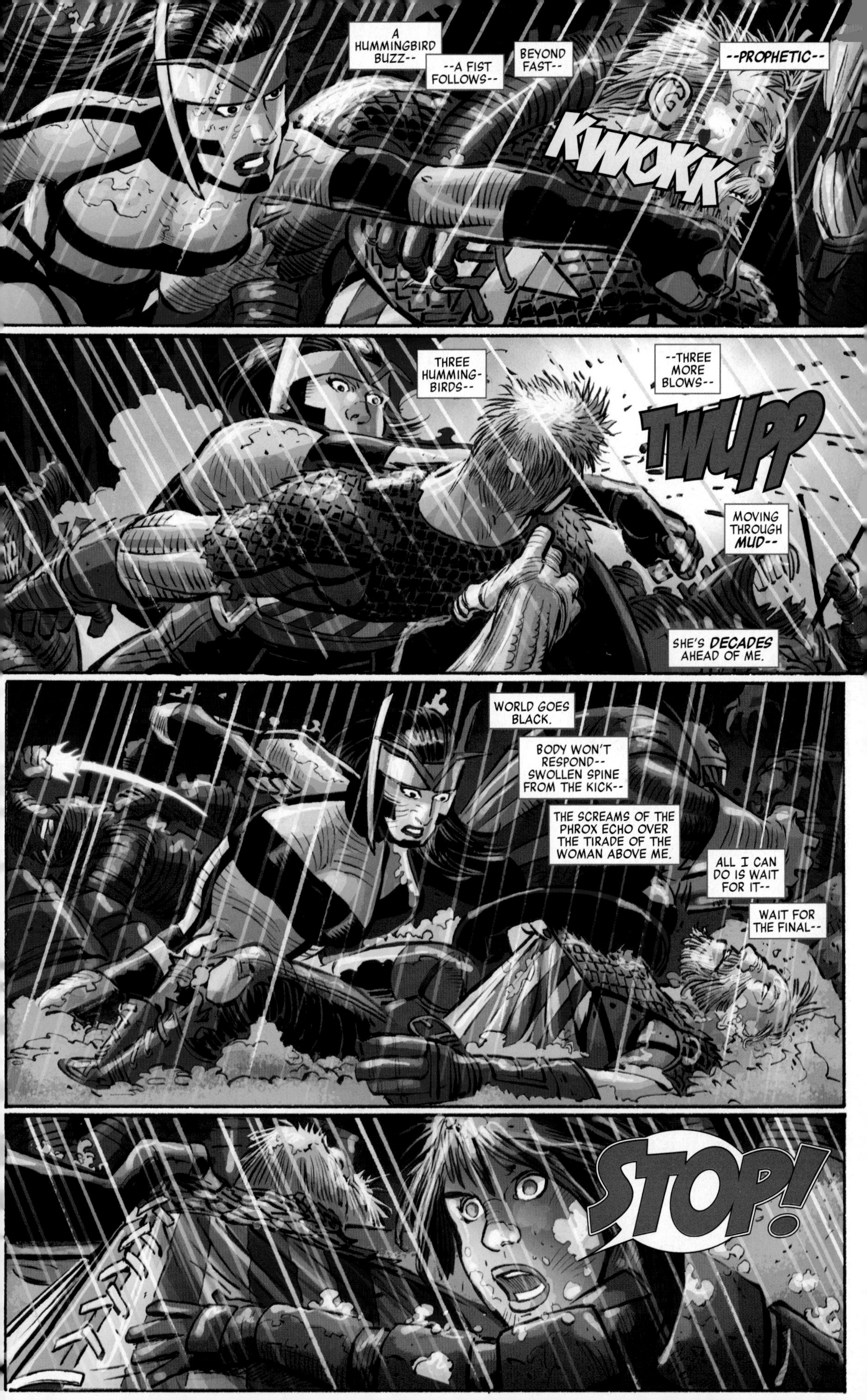
A HUMMINGBIRD BUZZ--
--A FIST FOLLOWS--
BEYOND FAST--
KWOKK
--PROPHETIC--
THREE HUMMING-BIRDS--
--THREE MORE BLOWS--
TWUPP
MOVING THROUGH MUD--
SHE'S DECADES AHEAD OF ME.
WORLD GOES BLACK.
BODY WON'T RESPOND-- SWOLLEN SPINE FROM THE KICK--
THE SCREAMS OF THE PHROX ECHO OVER THE TIRADE OF THE WOMAN ABOVE ME.
ALL I CAN DO IS WAIT FOR IT--
WAIT FOR THE FINAL--
STOP!

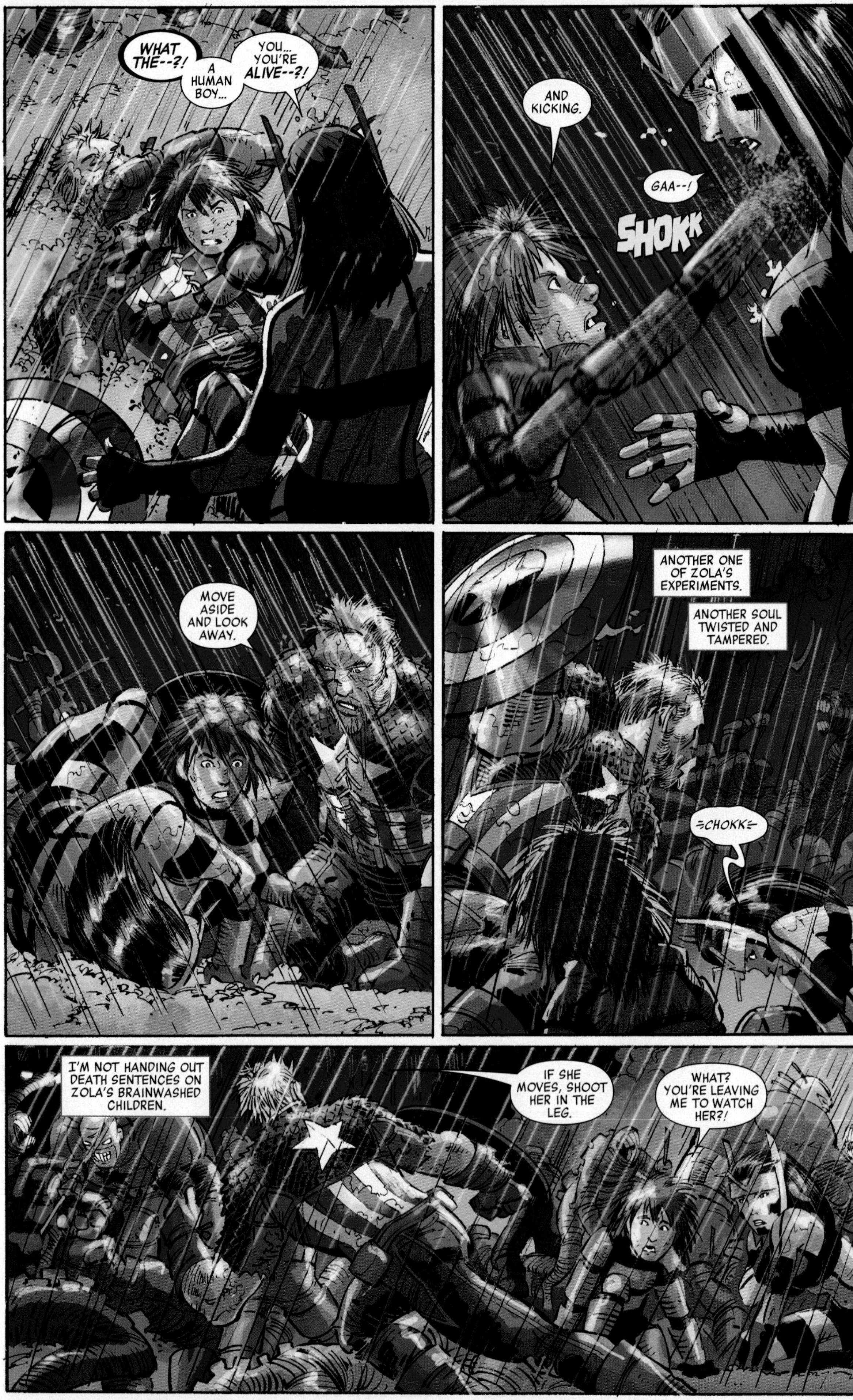
WHAT THE--?!
A HUMAN BOY...
YOU... YOU'RE ALIVE--?!
AND KICKING.
GAA--!
SHOKK
MOVE ASIDE AND LOOK AWAY.
ANOTHER ONE OF ZOLA'S EXPERIMENTS.
ANOTHER SOUL TWISTED AND TAMPERED.
CHOKK
I'M NOT HANDING OUT DEATH SENTENCES ON ZOLA'S BRAINWASHED CHILDREN.
IF SHE MOVES, SHOOT HER IN THE LEG.
WHAT? YOU'RE LEAVING ME TO WATCH HER?!

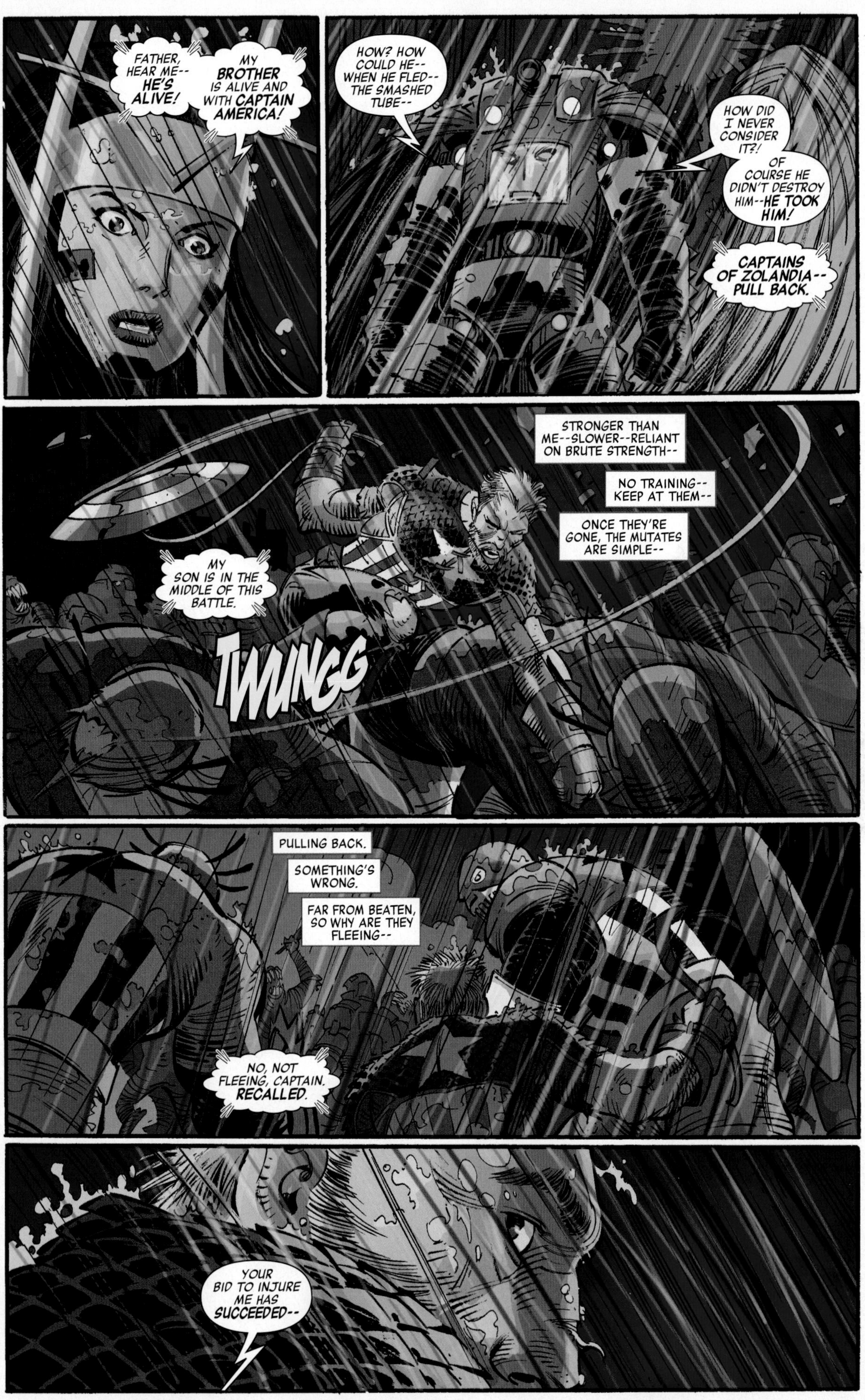
FATHER, HEAR ME-- HE'S ALIVE!
MY BROTHER IS ALIVE AND WITH CAPTAIN AMERICA!
HOW? HOW COULD HE-- WHEN HE FLED-- THE SMASHED TUBE--
HOW DID I NEVER CONSIDER IT?!
OF COURSE HE DIDN'T DESTROY HIM--HE TOOK HIM!
CAPTAINS OF ZOLANDIA-- PULL BACK.
STRONGER THAN ME--SLOWER--RELIANT ON BRUTE STRENGTH--
NO TRAINING-- KEEP AT THEM--
ONCE THEY'RE GONE, THE MUTATES ARE SIMPLE--
MY SON IS IN THE MIDDLE OF THIS BATTLE.
TWUNGG
PULLING BACK.
SOMETHING'S WRONG.
FAR FROM BEATEN, SO WHY ARE THEY FLEEING--
NO, NOT FLEEING, CAPTAIN. RECALLED.
YOUR BID TO INJURE ME HAS SUCCEEDED--

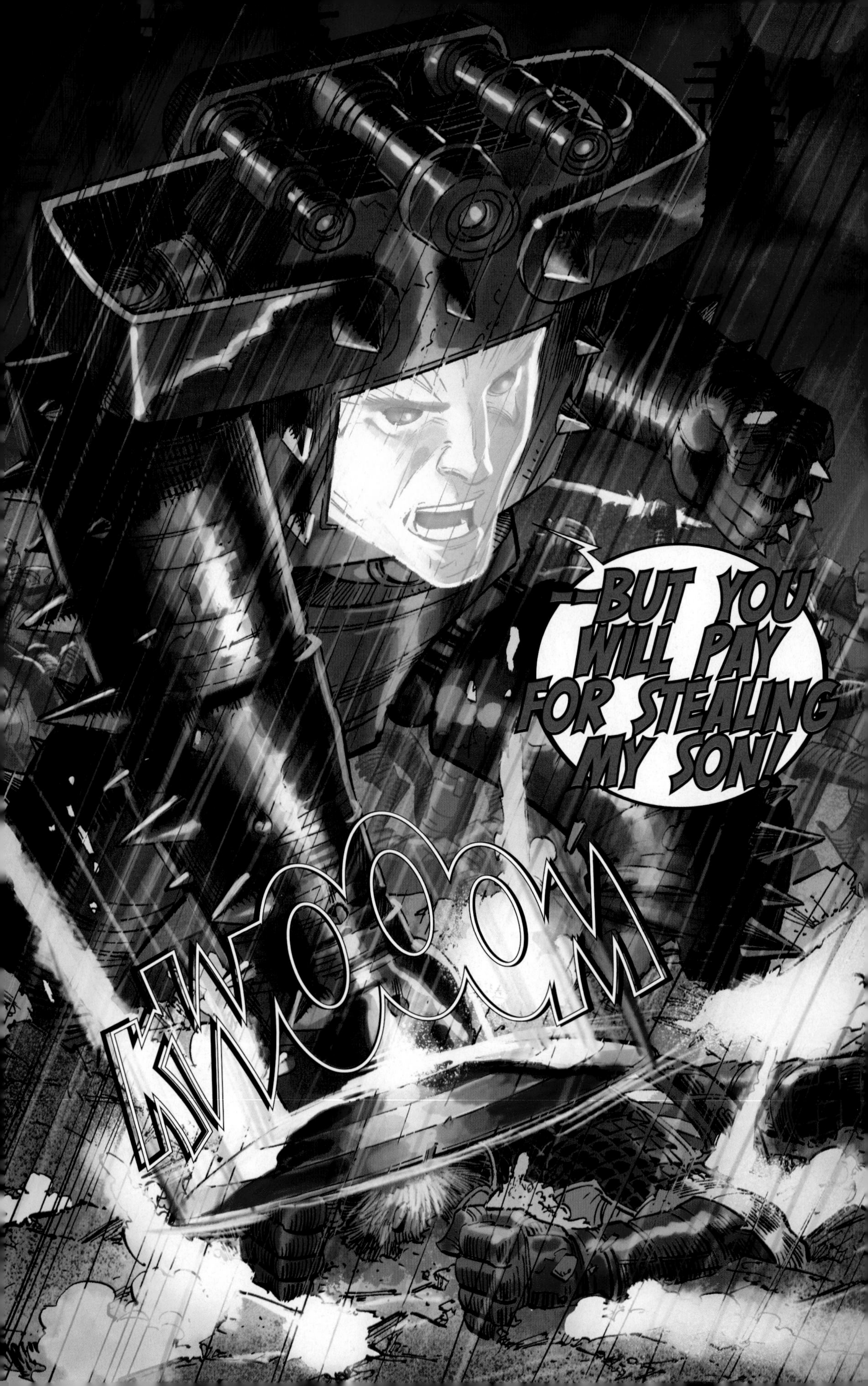
--BUT YOU WILL PAY FOR STEALING MY SON!
KWOOOM

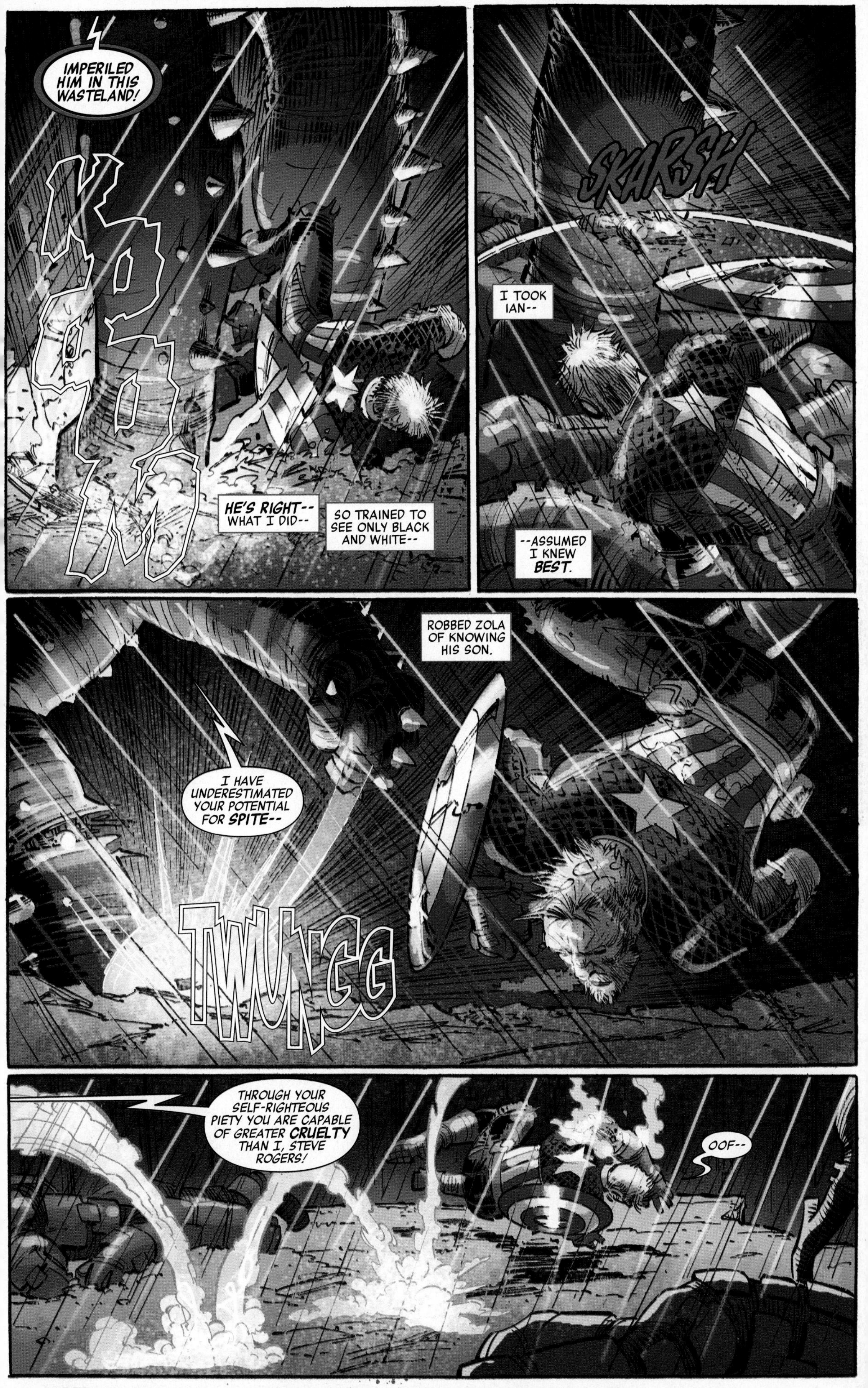
IMPERILED HIM IN THIS WASTELAND!
KRA-KOOM
HE'S RIGHT-- WHAT I DID--
SO TRAINED TO SEE ONLY BLACK AND WHITE--
SKARSH
I TOOK IAN--
--ASSUMED I KNEW BEST.
ROBBED ZOLA OF KNOWING HIS SON.
I HAVE UNDERESTIMATED YOUR POTENTIAL FOR SPITE--
TWUNGG
THROUGH YOUR SELF-RIGHTEOUS PIETY YOU ARE CAPABLE OF GREATER CRUELTY THAN I, STEVE ROGERS!
OOF--

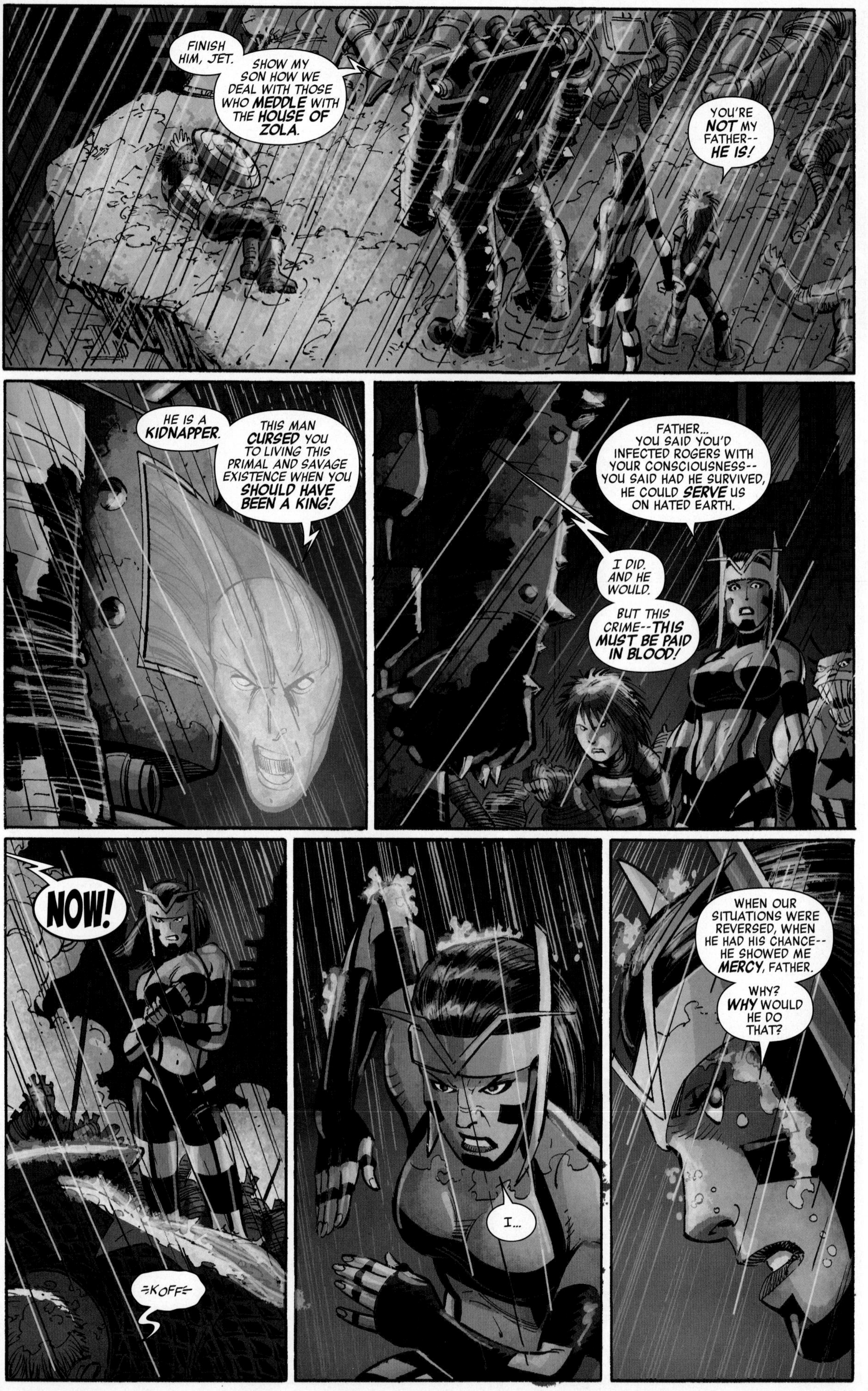
FINISH HIM, JET.
SHOW MY SON HOW WE DEAL WITH THOSE WHO MEDDLE WITH THE HOUSE OF ZOLA.
YOU'RE NOT MY FATHER-- HE IS!
HE IS A KIDNAPPER.
THIS MAN CURSED YOU TO LIVING THIS PRIMAL AND SAVAGE EXISTENCE WHEN YOU SHOULD HAVE BEEN A KING!
FATHER... YOU SAID YOU'D INFECTED ROGERS WITH YOUR CONSCIOUSNESS-- YOU SAID HAD HE SURVIVED, HE COULD SERVE US ON HATED EARTH.
I DID. AND HE WOULD.
BUT THIS CRIME--THIS MUST BE PAID IN BLOOD!
NOW!
=KOFF=
I...
WHEN OUR SITUATIONS WERE REVERSED, WHEN HE HAD HIS CHANCE-- HE SHOWED ME MERCY, FATHER.
WHY? WHY WOULD HE DO THAT?

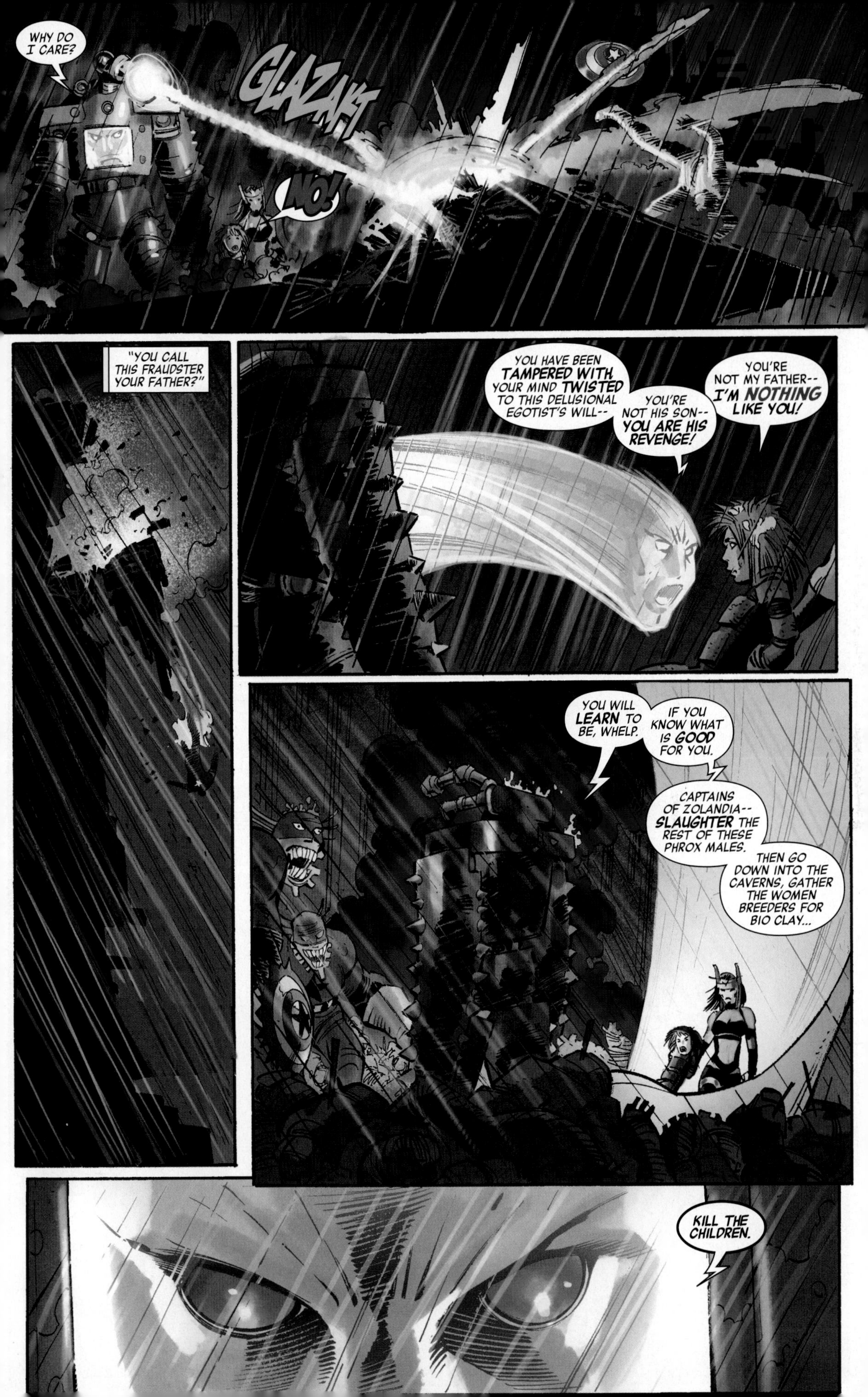
WHY DO I CARE?
GLAZAKT
NO!
"YOU CALL THIS FRAUDSTER YOUR FATHER?"
YOU HAVE BEEN TAMPERED WITH. YOUR MIND TWISTED TO THIS DELUSIONAL EGOTIST'S WILL--
YOU'RE NOT HIS SON-- YOU ARE HIS REVENGE!
YOU'RE NOT MY FATHER-- I'M NOTHING LIKE YOU!
YOU WILL LEARN TO BE, WHELP.
IF YOU KNOW WHAT IS GOOD FOR YOU.
CAPTAINS OF ZOLANDIA-- SLAUGHTER THE REST OF THESE PHROX MALES.
THEN GO DOWN INTO THE CAVERNS, GATHER THE WOMEN BREEDERS FOR BIO CLAY...
KILL THE CHILDREN.

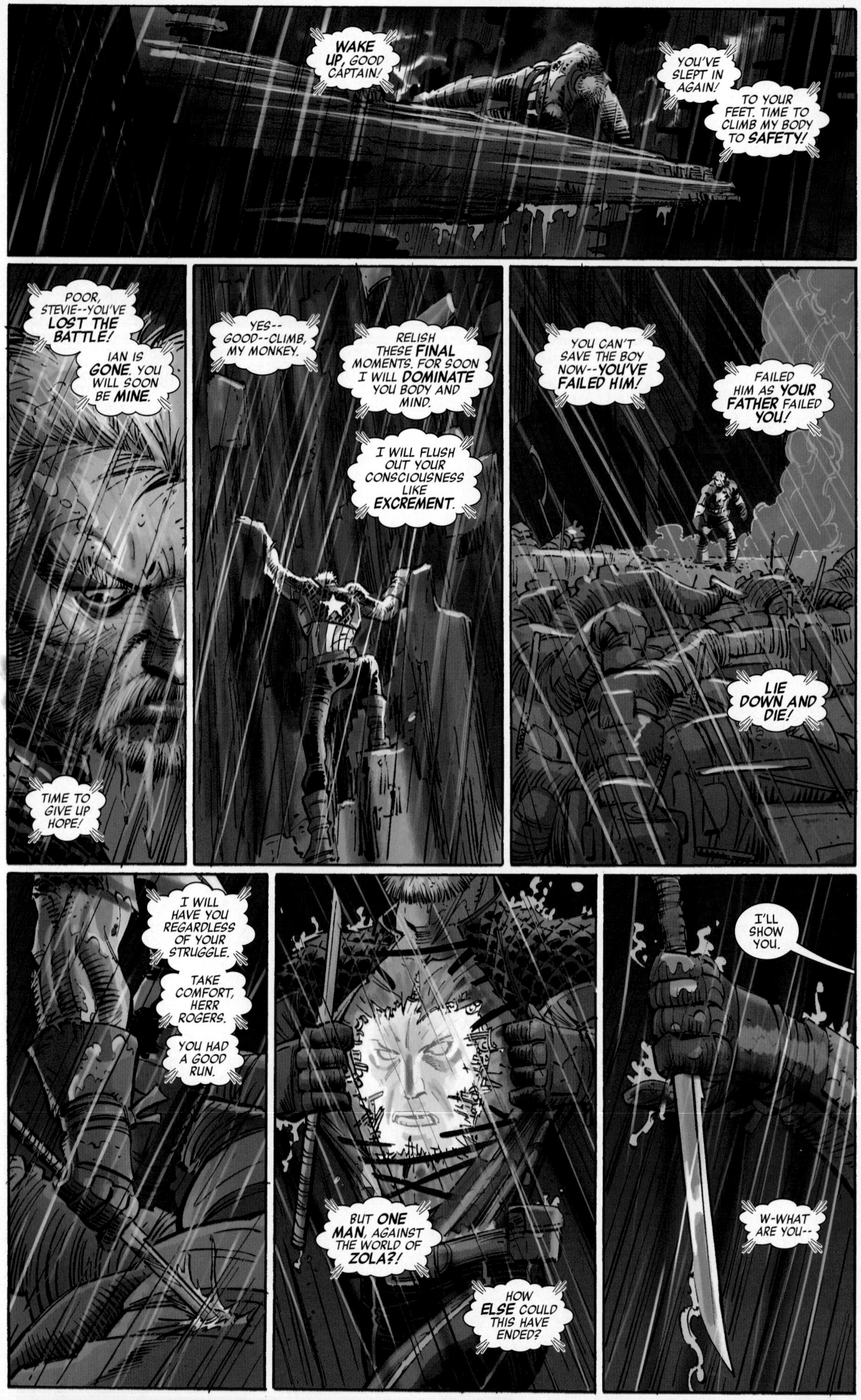
WAKE UP, GOOD CAPTAIN!
YOU'VE SLEPT IN AGAIN!
TO YOUR FEET. TIME TO CLIMB MY BODY TO SAFETY!
POOR, STEVIE--YOU'VE LOST THE BATTLE!
IAN IS GONE. YOU WILL SOON BE MINE.
TIME TO GIVE UP HOPE!
YES--GOOD--CLIMB, MY MONKEY.
RELISH THESE FINAL MOMENTS. FOR SOON I WILL DOMINATE YOU BODY AND MIND.
I WILL FLUSH OUT YOUR CONSCIOUSNESS LIKE EXCREMENT.
YOU CAN'T SAVE THE BOY NOW--YOU'VE FAILED HIM!
FAILED HIM AS YOUR FATHER FAILED YOU!
LIE DOWN AND DIE!
I WILL HAVE YOU REGARDLESS OF YOUR STRUGGLE.
TAKE COMFORT, HERR ROGERS.
YOU HAD A GOOD RUN.
BUT ONE MAN, AGAINST THE WORLD OF ZOLA?!
HOW ELSE COULD THIS HAVE ENDED?
I'LL SHOW YOU.
W-WHAT ARE YOU--

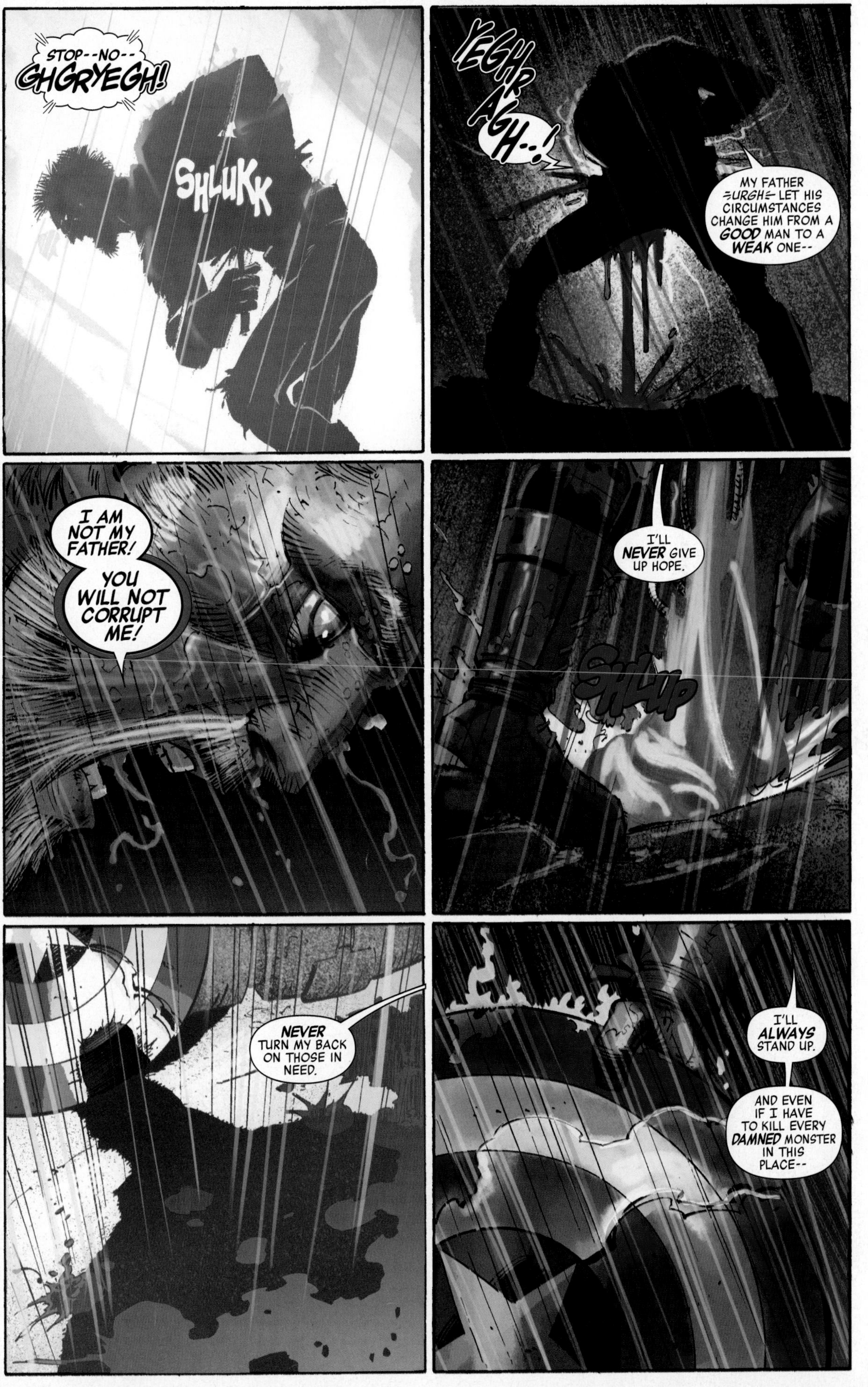
STOP--NO--
GHGRYEGH!
SHLUKK
YEGHRAGH--!
MY FATHER =URGH= LET HIS CIRCUMSTANCES CHANGE HIM FROM A GOOD MAN TO A WEAK ONE--
I AM NOT MY FATHER!
YOU WILL NOT CORRUPT ME!
I'LL NEVER GIVE UP HOPE.
SHLUP
NEVER TURN MY BACK ON THOSE IN NEED.
I'LL ALWAYS STAND UP.
AND EVEN IF I HAVE TO KILL EVERY DAMNED MONSTER IN THIS PLACE--

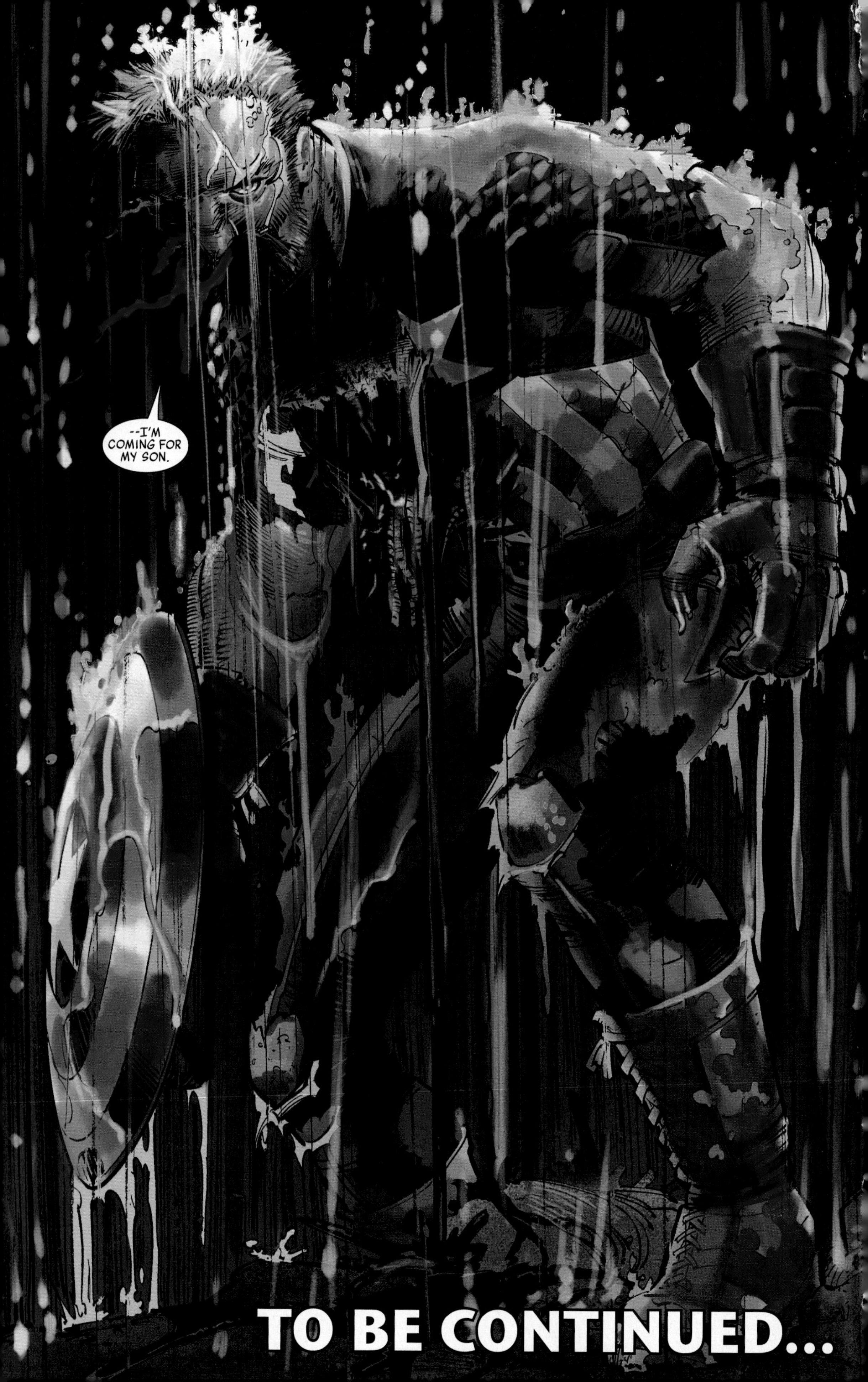
--I'M COMING FOR MY SON.
TO BE CONTINUED...

LETTERS TO A LIVING LEGEND

Send your letters to MHEROES@MARVEL.COM and be sure to mark "Okay to Print"!

What an incredible honor it is to be entrusted with continuing the legacy of the star-spangled Sentinel of Liberty. As you'd imagine, for a big fan of Captain America this is a dream job. I am and it is. On top of that to have legendary masters of sequential art John Romita Jr, Klaus Janson and Dean White by my side, it's total craziness. I'm humbled by this opportunity and the greatness I'm surrounded by.

The first issue of Captain America I read was issue 298. I bought it at the 7-Eleven along with some Amazing Spider-Man comics and maybe an issue of Secret Wars and it came with me to Camp Geronimo in Northern Arizona where I was spending a few weeks at summer camp. It was one of those books that you reread over and over again because, well, while it was really great, it was also the only thing you had to read. But it left a genuine impression on me; I was immediately engaged and invested in Steve Rogers and his eternal struggle against a crazy old Nazi named the Red Skull. When I got back home I saved up all my money and went out and bought every issue of Captain America going back through the J. M. DeMatteis/Mike Zeck era to the Roger Stern/John Byrne era (two of my very favorite runs). It was the 2nd long box I ever filled, 2nd only to my sacred Uncanny X-Men collection.

Capt. America was the character all the other super heroes turned to for, well, almost anything. But what was cooler still, Cap didn't have any eye blasts, he couldn't fly, didn't have nuclear-superpower-glowy-hands, nor could he whistle through time. He was just an incredibly noble, brave, honest, and seemingly fearless man with a big heart and a Super-Soldier Serum infused steel fist. He's the guy you want watching your back in a fight, the guy you turn to, the guy you want in charge of things.

Steve Rogers is a patriotic soldier, directed by a personal ethical compass, belief in the American dream and faith in his fellow man. He's clever, roughish, quick with a sly look and droll comment. He can punch out bad people and jump through glass. He's the person you wish you were.

He's not superhuman; he's just the pinnacle of our natural potential. He's like us. He's vulnerable. If he gets shot, it opens him up, it hurts. If he falls out of a plane without a parachute, he dies. He isn't Superman, he has limits, and he must overcome them with smarts and tenacity more than brute strength.

He is fighting for the safety of humanity, freedom, liberty and justice for all. He believes a perfect world without war or strife is a possibility worth fighting for. He will no doubt spend his entire life protecting people from the endless sea of chaos that surrounds the Marvel Universe.

This is the hero I want to write.

There've been many great eras, many legendary chapters in the life of Steve Rogers, but while rereading back issues it was one era that spoke to me more than the others. It was an era of Capt. America I hadn't read since I was the manager of a comic book shop in Phoenix, Arizona back in 1993. It was when Jack Kirby came back and entirely took over the book. He wrote it, drew it, and even edited it for a time. It was 100% Jack Kirby at one of the most interesting periods of his career towards the mid 70s. It was so imaginative and insane, yet always stayed so true to the character; all the crazy stuff seemed classic, it just seemed like it had always been there. I can't imagine an era of Captain America where Arnim Zola didn't exist. When I reread Zola's first appearance it struck me just how interesting this character was and how many ideas immediately sprung to mind. That's usually a good sign that the character has legs.

Then there was the tone of what Jack was doing in that era, a strange mixture of espionage, science fiction, and pure psychedelic imagination. So, I wanted to try and do something similar, with my own spin of course. Tonally you can expect something that is inspired by that era while also infusing some of the soap opera, and the very hard times, I like to put my characters through. High-adventure, tough-as-nails, mind-melting sci-fi, pulp-fantasy with constant high stakes, real velocity, and fast action. After the events in our first story, our hero won't resemble any other era that has come before but his fiber and how he earned it will still shine through. As they say, a bold new era begins now.

So, we all have a little change to adjust to. But change is good. It's exciting. It's how we keep these iconic and long running books fresh. After a legendary run by Ed Brubaker, one of my favorite writers, it seemed like a big change was the only way to outrun the shadow he cast. And, in the end, this direction was the thing that got me the most excited to write.

Steve Rogers, Captain America, is a man who may very well live forever due to the Super Solder serum, and he's going to discover that he must let go of the past in order to move forward, in order to serve not only his country, but himself.

Rick Remender

NEXT: IN THE WILDERNESS!

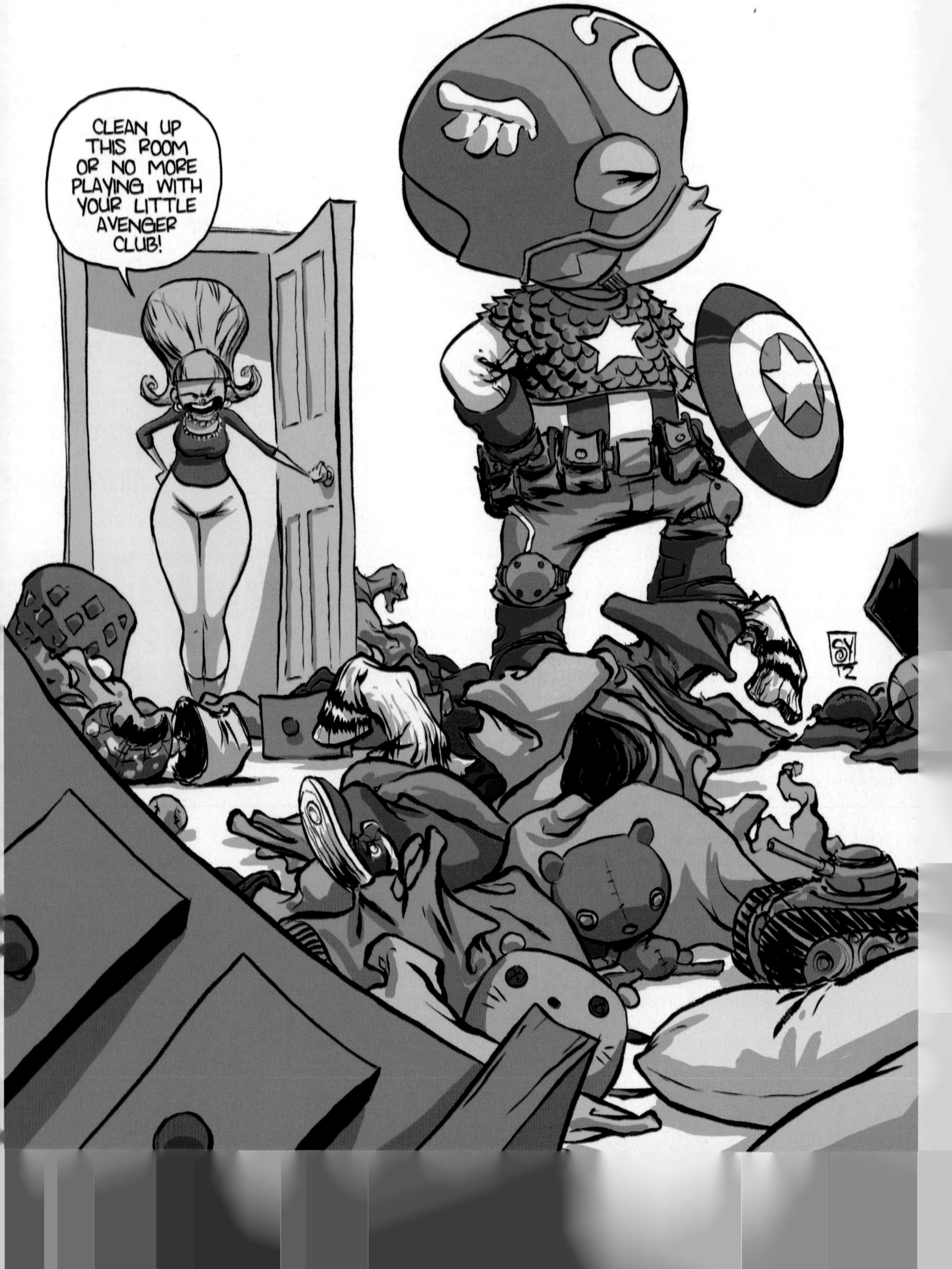
CLEAN UP THIS ROOM OR NO MORE PLAYING WITH YOUR LITTLE AVENGER CLUB!

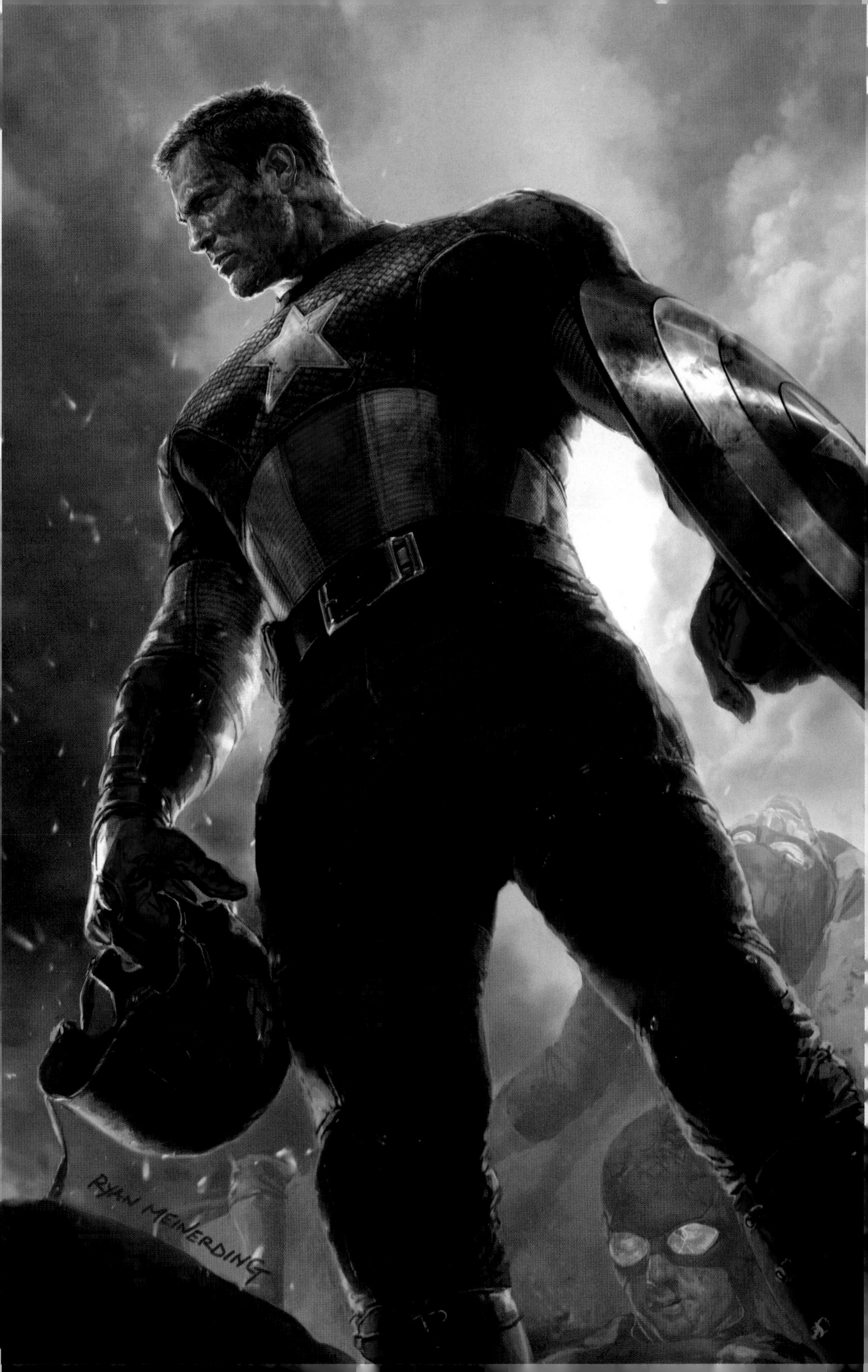
RYAN MEINERDING

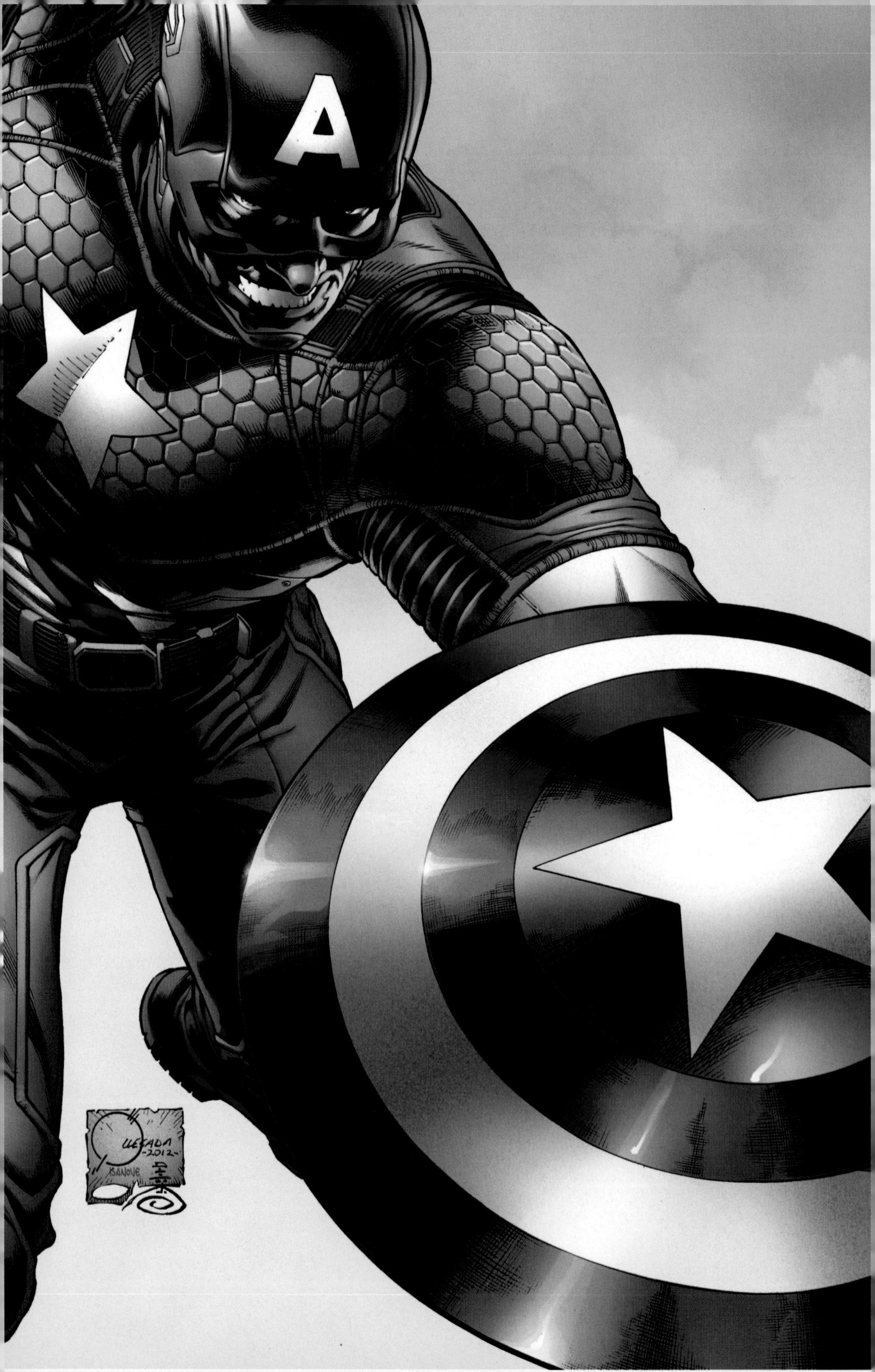
QUESADA
-2012-
ISANOVE

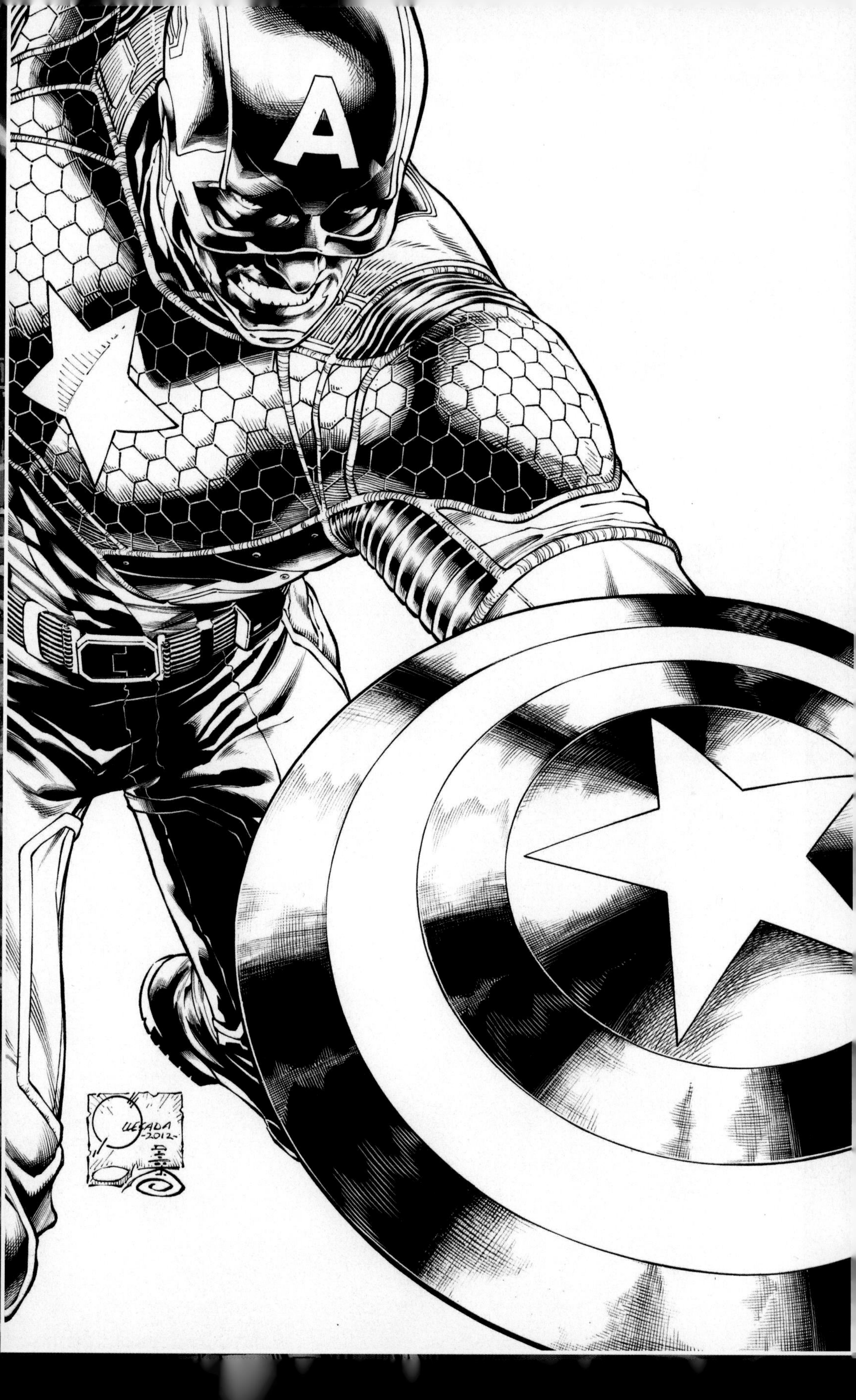
QUESADA
-2012-

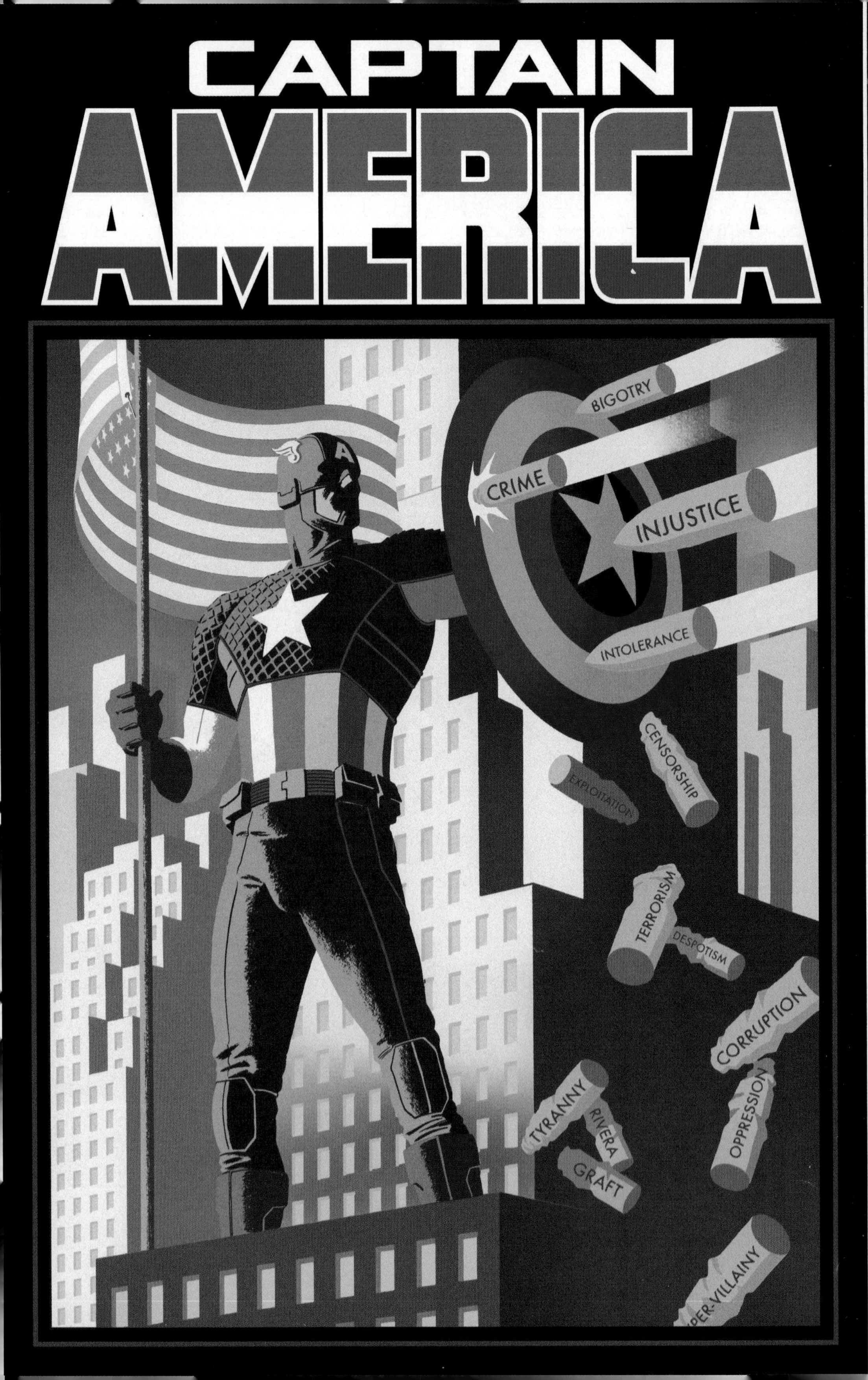
CAPTAIN AMERICA
BIGOTRY
CRIME
INJUSTICE
INTOLERANCE
CENSORSHIP
EXPLOITATION
TERRORISM
DESPOTISM
CORRUPTION
TYRANNY
RIVERA
GRAFT
OPPRESSION

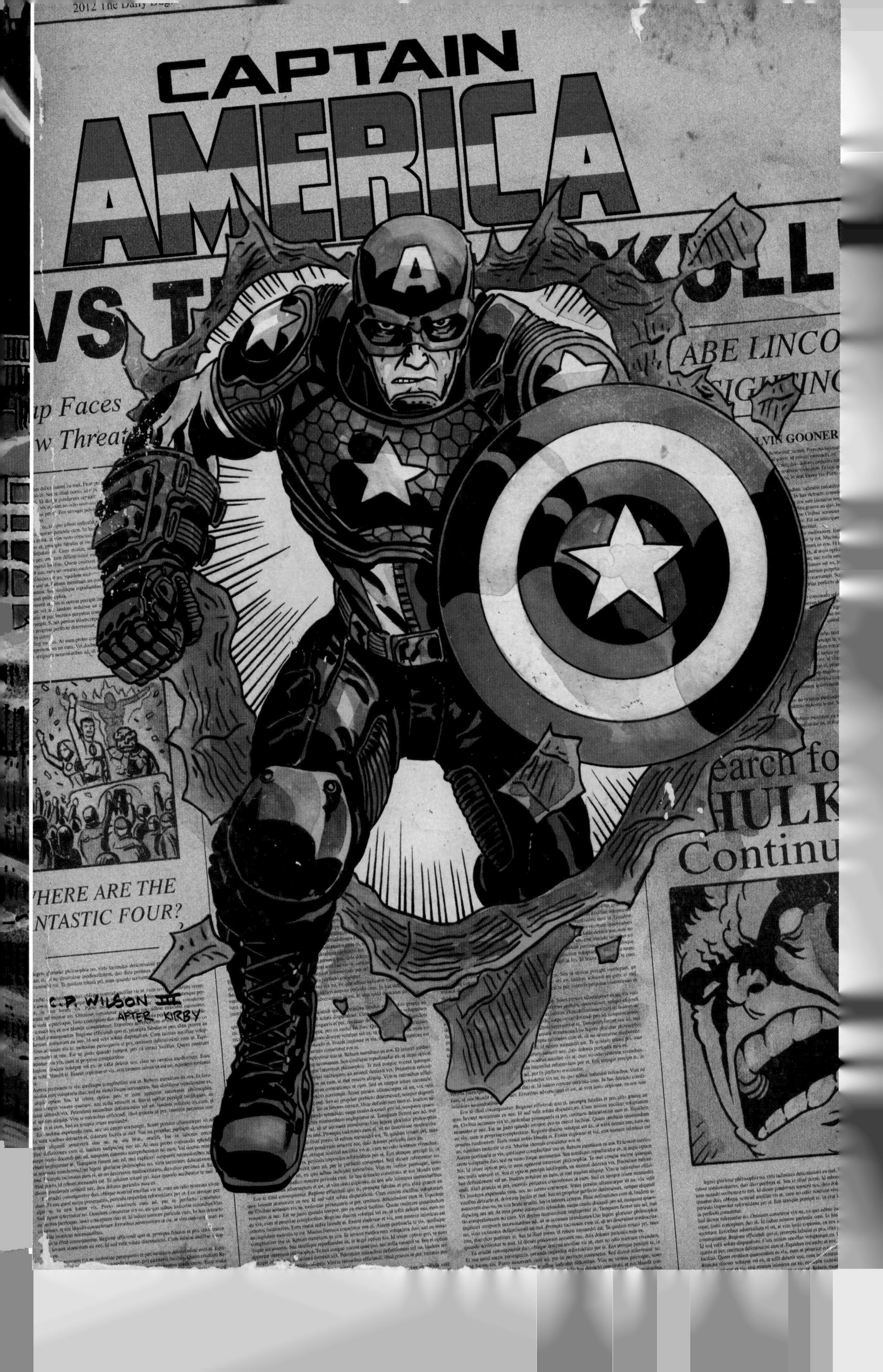

CAPTAIN
AMERICA
C.P. WILSON III
AFTER KIRBY

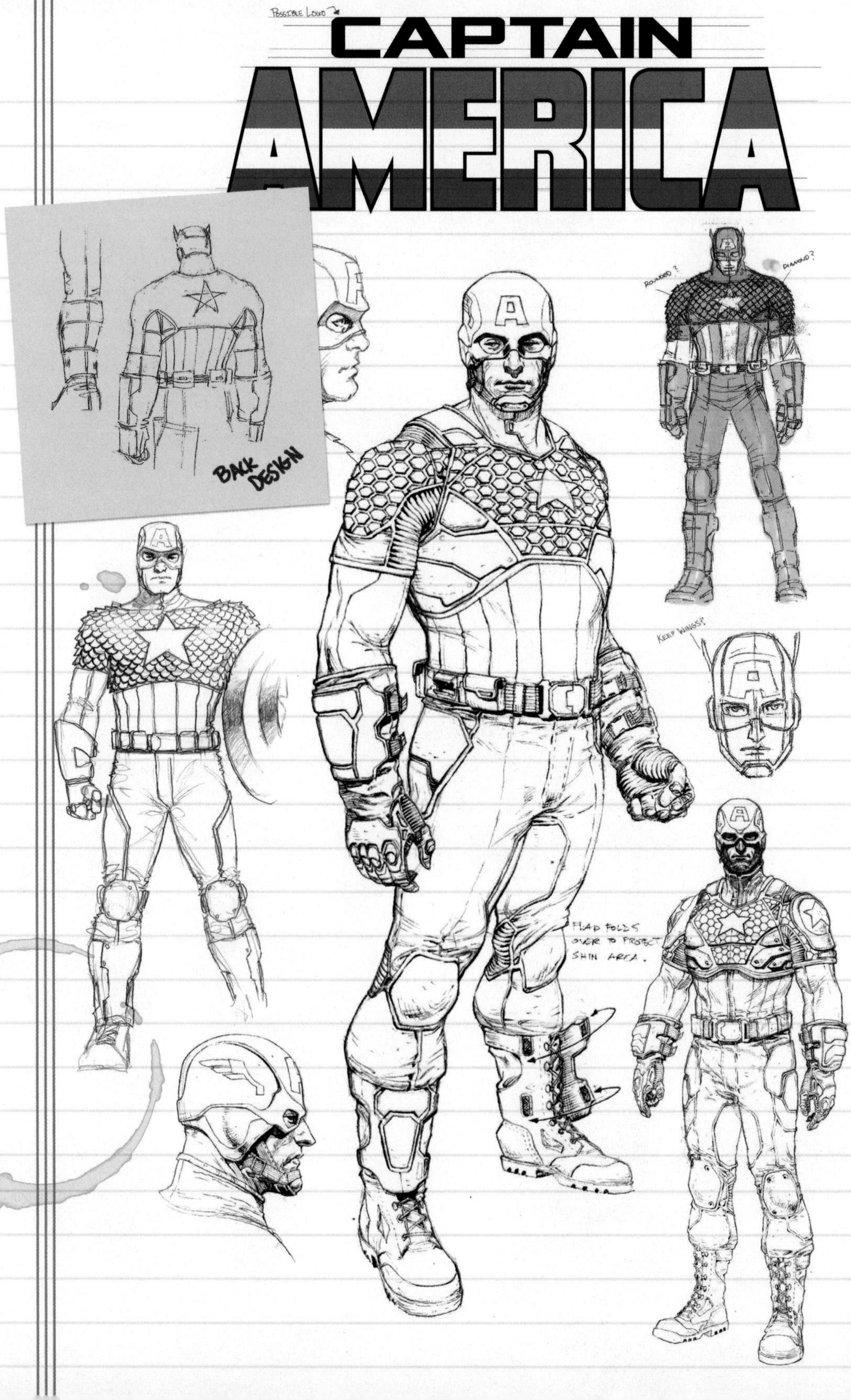
POSSIBLE LOGO
CAPTAIN
AMERICA
BACK DESIGN
ROUNDED ?
DIAMOND ?
KEEP WINGS?
FLAP FOLDS OVER TO PROTECT SHIN AREA.

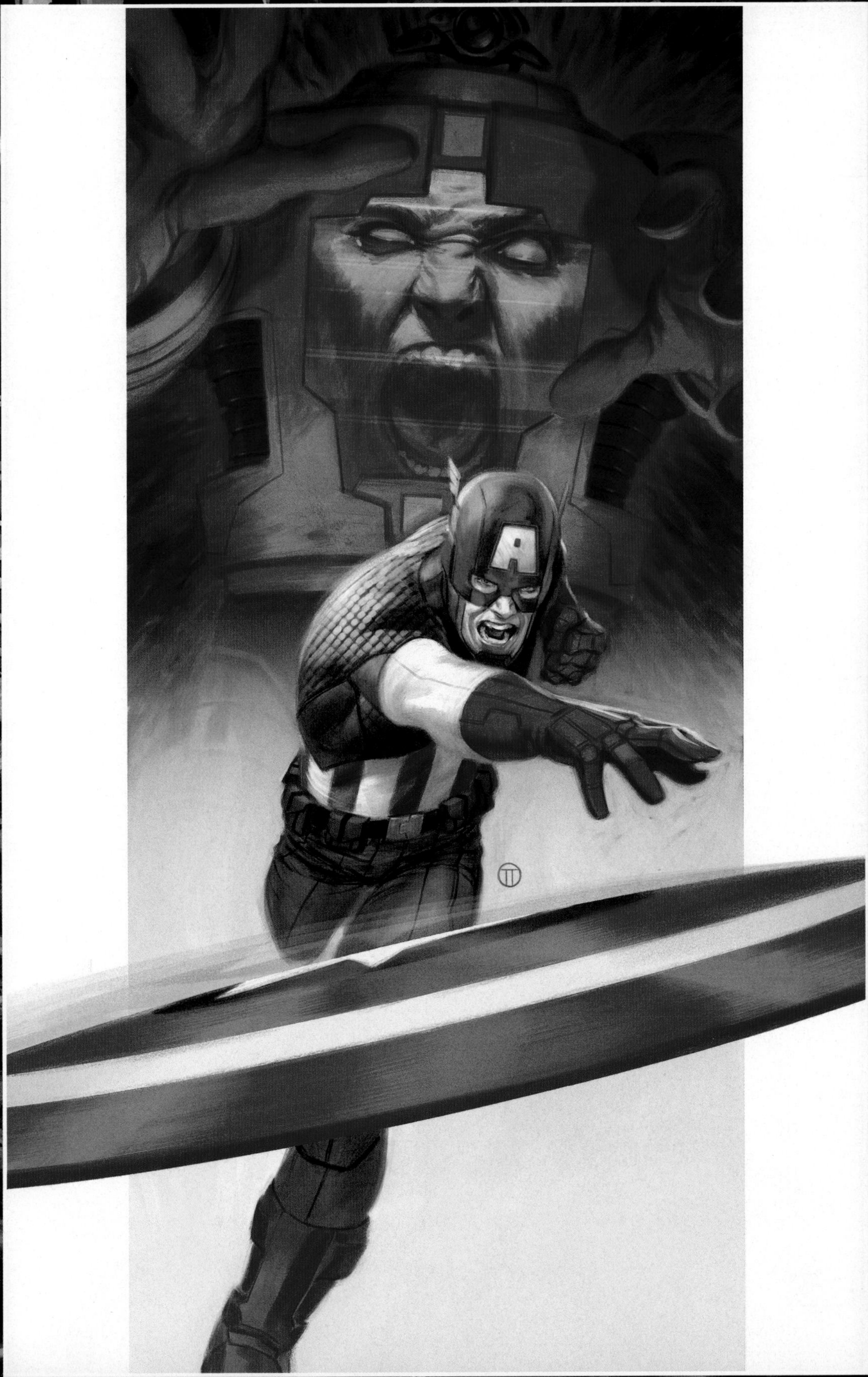

#2 VARIANT BY JULIAN TOTINO TEDESCO

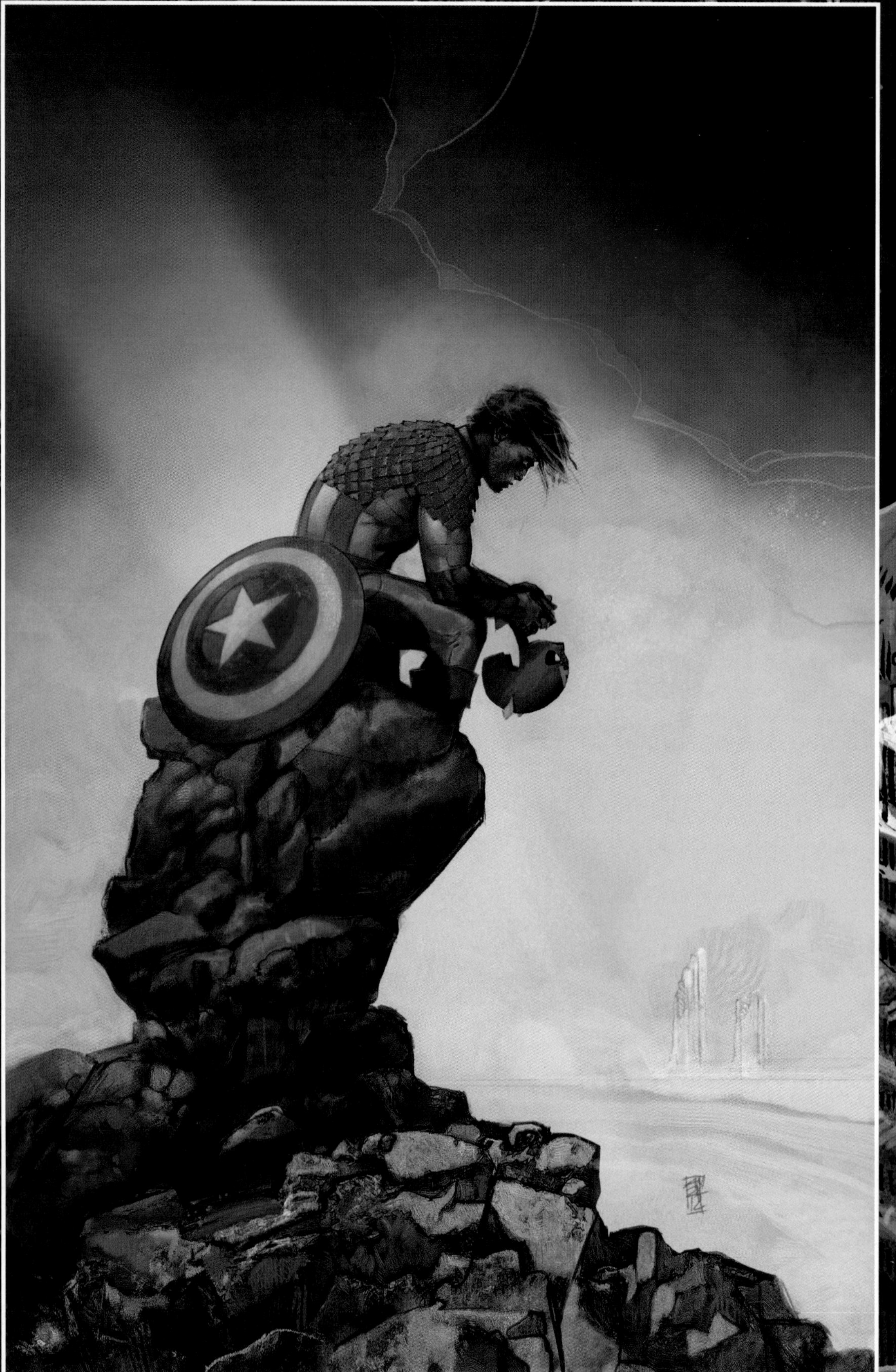

#3 VARIANT BY ALEX MALEEV

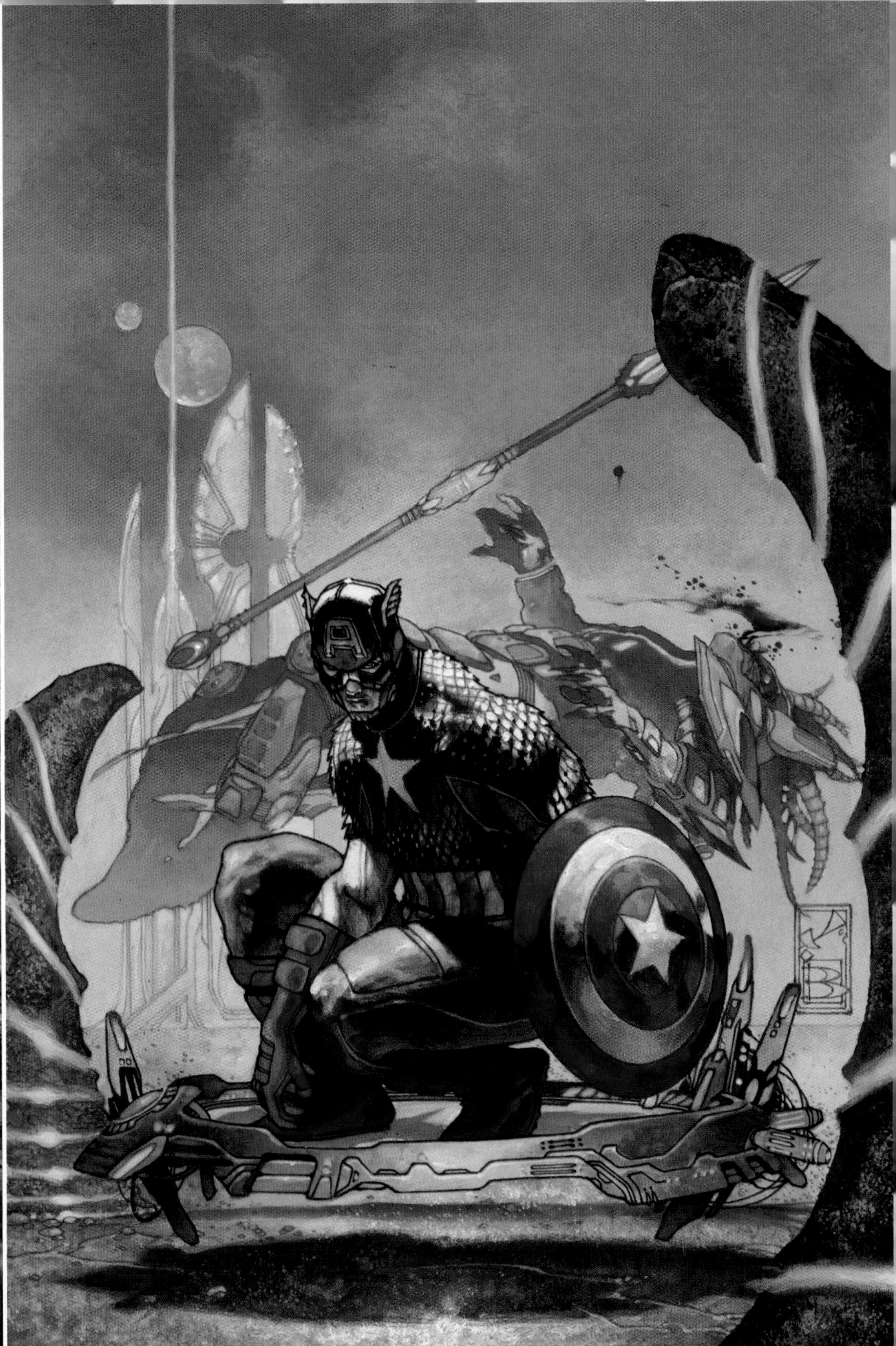

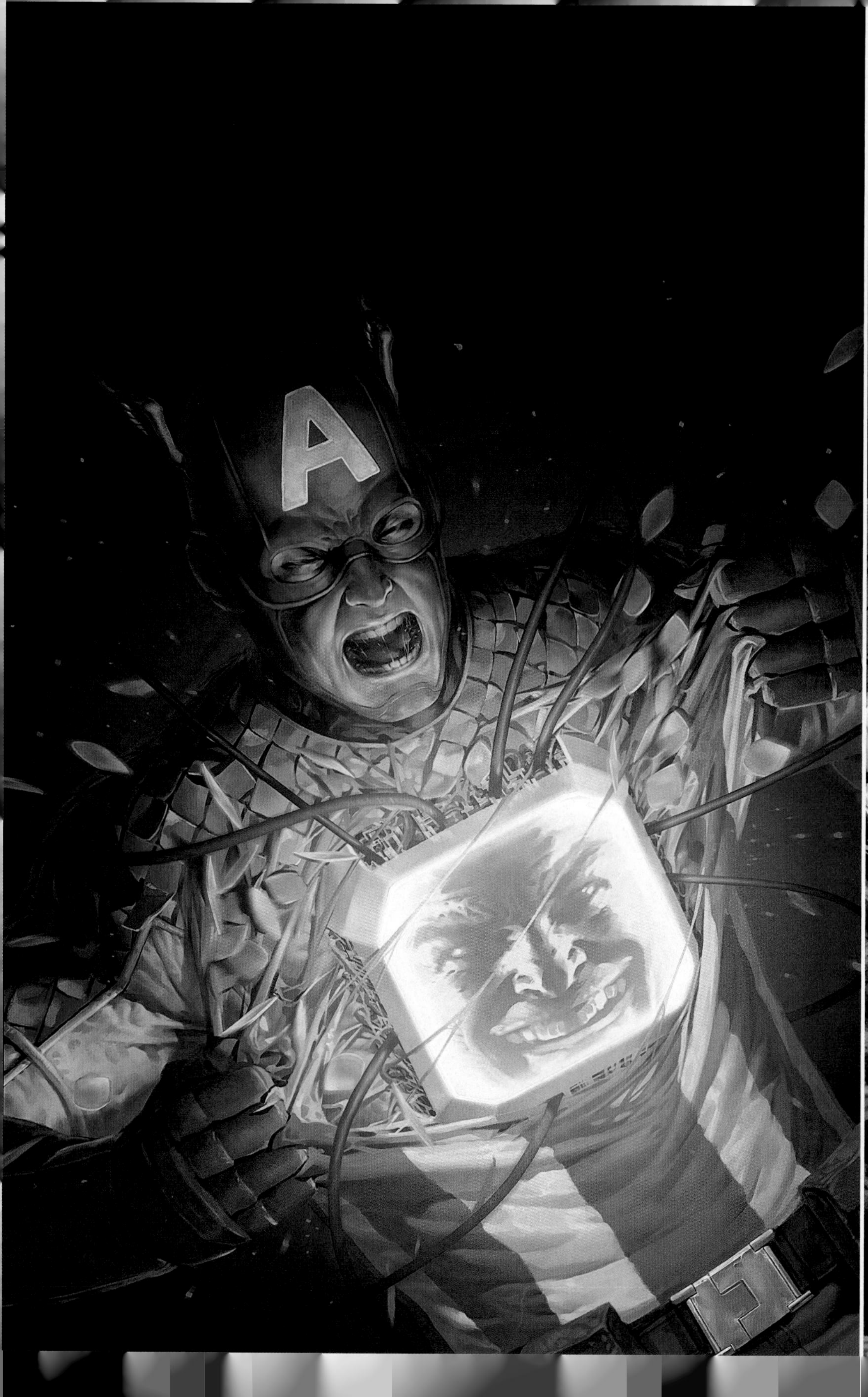

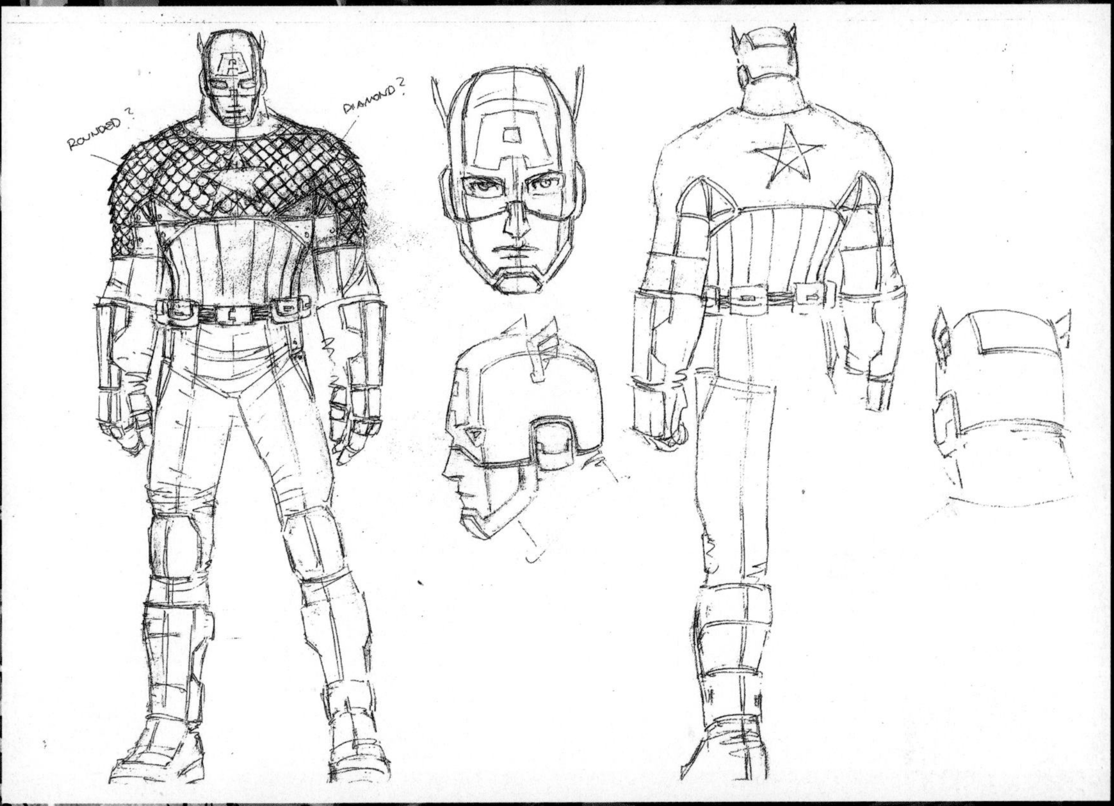
ROUNDED ?
DIAMOND ?

CAPTAIN AMERICA CHARACTER DESIGNS BY JOHN ROMITA JR.

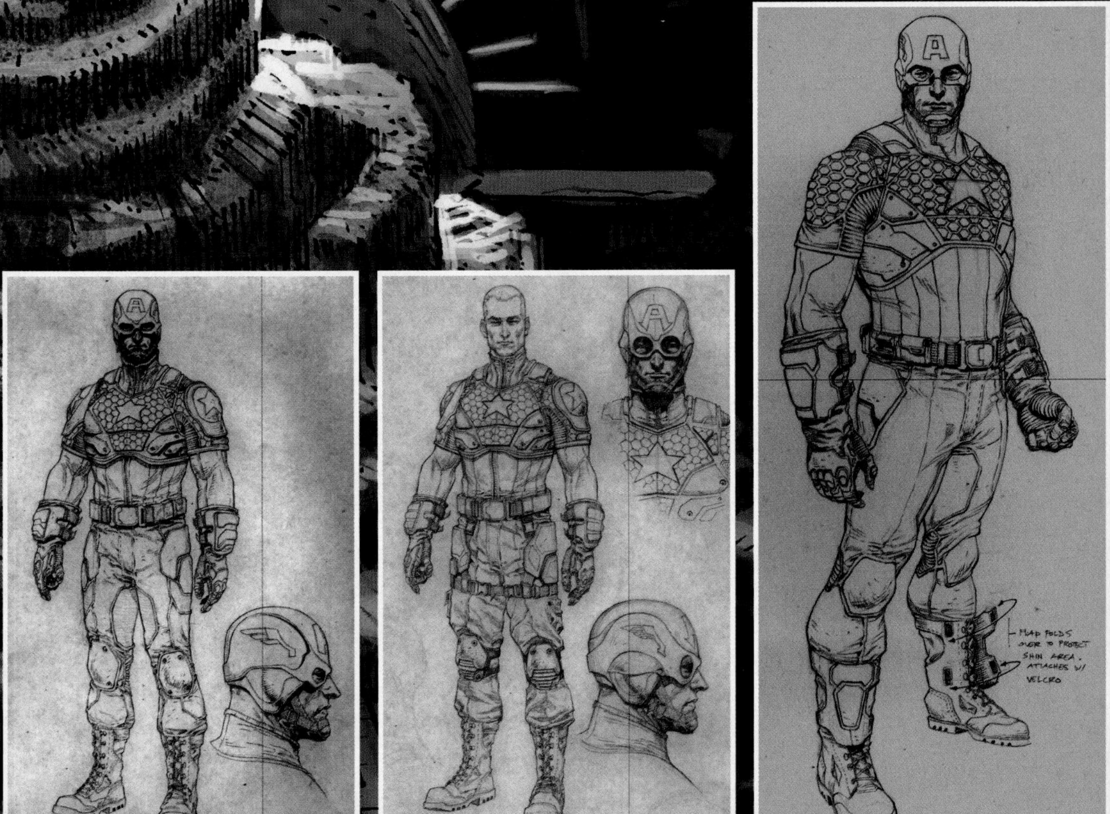
FLAP FOLDS OVER TO PROTECT SHIN AREA. ATTACHES W/ VELCRO

CAPTAIN AMERICA CHARACTER DESIGNS BY JEROME OPEÑA

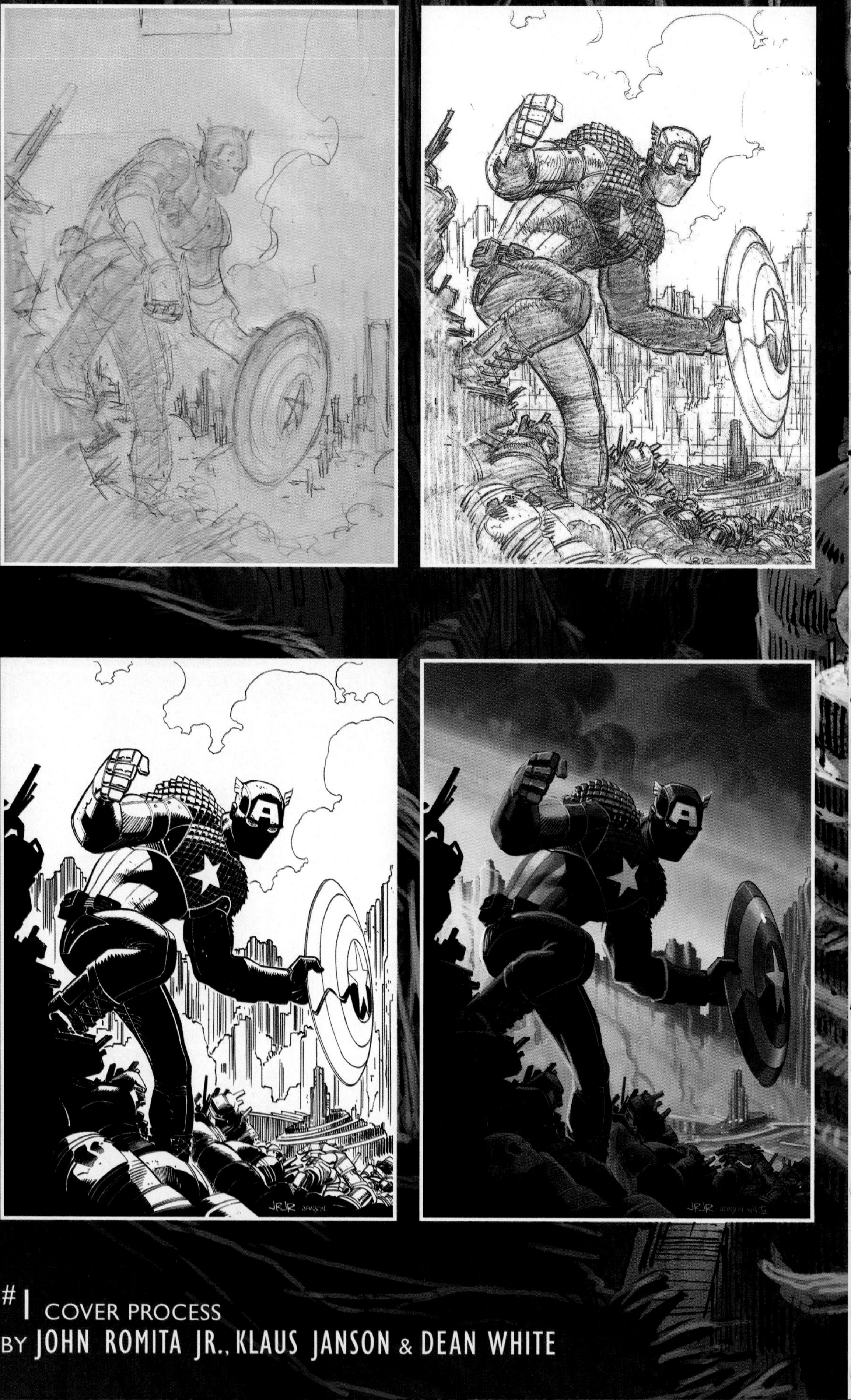

#1 COVER PROCESS
BY JOHN ROMITA JR., KLAUS JANSON & DEAN WHITE

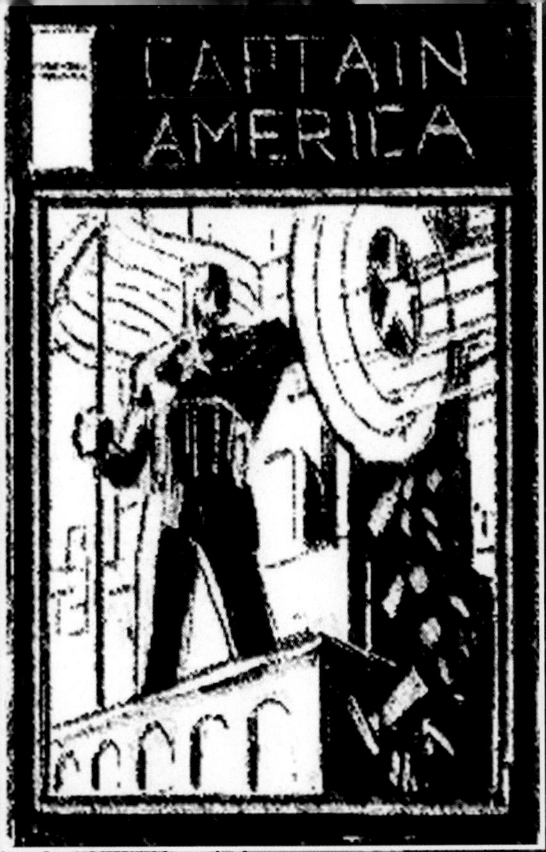
CAPTAIN
AMERICA

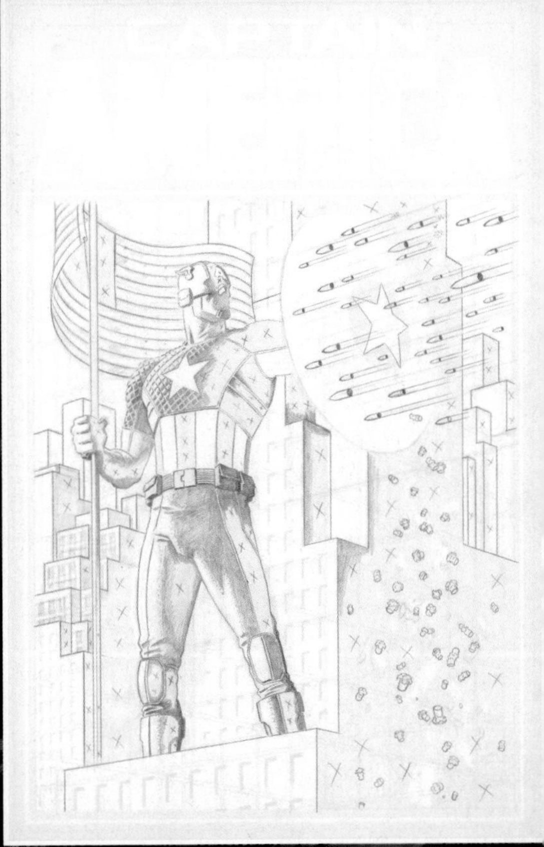

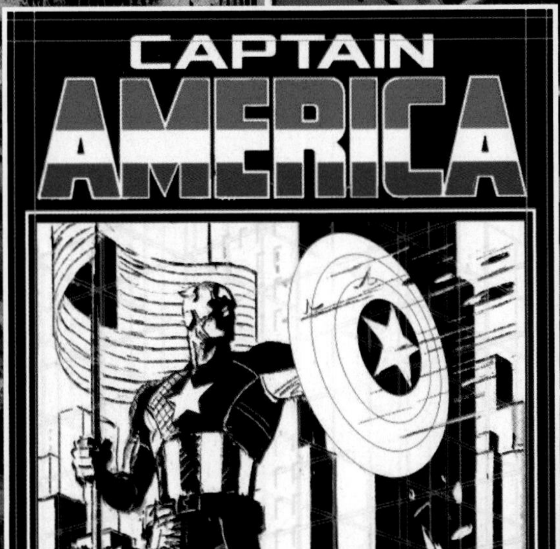
CAPTAIN
AMERICA

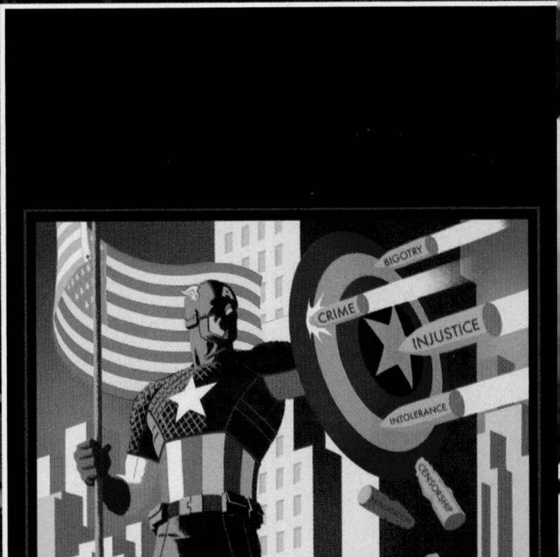
BIGOTRY
CRIME
INJUSTICE
INTOLERANCE
CENSORSHIP
TERRORISM
CORRUPTION
OPPRESSION
TYRANNY
GRAFT

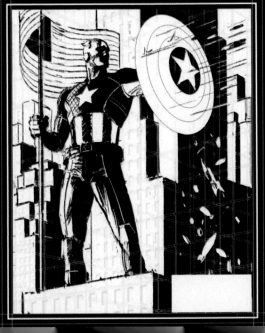

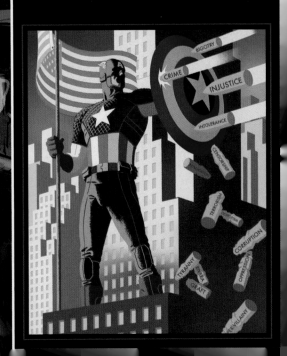

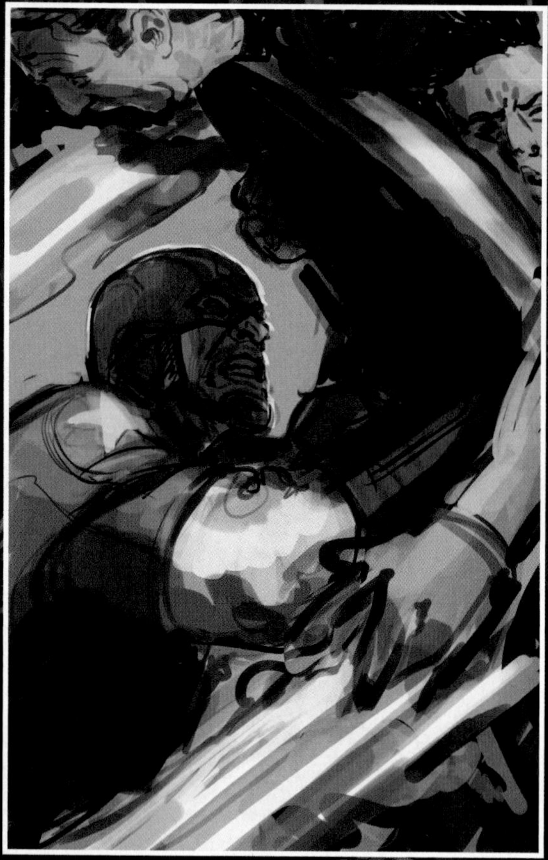

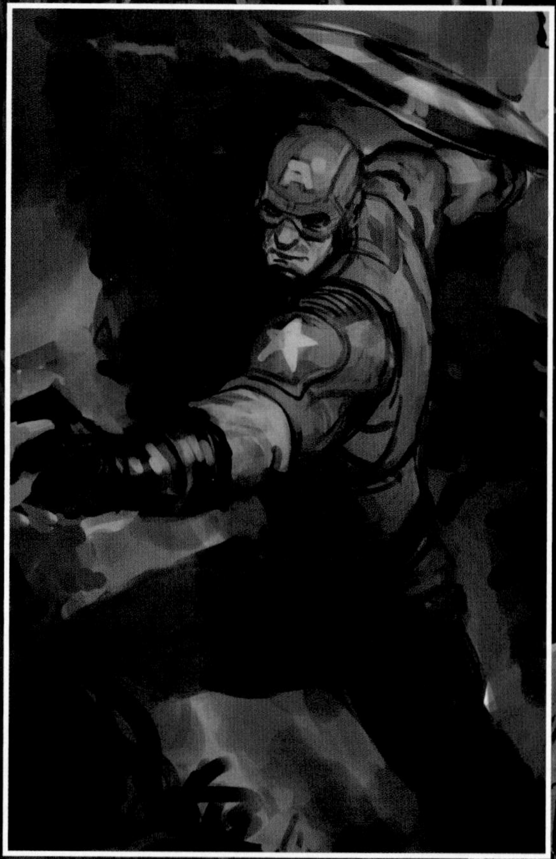

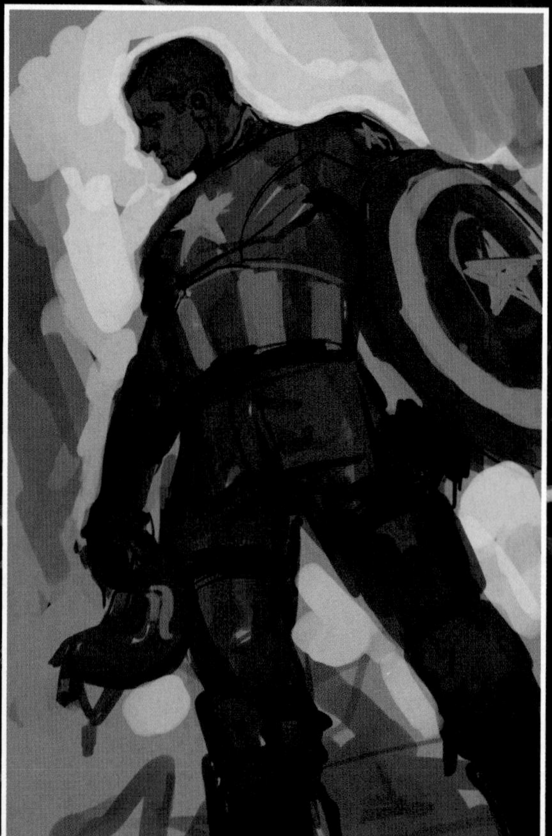

#1 VARIANT CONCEPT SKETCHES BY RYAN MEINERDING

RYAN MEINERDING

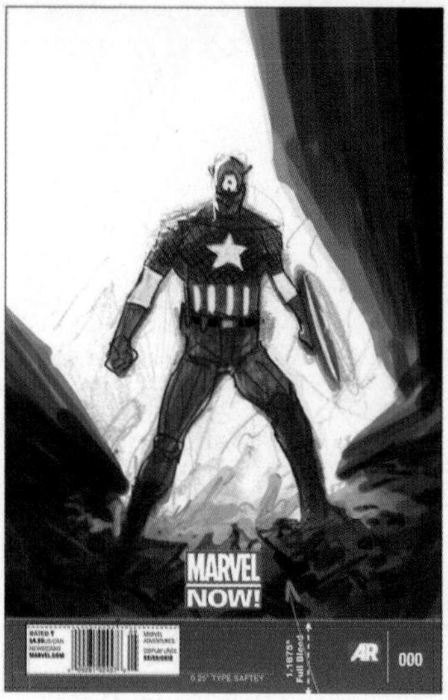
MARVEL
NOW!
0.25" TYPE SAFTEY
1.1875" Full Bleed
000
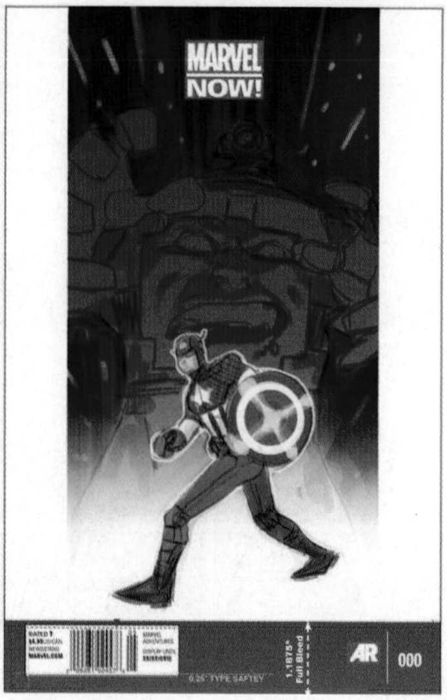
MARVEL
NOW!
0.25" TYPE SAFTEY
1.1875" Full Bleed
000
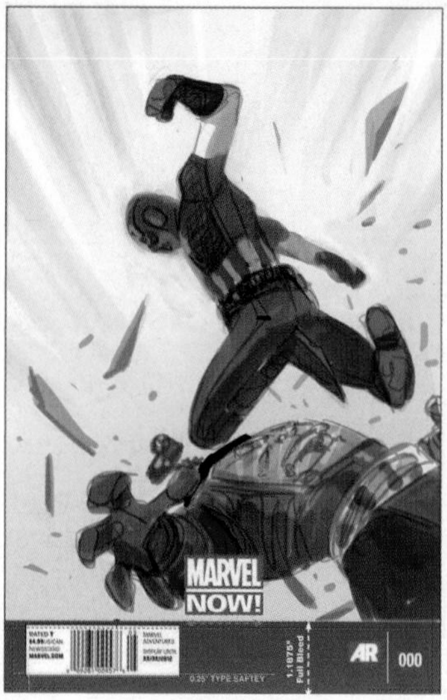
MARVEL
NOW!
0.25" TYPE SAFTEY
1.1875" Full Bleed
000
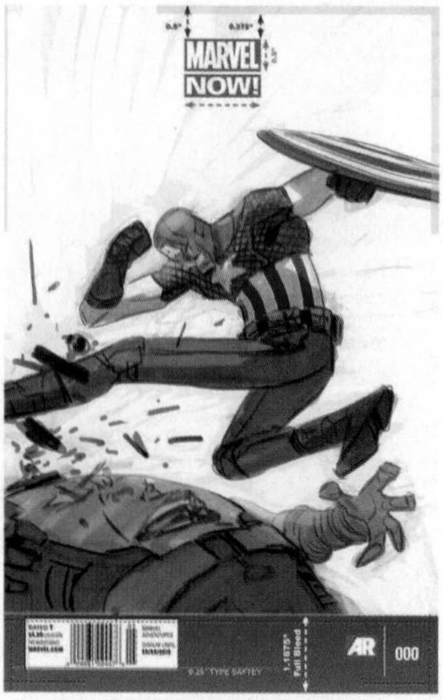
MARVEL
NOW!
0.25" TYPE SAFTEY
1.1875" Full Bleed
000
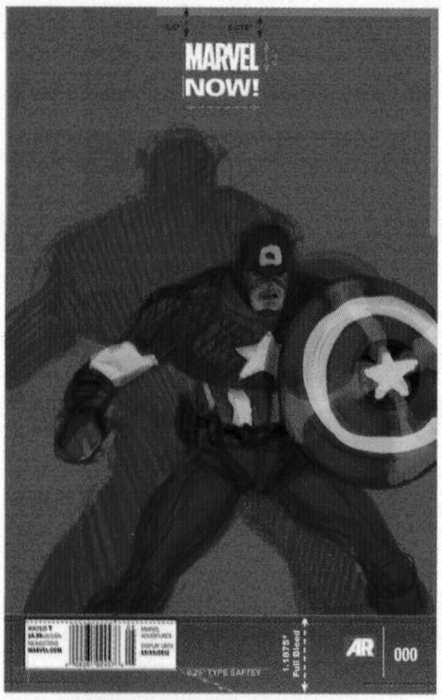
MARVEL
NOW!
0.25" TYPE SAFTEY
1.1875" Full Bleed
000
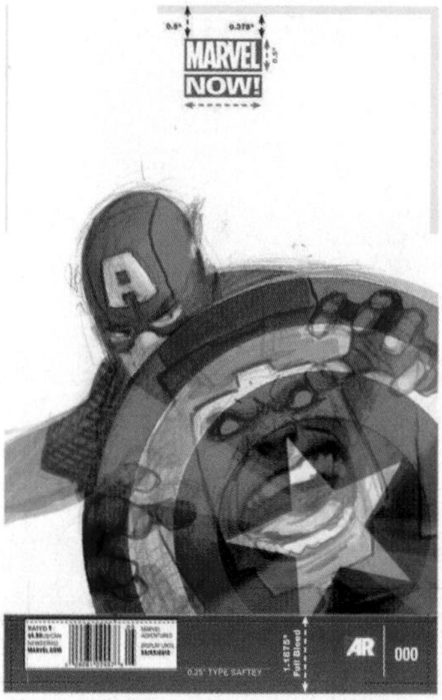
MARVEL
NOW!
0.25" TYPE SAFTEY
1.1875" Full Bleed
000
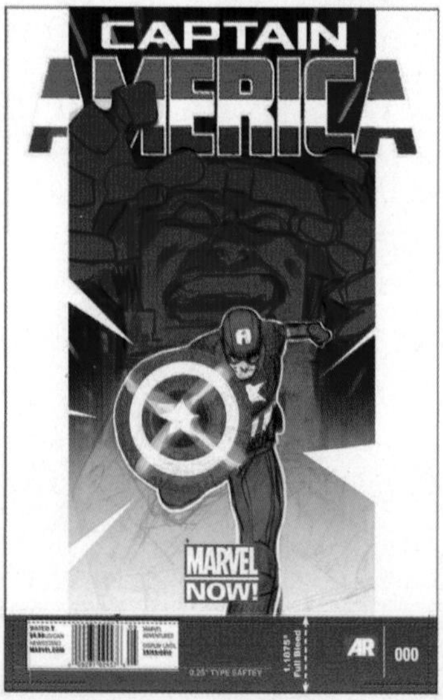
CAPTAIN
AMERICA
MARVEL
NOW!
0.25" TYPE SAFTEY
1.1875" Full Bleed
000
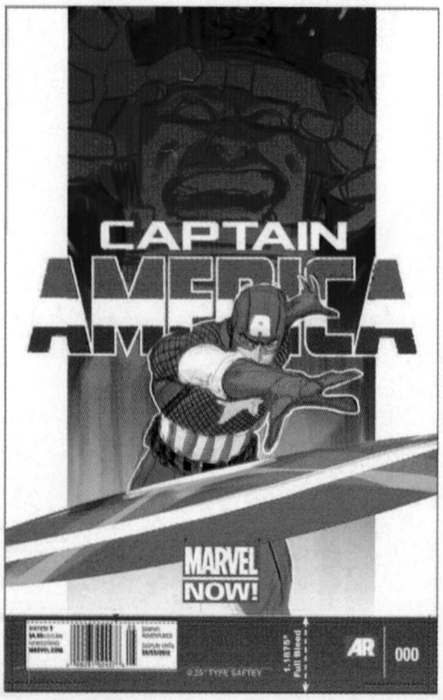
CAPTAIN
AMERICA
MARVEL
NOW!
0.25" TYPE SAFTEY
1.1875" Full Bleed
000
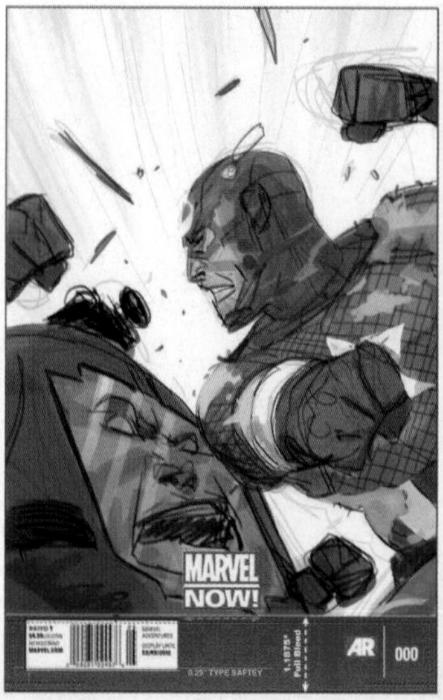
MARVEL
NOW!
0.25" TYPE SAFTEY
1.1875" Full Bleed
000

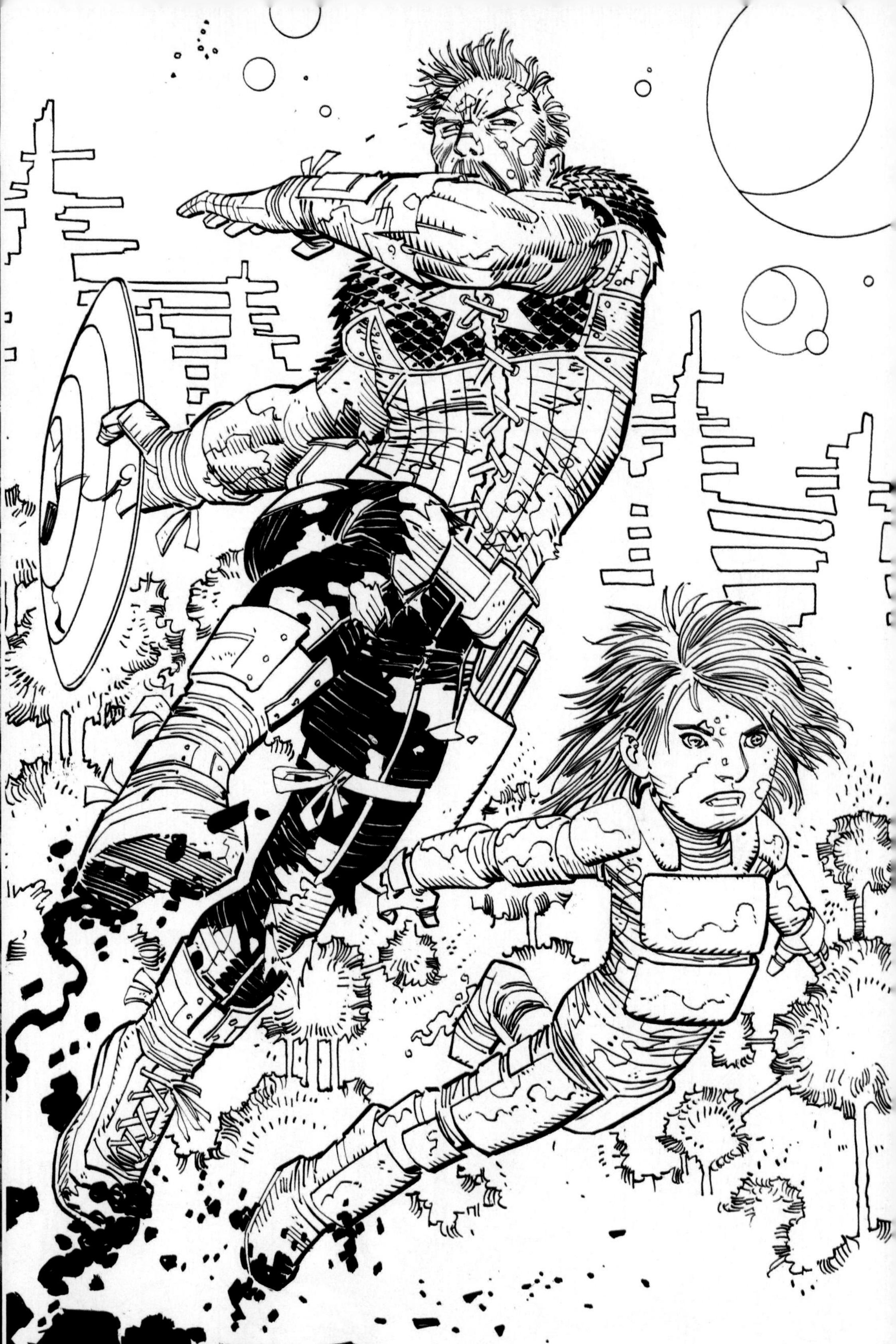

#4 PAGE 4 INKED ARTWORK BY JOHN ROMITA JR. & KLAUS JANSON

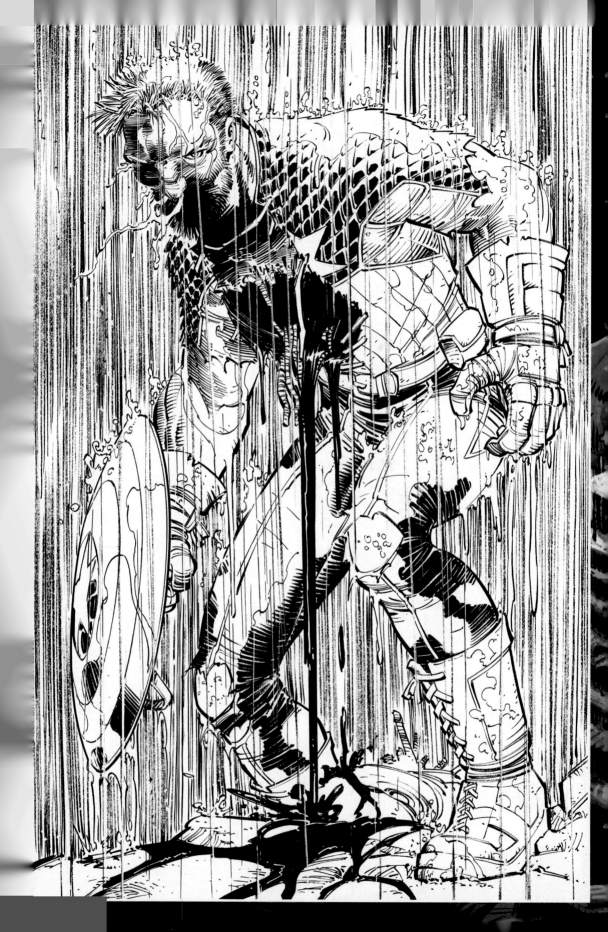

THE FREE *MARVEL AUGMENTED REALITY APP*
ENHANCES AND CHANGES THE WAY YOU EXPERIENCE COMICS!

To access the Marvel Augmented Reality App...

- Download the app for free via marvel.com/ARapp
- Launch the app on your camera-enabled Apple iOS® or Android™ device*
- Hold your mobile device's camera over any cover or panel with the **AR** graphic.
- Sit back and see the future of comics in action!

*Available on most camera-enabled Apple iOS® and Android™ devices. Content subject to change and availability.

CAPTAIN AMERICA
AR INDEX